Seventeenth-C

|२|०|२५

LONGMANS' ENGLISH SERIES

This new series includes both period anthologies and selections from the work of individual authors. The introductions and notes have been based upon the most up-to-date criticism and scholarship and the editors have been chosen for their special knowledge of the material.

General Editor *Maurice Hussey*

Seventeenth-Century Prose

An Anthology Selected and Edited by

Brian Vickers

Longman

LONGMANS, GREEN AND CO LTD

London and Harlow

Associated companies, branches and representatives throughout the world

*Introduction and Notes © Longmans, Green and Co Ltd 1969
First published 1969
Second Impression 1974*

*Printed in Great Britain by
Compton Printing Ltd, Aylesbury*

ISBN 0582 34 164 7

THE EDITOR

Dr Brian Vickers was educated at St Marylebone Grammar School
and Trinity College, Cambridge. He is a University Assistant Lecturer in English at Cambridge, and Fellow and Director of Studies
in English at Downing College. He has written: *The Artistry of
Shakespeare's Prose* (Methuen, 1968), *Francis Bacon and Renaissance
Prose* (Cambridge, 1968); has edited Henry Mackenzie's novel *The
Man of Feeling* (Oxford English Novels, 1967), and has edited and
contributed to *The World of Jonathan Swift* (Blackwell, 1968).

For St Marylebone Grammar School
and in Memory of Philip Wayne
Headmaster 1924–54

Contents

CONTENTS

Acknowledgements

We are grateful to the following for permission to reproduce copyright material:

Basil Blackwell & Mott Ltd for adapted extracts from *Leviathan* by Hobbes, ed. Michael Oakeshott; editor and Cambridge University Press for adapted extracts from *Religio Medici* by Browne, ed. James Winny; Cambridge University Press for adapted extracts from *Hydrotaphia* (non-burial), ed. W. Murison; Clarendon Press for adapted extracts from *The Centuries* by Thomas Traherne, ed. B. Dobell; J. M. Dent & Sons Ltd and E. P. Dutton & Co. Inc. for adapted extracts from *Of Dramatic Poesy and other Critical Essays* by Dryden, ed. George Watson (Everyman's Library).

Introduction

'Seventeenth-Century Prose' is a convenient label but one which does not define its subject (in the sense that 'Shakespearian' or 'Keatsian' may refer to certain qualities unique to those writers). It is a label of chronology not of genre, and it not only conceals within the limit of one century an enormous range of styles in prose but also includes a major revolution in the theory and practice of prose style brought about in the 1660s by a complex of forces, of which the best known is the Royal Society. The new style favoured in the last third of this century and through most of the following one was antipathetic to the 'old style', but its own tenets are generally agreed to have resulted in the weakening of the imaginative powers of prose, and although this anthology charts the reaction and includes examples of the admired new model style in Dryden, the bulk of its space is given to that style which was thought to have been superseded. By 'that style' I mean what might be called Renaissance prose, and although critical labels can obscure as much as they define this does seem an accurate description of the attitude to prose that persisted in English from Sir Thomas More to Milton. The English Renaissance was just as much concerned in re-claiming classical models for literature as were the revivals of Humanism on the Continent, and it seems to have surpassed both Italy and France in the production of great works in prose. But it was a revival which did not move steadily: the brilliant example of Sir Thomas More's mastery in both Latin and English prose produced no immediate development (nor did several other literary innovations in the unhappy reign of Henry VIII) and it was not until the mid-century, with the work of Roger Ascham (*Toxophilus*, 1545; *The Scholemaster*, 1570), that prose in the vernacular attained any clarity or shape. Ascham's reforms were carried on by an unlikely source, Lyly's romantic novel *Euphues* (1578; Part 2, 1580), which, despite its stereotyped characterization and pretentious use of recondite 'natural history' gave an influential demonstration of the degree to which English syntax could be organized in symmetrical series, and although Euphuism was an impracticable model the type of logical analysis produced by its patterning had a salutary effect.[1] The speed and range of the development of prose under Elizabeth can be seen by the great achievements of Hooker, Sidney, and Nashe, three writers who could hardly be more different.

Lyly's influence was also strong in the theatre, and although the huge topic of prose in Elizabethan and Jacobean drama lies outside the scope of this anthology reference must at least be made to the two greatest writers of dramatic prose, Shakespeare and Jonson.[2] The contrast between them is in part that between the old and the new styles: Shakespeare retains the traditional Ciceronian symmetries of syntax whose potential Lyly had demonstrated, while Jonson strives almost consciously for a non-symmetrical style, a more realistic representation of normal speech, and adds to it a studiously precise yet vigorous imitation of actual speech-habits. Shakespeare is no less able to re-create character through prose style, and excels Jonson in the variety and flexibility of his prose, using the movement between verse and prose for many subtle changes of level and mood, and applying the traditional devices to an unlimited range of dramatic situations. Shakespeare, using the prose of Art, is free to create within it; Jonson, being closer to Nature, is more tied by it.

Although the contrast between their styles is mainly that between very individual writers making their own artistic choices Jonson does point the way to the seventeenth century in his development of the prose of ideas, from the critical discussions of literature in his inductions and prologues (and within the plays themselves) to the sections of criticism in his notebook, *Timber, or Discoveries*. An obvious but important superiority of prose written after about 1600 to that written before lies in its ability to handle abstract issues in a compelling way. Seventeenth-century prose as represented in this anthology or elsewhere is remarkable for its control of both witty and serious modes, and is more impressive in the latter style. Important

[1] A valuable assessment of this influence is given by C. S. Lewis in his *Oxford History of English Literature in the Sixteenth Century*, O.U.P., 1954, and a more detailed study is that of G. K. Hunter, *John Lyly: the Poet as Courtier*, Routledge, 1962.

[2] See B. W. Vickers, *The Artistry of Shakespeare's Prose*, Methuen, 1968, and J. A. Barish, *Ben Jonson and the Language of Prose Comedy*, Harvard, 1960.

intellectual issues such as the relationships between man and God, between the individual and society, within the individual's moral and psychological states, the function of literature (scholarship, censorship, criticism)—these were all treated at a high intellectual level as can be seen from this anthology. Such topics were of course discussed in Elizabethan prose but, with the exception of Hooker, not in any memorable way; now abstract issues are handled in a fresh and concrete manner, for prose itself is now a medium with both flexibility and intensity —is, in a word, poetic.

Poetry and prose

It is always difficult to explain why literature should suddenly blossom in a particular country at a particular time, but one very good reason why English prose in the Renaissance reached these heights is that it absorbed the lessons of classical prose and applied them to the vernacular with imagination and energy in experiment. The classical models both in theory and practice encouraged the development of the two great resources of prose, imagery and structure of syntax: that is, equal shape in the length, structure, rhythms, and even the sound of cor-responding clauses and sentences. These twin resources might today be thought to belong to poetry, but in Greece and Rome as in Renaissance England prose *was* 'poetic': at a very early stage Greek oratory had appropriated for prose the rhetorical figures (including metaphor) which were originally used for poetry, and the idea persisted until the end of the seventeenth century that prose and poetry were of basically equal artistic status, the only difference being that poetry had the added complication of metrics (and to some critics the irregular rhythmic patterning of prose seemed more difficult). Thus the modern reader, brought up on the idea that poetry and prose are differentiated not merely by their shape on the page but by their whole imaginative resources—differentiated to the point that they are now almost antithetical—that reader must now think himself back into the earlier frame of mind and read Renaissance prose as if it were poetry. The closeness of poetry to prose has been demonstrated by E. R. Curtius[1] among others, and of the many statements of the relationship which could be

[1] In his great book, *European Literature and the Latin Middle Ages*, Routledge, 1953 (paperback edition, Harper Torchbooks, 1963), especially Chapter 8.

quoted two must suffice: in 1513, Erasmus writing to a friend, confessed that 'What especially delights me is a rhetorical poem and a poetical oration, in which you can see the poetry in the prose and the rhetorical expression in the poetry', and in 1700 Dryden recorded in his *Preface to the Fables* that even at his age 'thoughts, such as they are, come crowding in so fast upon me that my only difficulty is to choose or reject, to run them into verse or to give them the other harmony of prose'. It is no accident that then, as in no other period before or since, the greatest poets of the age were also among the greatest prose writers: Sidney, Shakespeare, Jonson, Ralegh, Donne, and Milton.

Metaphor

Of the two 'poetic' resources imagery will be the more familiar today and will need less background information. The validity of using imagery in prose was first stated clearly by Aristotle in his *Rhetoric*: metaphor 'is most important both in poetry and in prose. But the orator must devote the greater attention to them in prose, since the latter has fewer resources than verse' (III, ii, 8). Thus in prose, metaphor has the same properties that it has in poetry: it sets the matter 'vividly before the eyes'; it can be used to make a topic look either admirable or ridiculous; it appeals to the emotions and helps persuasion; and it should not be too far-fetched. Latin rhetoricians repeat Aristotle's injunctions, and for one example only we turn to Quintilian's great *Institutes of Oratory* where metaphor is held to be not only valid in prose but is 'the supreme ornament of oratory' (VIII, ii, 6) and has the power to illuminate and convince. The Elizabethan rhetoricians carry on this tradition, even giving metaphors and similes the status of arguments because of their force in persuasion: again one example must serve for many, Puttenham's ruling that: 'As well to a good maker and Poet as to an excellent persuader in prose, the figure of *Similitude* is very necessary, by which we not onely bewtifie our tale, but also very much enforce and enlarge it. I say enforce because no one thing more prevaileth with all ordinary judgements than persuasion by *similitude*.' The 'excellent persuaders in prose' of the Renaissance certainly applied the principle, and for wit, imagination, and emotional effect they often come close to the poets and dramatists.

4

The shape of prose

Syntactical symmetry, the second major resource of prose in
this period, had equally ancient and distinguished advocates,
but here the tradition had been so well established in Greece
and Rome that there was little need for theoretical approval
beyond urging that prose might use all the figures of rhetoric.
It is not necessary to know the technicalities of rhetoric to
appreciate the effects attainable by means of balance and parallelism. While a work which uses these means for every sentence
would soon pall (as indeed *Euphues* does) if used at strategic
moments they can greatly reinforce meaning, and the most
famous of orators, Cicero, employed them with great force:

> Soleo saepe ante oculos ponere,
> idque libenter crebris usurpare sermonibus,
> omnes nostrorum imperatorum,
> omnes exterarum gentium potentissimorumque populorum,
> omnes regum clarissimorum res gestas
> cum tuis nec contentionum magnitudine
> > nec numero proeliorum
> > nec varietate regionum
> > nec celeritate conficiendi
> > nec dissimilitudine bellorum posse conferri,
> > nec vero disiunctissimas terras citius passibus
> > > cuiusquam potuisse peragrari,
> > quam tuis non dicam cursibus,
> > > sed victoriis lustratae sunt.
> > > *(Pro Marcello,* 5)

Even without translating that example we can see how the unexpected recurrence of sound and shape give an extra dimension
to the sense, and suddenly introduce the valuable weapon of
tempo: by accelerating or slowing down the movement the
writer can achieve a variety of effects, from a slow build-up to
a surprise reversal.

The tradition of syntactical symmetry in prose persists in
Latin from the classical period through the Middle Ages to the
Renaissance, and in the vernacular it is found in medieval English as well as throughout the sixteenth and seventeenth centuries. Thus the writers anthologized here make constant imaginative use of structure to point up sense: in his essay 'On

Friendship' Bacon sets two sensitive images within a symmetrical frame which postpones the subject of the sentence until the end and creates a fine effect of tension and release:

> For a crowd is not company;
>   and faces are but a gallery of pictures;
>   and talk   but a tinkling cymbal,
>   where there is no love.

A more complex but equally effective use of symmetrical structure can be taken from a passage in Ralegh's *Preface* not excerpted here, where he writes his own bitter version of the traditional Renaissance discussion of the relative advantages of Virtue and Fortune:

> For, seeing it is a thing exceeding rare to distinguish
>   Virtue and Fortune; the most impious (if prosperous)
> have ever been applauded; the most virtuous (if unprosper-
>   ous)
> have ever been despised.
>   For, as Fortune's man rides the horse,
>   so Fortune herself rides the man. Who,
>   when he is descended and on foot,
>   the man taken from his beast,
>   and Fortune   from the man,
>   a base groom beats the one,
>   and a bitter contempt spurns at the other,
>   with equal liberty.

There the riddling contortions of the sense (the counters marked 'Fortune', 'Man', 'Beast' being moved about like so many chessmen) are set against the almost mathematical symmetry of syntax with the effect that the unpredictable but fatal ends of him who follows Fortune are both exposed and enacted. A third and last example of this resource comes from a sermon by Donne, where symmetry is used to build up to an apparent climax which proves to be the undermining of the whole structure of human sin:

> some reclinations, some retrospects we have,
> a little of Lot's wife is in us,
> a little sociableness, and conversation,
> a little point of honour,

6

not to be false to former promises,
a little false gratitude and thankfulness,
in respect of former obligations,
a little of the compassion and charity of Hell ...

The let-down of the last clause here is almost a giving-in to despair, a deliberate ebbing-out of optimism about man, and the syntactical progression both fits and extends the sense.

Even from this brief discussion it is evident that syntactical symmetry is a weapon of considerable range and force in prose, and although it cannot approach the subtleties of metrics in poetry, it is undeniably an artistic resource which, like imagery, can 'enlarge and enforce' sense. But the revolution in attitudes to prose which finally produced the manifesto of the Royal Society had among its main targets both of these resources: the ideal prose style from 1667 onwards was one without imagery and without syntactical effects of any kind. These 'peculiarities' were ironed out, and the result is a flat, smooth, neutral type of prose, but one which is also colourless, tasteless, and one-dimensional. To use a metaphor which would seem to them suspect, where they found wine—with all its variety of colour and taste—they left water. Happily, revolutions in literary theory are less thoroughgoing than those in politics, and enough traces of imagery are left even in those who most abused it to make our reading experience of them not entirely neutral. Some of the stages in this revolution will be charted below, but meanwhile and for the first four-fifths of this book we are presented with Renaissance prose before the drought.

I
Sir Francis Bacon
1561–1626

In the seventeenth century not all roads led to Rome, but most of them led from Bacon. No Englishman has ever had such a great influence on his own nation, and certainly none ever had such a standing abroad: he dominated so many spheres during his life (philosophy, science, law, politics, historiography) and after his death he was claimed as the leader of several movements. The most important of these was the growth of science, and even though his own deficiencies as a scientist were less evident then than they are today, the often misleading details of his proposed reforms in science and technology were obscured by the excitement produced by his accurate general diagnosis and prophecy of the future of science. Bacon saw clearly the need to free science from the uncritical subservience to Aristotle which persisted through the Middle Ages and into the Renaissance, and a large part of his energy was devoted to breaking the shackles of reverence for the past: he initiates the battle between the Ancients and Moderns in the seventeenth century and it is thanks to him that the Moderns won it. Having destroyed previous systems new ones had to be built, and although he made grave mistakes, such as ignoring mathematics, Bacon was historically correct in urging that the new science should be based totally on experimentation and a rigorously controlled method. His further proposals for cooperation (best seen in the scientific academy outlined in his *New Atlantis*) had an immediate result in the founding of the Royal Society, which claimed him as its spiritual begetter, and showed in the writings of its members an unlimited veneration for (in Cowley's words) the 'Moses' who 'led us forth at last' to 'the blest promised Land'.

But Bacon is not to be limited to the development of experimental science. In a famous letter which he wrote at the age of thirty-two he proclaimed that:

I have taken all knowledge to be my province; and if I could purge it of two sorts of rovers,[1] whereof the one with

[1] Rovers: random, haphazard traditions; misleading directions.

8

SIR FRANCIS BACON

frivolous disputations, confutations, and verbosities, the other with blind experiments and auricular traditions and impostures, hath committed so many spoils, I hope I should bring in industrious observations, grounded conclusions, profitable inventions and discoveries.

There the two parts of his reforms—one destructive, one constructive—are already announced, and the whole second half of his life was devoted to giving them form. Bacon certainly inspected the whole province of knowledge, and in *The Advancement of Learning* he set himself the double task of review and recommendation: in Book I he was to set out 'the excellency of knowledge and learning' and to defend it from the many attacks it had received in the Renaissance; in Book II, he wrote (with a characteristically fluent series of images) he was to make 'a general and faithful perambulation of learning, with an inquiry what parts thereof lie fresh and waste, and not improved and converted by the industry of man; to the end that such a plot made and recorded to memory may both minister light to any public designation, and also serve to excite voluntary endeavours'. The survey is carried out with great penetration along a very wide scale of knowledge, and whatever the weaknesses of Bacon's own scientific projects there can be no doubt about his supremacy as a critic of extant systems.

Part of the scope of his 'Defence of Learning' in Book I was the exposure of the discredits brought upon intellectual endeavours by the weaknesses of learned men themselves, and the central section is made up of the attacks on medieval scholasticism and on Renaissance Ciceronianism (excerpted here). The decline of scholasticism presented the strange sight of a watertight body of learning, to which nothing could be added, being continually varied into slightly new forms but with no hope of progress: Aristotle was both canonized and embalmed. Ciceronianism showed the equally stagnant and trivial purpose of cultivating the ornament of language at the expense of meaning, of limiting vocabulary to words and even case-endings used by Cicero. It was thus immediately debarred from discussing Christianity, as Erasmus pungently showed, because it used only pagan words, and it was equally incapable of discussing modern science. Bacon seizes on the absurdities of both systems, and makes them appear banal, ludicrous, and

9

most serious, stultifying. His other great critique of extant errors and inconsistencies is directed against the very cognitive processes themselves, the innate fallacies in thought and language to which the human mind is prone, which he called, again with an illuminating image, 'the Idols of the Tribe', things that we worship, without realizing it, by our unalterable human nature. This analysis is fully expounded in his greatest scientific work, the *Novum Organum* or 'New Instrument of the Sciences' (1620), but it is sufficiently clarified in the *Advancement of Learning* to make it worth studying, especially in the vigour of his English.

The *Essays* (1597; 1612; 1625) are the most misunderstood of Bacon's works. They have suffered from being read with the same expectations that are brought to the essay as developed after Montaigne, the whimsical, relaxed, discursive tradition that runs from Addison to Charles Lamb and beyond, and they are thus found too 'humourless' or 'non-personal'. The truth is that they belong to several quite different traditions: at one level they resemble the 'Advice to Princes' literature, in its new, sharp form after Machiavelli and Guicciardini, replete with dispassionate precepts for political success; at another level they share the conduct-books' interest in guiding personal behaviour in matters ranging from ethics to conversation and managing your purse (in the 1625 edition they have the subtitle, 'Essays, or Counsels, Civil and Moral'); finally, most important, and least understood, they fit Bacon's own scientific scheme. In Book II of the *Advancement of Learning* Bacon came to 'moral knowledge', and divided it into two parts: the 'Exemplar of Good' (ethics, morality), which he finds to have been adequately handled, and the 'Culture of the Mind' which is deficient, particularly in formal philosophy, such as Aristotle's, though, he says, the poets and dramatists have incidentally given good examples. He subdivides this topic into three sections, and it is easily seen that the recommendations made under each in 1605 were carried out in the *Essays* of 1625. The first head is the 'complexions and constitutions' of the mind, that is the determining influences upon the human personality whether caused by heredity or environment, such things as age, health and sickness, beauty, nobility, prosperity, adversity, and so on: in 1625 he includes essays 'Of Youth and Age', 'Of Beauty', 'Of Deformity', 'Of Nobility', 'Of Riches', 'Of

Adversity', and others. And the same holds both for the other two sections, the diseases of the mind ('Of Anger', 'Of Envy') and its cures ('Of Custom and Education', 'Of Nature in Men'), as for the other main section on Civil Knowledge, which produced such essays as 'Of Negotiating', 'Of Factions', 'Of Followers and Friends'. Thus, far from the *Essays* being a series of random jottings on topics which just came into his head, they have a logical place in a larger scheme, and form pioneering attempts to define the influence on man of causes which we might now discuss under psychology, sociology, political theory. The qualities of Bacon's mind that I have emphasized in this selection from the *Essays* are those often denied him by critics who confuse the dispassionate precepts of Italian statecraft with their own distorted visions of Bacon's character: he can be seen here concerned with distinguishing between political expediency and moral obligations, and giving his vote for charity and truth.

That has been perhaps the minimum information needed to understand the purpose of Bacon's writing in his two greatest English works. As for the quality of that writing, it makes vigorous use of the two main resources of Renaissance prose, especially in the attack on decadent learning. Syntactical symmetry is used for sarcastic emphasis, for prolonging the catalogue of vanity in things and persons so that we catch the full force of the condemnation, and to the parallelism is added the mocking echoes in the suffixes:

these three distempers (as I may term them) of learning;
    the first,   fantastical learning;
  the second, contentious learning;
  and the last,   delicate learning;
             vain imaginations,
             vain altercations,
        and vain affectations;
    and with the last I will begin.

Having lulled us into passivity by parodying the self-admiring eloquence of this school Bacon startles us by shooting off on an unexpected direction. The same exploitation of stylistic contrast is used in the brilliant passage where Bacon caps his analysis of the various causes which combined to produce

Ciceronianism by describing the effect which it had on prose, and by widening the initial distinction between 'words' and 'matter' he allows the section amplifying 'words' to grow more and more expansive and self-indulgent and then sharply contrasts it with the real virtues of 'matter'. In this decadent style men began to hunt:

> more after words than matter; and
> more after the choiceness of the phrase, and
>> the round and clean composition of the sentence,
>> and the varying and illustration of their works with
>>> tropes   and figures
> than after the weight   of matter,
>> worth   of subject,
>> soundness of argument,
>> life   of invention, or
>> depth   of judgement.

Again the sound and structure imitate and enforce the sense, expanding within a fixed frame to the ever looser state of the first main clause, and then contracting to the unexpectedly sharp recurrence of identical structure in the second clause. Syntactical symmetry helps to make the point on two planes, and Bacon uses the device for many subtle and different ends, as a careful reading of the excerpts from both works will show.

Imagery is an even more effective weapon in Bacon's hands. The schoolmen[1] are comprehensively annihilated by metaphor, starting from the damaging analogy between the process by which 'many substances in nature which are solid do putrefy and corrupt into worms', and the suggested equally inevitable process by which the schoolmen reduce knowledge to 'vermiculate questions'. From worms Bacon moves to spiders, the metaphor now being based on the limited diet and restricted working-space common to both those insects and to the schoolmen: 'Their wits being shut up in the cells of a few authors ... as their persons were shut up in the cells of monasteries and colleges; ... did out of no great quantity of matter, and in-

---

[1] The scholars who, from about the ninth to the fourteenth century, treat of logic, metaphysics, and theology as taught in the medieval 'schools' or universities. To the forward-looking minds of the Renaissance medieval scholasticism represented all that was sterile and incapable of growth.

finite agitations of wit, spin out unto us those laborious webs of learning which are extant in their books.'

Bacon's sarcastic wit takes the image yet further, down even to mock-serious considerations of 'the fineness of thread and work'. He seems to be drawing on an inexhaustible well of analogy here, fixing the schoolmen in amber, then matching the fragility of their work with the triviality of their controversial tactics, which consisted in breaking up single sticks (how easy!) instead of dealing with the whole issue, a short-sightedness which is developed further by the image of the tiny candle as against a 'branching candlestick of lights', before the final collapse of scholasticism into a mob of monsters barking around the loins of knowledge. There is great verve in the writing throughout this section, not least in the wit shown by the puns on words like 'breeding' and 'descend', puns which in turn produce more images. Already some of the characteristics of Bacon's imagery stand out: his basing of an analogy on indisputable natural phenomena—food *will* decay, it *is* easier to break single sticks than the whole bundle; his giving the images concrete localization—the insects and monsters of this sequence are almost tangible; and his moving from image to image by an associative rather than a logical process—*fragility* was one quality in common in several of the schoolmen's activities, *futility* or *fruitlessness* another.

But Bacon is not only a critic. His use of imagery is illuminating even in fairly neutral contexts (such as the discussion of innate fallacies) and it can extend to praise and enthusiasm on a worthy theme, especially in that great passage in praise of Letters which closes Book I of the *Advancement of Learning*, where we see how his application of imagery to an argument (a perfectly normal application, according to classical and Renaissance theory and practice, although mistaken by some modern critics for a misuse of metaphor) not only lights up the immediate context but casts illumination both forwards and backwards. How simple and yet how compelling is his analogy for the way in which the unlearned man, deprived of the educative power of knowledge, stays as he has always been: 'The good parts he hath he will learn to shew to the full and use them dexterously, but not much to increase them: the faults he hath he will learn how to hide and colour them, but not much to amend them; like an ill mower, that mows on still and never whets his scythe.'

Even more impressive is the sequence of metaphors for the immortality of learning, which, Bacon claims, is 'more durable than the monuments of power or of the hands', for: 'the images of men's wits and knowledge remain in books, exempted from the wrong of time and capable of perpetual renovation. Neither are they fitly to be called images, because they generate still, and cast their seeds in the minds of others, provoking and causing infinite actions and opinions in succeeding ages.' Few celebrations of learning are as eloquent as this, and none dare risk the wry and offhand conclusion which follows it and somehow makes it seem more eloquent.

In the *Essays* comparable qualities of imagination are shown both in syntax and in metaphor, if on a smaller time scale due to the shorter separate series of structures. Indeed, the condensed nature of the treatment and the fact that Bacon sometimes used aphorisms here as a means of embodying experience in an authoritative and applicable form results in a densely packed type of writing with much serious wit operating intensely, almost between the sentences. Anne Righter has well said that the 1625 edition: 'is an accumulation of disparate pieces as difficult to generalize about, or to connect internally, as Donne's *Songs and Sonets*, and it is to be read in a not dissimilar fashion',[1] and her own analysis of 'Of Truth' brings out well the elliptical, surprising, unpredictable nature of the development within so many of the *Essays*. The use of imagery is particularly imaginative in that essay, but a sensitive and evocative application of metaphor is a frequent discovery: thus in arguing that 'Prosperity is the blessing of the Old Testament; Adversity is the blessing of the New' Bacon makes a distinction: 'Yet even in the Old Testament, if you listen to David's harp you shall hear as many hearse-like airs as carols; and the pencil of the Holy Ghost hath laboured more in describing the affliction of Job than the felicities of Solomon.' There the thought is embodied in the imagery, and could only be extracted from it by a prose paraphrase which would crudify the imaginative effect. At the other end of the human and moral scale his description of the sole useful function of *misanthropi* is equally concrete

[1] 'Francis Bacon', in *The English Mind*, ed. H. S. Davies and G. Watson, C.U.P., 1964.

and ingenious: 'Such dispositions are the very errors of human
nature; and yet they are the fittest timber to make great politiques of; like to knee timber, that is good for ships, that are
ordained to be tossed; but not for building houses, that shall
stand firm.' Again the image is more exact and illuminating
(and emotionally balanced) than pure statement could have
been. Bacon's dominance over the seventeenth century was not
fortuitous: only Shakespeare exceeds him in range or depth of
imagination and expressiveness.

From *The Advancement of Learning*

[*Decadent Knowledge*] Now I proceed to those errors and vanities
which have intervened amongst the studies themselves of the
learned; which is that which is principal and proper to the present argument; wherein my purpose is not to make a justification of the errors, but, by a censure and separation of the errors,
to make a justification of that which is good and sound, and to
deliver that from the aspersion of the other. For we see that it
is the manner of men to scandalize and deprave that which
retaineth the state and virtue, by taking advantage upon that
10 which is corrupt and degenerate: as the Heathens in the primitive church used to blemish and taint the Christians with the
faults and corruptions of heretics. But nevertheless I have
no meaning at this time to make any exact animadversion
of the errors and impediments in matters of learning which
are more secret and remote from vulgar opinion; but only
to speak unto such as do fall under, or near unto, a popular
observation.

There be therefore chiefly three vanities in studies, whereby
learning hath been most traduced. For those things we do
20 esteem vain, which are either false or frivolous, those which
either have no truth or no use: and those persons we esteem
vain, which are either credulous or curious; and curiosity is
either in matter or words: so that in reason as well as in experience, there fall out to be these three distempers (as I may term
them) of learning; the first, fantastical learning; the second,
contentious learning; and the last, delicate learning; vain
imaginations, vain altercations, and vain affectations; and with
the last I will begin. Martin Luther, conducted (no doubt) by
an higher Providence, but in discourse of reason finding what

a province he had undertaken against the Bishop of Rome and the degenerate traditions of the church, and finding his own solitude, being no ways aided by the opinions of his own time, was enforced to awake all antiquity, and to call former times to his succors to make a party against the present time; so that the ancient authors, both in divinity and in humanity, which had long time slept in libraries, began generally to be read and revolved. This by consequence did draw on a necessity of a more exquisite travail in the languages original wherein those
10 authors did write, for the better understanding of those authors and the better advantage of pressing and applying their words. And thereof grew again a delight in their manner of style and phrase, and an admiration of that kind of writing; which was much furthered and precipitated by the enmity and opposition that the propounders of those (primitive but seeming new) opinions had against the schoolmen; who were generally of the contrary part, and whose writings were altogether in a differing style and form; taking liberty to coin and frame new terms of art to express their own sense and to avoid circuit of
20 speech, without regard to the pureness, pleasantness, and (as I may call it) lawfulness of the phrase or word. And again, because the great labour then was with the people, (of whom the Pharisees were wont to say, *Execrabilis ista turba, quæ non novit legem,*) [the wretched crowd that has not known the law,] for the winning and persuading of them, there grew of necessity in chief price and request eloquence and variety of discourse, as the fittest and forciblest access into the capacity of the vulgar sort. So that these four causes concurring, the admiration of ancient authors, the hate of the schoolmen, the exact
30 study of languages, and the efficacy of preaching, did bring in an affectionate study of eloquence and copie of speech, which then began to flourish. This grew speedily to an excess; for men began to hunt more after words than matter; and more after the choiceness of the phrase, and the round and clean composition of the sentence, and the sweet falling of the clauses, and the varying and illustration of their works with tropes and figures, than after the weight of matter, worth of subject, soundness of argument, life of invention, or depth of judgment. Then grew the flowing and watery vein of Osorius, the
40 Portugal bishop, to be in price. Then did Sturmius spend such infinite and curious pains upon Cicero the orator and Hermo-

16

genes the rhetorician, besides his own books of periods and imitation and the like. Then did Car of Cambridge, and Ascham, with their lectures and writings, almost deify Cicero and Demosthenes, and allure all young men that were studious unto that delicate and polished kind of learning. Then did Erasmus take occasion to make the scoffing echo; *Decem annos consumpsi legendo Cicerone*, [I have spent ten years in reading Cicero:] and the echo answered in Greek, *one, Asine* [thou ass]. Then grew the learning of the schoolmen to be utterly despised as barbar-
10 ous. In sum, the whole inclination and bent of those times was rather towards copie than weight.

Here therefore [is] the first distemper of learning, when men study words and not matter: whereof though I have represented an example of late times, yet it hath been and will be *secundum majus et minus* [more or less] in all time. And how is it possible but this should have an operation to discredit learning, even with vulgar capacities, when they see learned men's works like the first letter of a patent or limned book; which though it hath large flourishes, yet it is but a letter? It seems to me that
20 Pygmalion's frenzy is a good emblem or portraiture of this vanity: for words are but the images of matter; and except they have life of reason and invention, to fall in love with them is all one as to fall in love with a picture.

But yet notwithstanding it is a thing not hastily to be condemned, to clothe and adorn the obscurity even of philosophy itself with sensible and plausible elocution. For hereof we have great examples in Xenophon, Cicero, Seneca, Plutarch, and of Plato also in some degree; and hereof likewise there is great use; for surely to the severe inquisition of truth, and the deep pro-
30 gress into philosophy, it is some hinderance; because it is too early satisfactory to the mind of man, and quencheth the desire of further search, before we come to a just period; but then if a man be to have any use of such knowledge in civil occasions, of conference, counsel, persuasion, discourse, or the like; then shall he find it prepared to his hands in those authors which write in that manner. But the excess of this is so justly contemptible, that as Hercules, when he saw the image of Adonis, Venus' minion, in a temple, said in disdain, *Nil sacri es,* [you are no divinity;] so there is none of Hercules' followers in
40 learning, that is, the more severe and laborious sort of inquirers into truth, but will despise those delicacies and affectations, as

indeed capable of no divineness. And thus much of the first
disease or distemper of learning.

The second, which followeth, is in nature worse than the
former; for as substance of matter is better than beauty of
words, so contrariwise vain matter is worse than vain words:
wherein it seemeth the reprehension of St. Paul was not only
proper for those times, but prophetical for the times following;
and not only respective to divinity, but extensive to all knowledge: *Devita profanas vocum novitates, et oppositiones falsi nominis*
10 *scientiæ*: [shun profane novelties of terms and oppositions of
science falsely so called]. For he assigneth two marks and
badges of suspected and falsified science; the one, the novelty
and strangeness of terms; the other, the strictness of positions,
which of necessity doth induce oppositions, and so questions
and altercations. Surely, like as many substances in nature which
are solid do putrefy and corrupt into worms, so it is the property of good and sound knowledge to putrefy and dissolve into
a number of subtile, idle, unwholesome, and (as I may term
them) vermiculate questions, which have indeed a kind of
20 quickness and life of spirit, but no soundness of matter or
goodness of quality. This kind of degenerate learning did chiefly reign amongst the schoolmen; who having sharp and strong
wits, and abundance of leisure, and small variety of reading;
but their wits being shut up in the cells of a few authors (chiefly
Aristotle their dictator) as their persons were shut up in the
cells of monasteries and colleges; and knowing little history,
either of nature or time; did out of no great quantity of matter,
and infinite agitation of wit, spin out unto us those laborious
webs of learning which are extant in their books. For the wit and
30 mind of man, if it work upon matter, which is the contemplation of the creatures of God, worketh according to the stuff,
and is limited thereby; but if it work upon itself, as the spider
worketh his web, then it is endless, and brings forth indeed cobwebs of learning, admirable for the fineness of thread and work,
but of no substance or profit.

This same unprofitable subtility or curiosity is of two sorts;
either in the subject itself that they handle, when it is a fruitless
speculation or controversy, (whereof there are no small number both in divinity and philosophy), or in the manner or
40 method of handling of a knowledge; which amongst them was
this; upon every particular position or assertion to frame ob-

jections, and to those objections, solutions; which solutions were for the most part not confutations, but distinctions: whereas indeed the strength of all sciences is, as the strength of the old man's faggot, in the bond. For the harmony of a science, supporting each part the other, is and ought to be the true and brief confutation and suppression of all the smaller sort of objections; but on the other side, if you take out every axiom, as the sticks of the faggot, one by one, you may quarrel with them and bend them and break them at your pleasure: so that
10 as was said of Seneca, *Verborum minutiis rerum frangit pondera*, [that he broke up the weight and mass of the matter by verbal points and niceties]; so a man may truly say of the schoolmen, *Quæstionum minutiis scientiarum frangunt soliditatem;* [they broke up the solidity and coherency of the sciences by the minuteness and nicety of their questions]. For were it not better for a man in a fair room to set up one great light, or branching candle-stick of lights, than to go about with a small watch candle into every corner? And such is their method, that rests not so much upon evidence of truth proved by arguments, authorities,
20 similitudes, examples, as upon particular confutations and solutions of every scruple, cavillation, and objection; breeding for the most part one question as fast it solveth another; even as in the former resemblance, when you carry the light into one corner, you darken the rest: so that the fable and fiction of Scylla seemeth to be a lively image of this kind of philosophy or knowledge; which was transformed into a comely virgin for the upper parts; but then *Candida succinctam latrantibus inguina monstris*, [there were barking monsters all about her loins]: so the generalities of the schoolmen are for a while
30 good and proportionable; but then when you descend into their distinctions and decisions, instead of a fruitful womb for the use and benefit of man's life, they end in monstrous alter-cations and barking questions. So as it is not possible but this quality of knowledge must fall under popular contempt, the people being apt to contemn truth upon occasion of controver-sies and altercations, and to think they are all out of their way which never meet: and when they see such digladiation about subtilities and matter of no use nor moment, they easily fall upon that judgment of Dionysius of Syracusa, *Verba ista sunt*
40 *senum otiosorum,* [it is the talk of old men that have nothing to do].
Notwithstanding certain it is, that if those schoolmen to their

great thirst of truth and unwearied travail of wit had joined variety and universality of reading and contemplation, they had proved excellent lights, to the great advancement of all learning and knowledge. But as they are, they are great undertakers indeed, and fierce with dark keeping; but as in the inquiry of the divine truth their pride inclined to leave the oracle of God's word and to vanish in the mixture of their own inventions, so in the inquisition of nature they ever left the oracle of God's works and adored the deceiving and deformed images which
10 the unequal mirror of their own minds or a few received authors or principles did represent unto them. And thus much for the second disease of learning.

For the third vice or disease of learning, which concerneth deceit or untruth, it is of all the rest the foulest; as that which doth destroy the essential form of knowledge, which is nothing but a representation of truth: for the truth of being and the truth of knowing are one, differing no more than the direct beam and the beam reflected. This vice therefore brancheth itself into two sorts; delight in deceiving, and aptness to be
20 deceived; imposture and credulity; which, although they appear to be of a diverse nature, the one seeming to proceed of cunning, and the other of simplicity, yet certainly they do for the most part concur: for as the verse noteth,

> Percontatorem fugito, nam garrulus idem est,

an inquisitive man is a prattler, so upon the like reason a credulous man is a deceiver. . . .

[*The Advantages of Knowledge*] To proceed now from imperial and military virtue to moral and private virtue: first, it is an assured truth which is contained in the verses,

30
> Scilicet ingenuas didicisse fideliter artes
> Emollit mores, nec sinit esse feros;

[a true proficiency in liberal learning softens and humanises the manners]. It taketh away the wildness and barbarism and fierceness of men's minds: but indeed the accent had need be upon *fideliter:* [it must be a *true* proficiency]: for a little superficial learning doth rather work a contrary effect. It taketh away all levity, temerity, and insolency, by copious suggestion of all doubts and difficulties, and acquainting the mind to balance

reasons on both sides, and to turn back the first offers and conceits of the mind, and to accept of nothing but examined and tried. It taketh away vain admiration of any thing, which is the root of all weakness. For all things are admired, either because they are new, or because they are great. For novelty, no man that wadeth in learning or contemplation throughly, but will find that printed in his heart *Nil novi super terram:* [there is nothing new under the sun]. Neither can any man marvel at the play of puppets, that goeth behind the curtain and adviseth
10 well of the motion. And for magnitude, as Alexander the Great after that he was used to great armies and the great conquests of the spacious provinces in Asia, when he received letters out of Greece of some fights and services there, which were commonly for a passage or a fort or some walled town at the most, he said, *It seemed to him that he was advertised of the battles of the frogs and the mice, that the old tales went of:* so certainly if a man meditate much upon the universal frame of nature, the earth with men upon it (the divineness of souls except) will not seem much other than an ant-hill, whereas some ants carry corn,
20 and some carry their young, and some go empty, and all to and fro a little heap of dust. It taketh away or mitigateth fear of death or adverse fortune; which is one of the greatest impediments of virtue and imperfections of manners. For if a man's mind be deeply seasoned with the consideration of the mortality and corruptible nature of things, he will easily concur with Epictetus, who went forth one day and saw a woman weeping for her pitcher of earth that was broken, and went forth the next day and saw a woman weeping for her son that was dead; and thereupon said, *Heri vidi fragilem frangi, hodie vidi mortalem*
30 *mori:* [yesterday I saw a brittle thing broken, to-day a mortal dead]. And therefore Virgil did excellently and profoundly couple the knowledge of causes and the conquest of all fears together, as *concomitantia.*

> Felix qui potuit rerum cognoscere causas,
> Quique metus omnes et inexorabile fatum
> Subjecit pedibus, strepitumque Acherontis avari.

> [Happy the man who doth the causes know
> Of all that is: serene he stands, above
> All fears; above the inexorable Fate,
40 And that insatiate gulph that roars below.]

It were too long to go over the particular remedies which learning doth minister to all the diseases of the mind; sometimes purging the ill humours, sometimes opening the obstructions, sometimes helping digestion, sometimes increasing appetite, sometimes healing the wounds and exulcerations thereof, and the like; and therefore I will conclude with that which hath *rationem totius*; which is, that it disposeth the constitution of the mind not to be fixed or settled in the defects thereof, but still to be capable and susceptible of growth and reformation.

10 For the unlearned man knows not what it is to descend into himself or to call himself to account, nor the pleasure of that *suavissima vita, indies sentire se fieri meliorem,* [to feel himself each day a better man than he was the day before]. The good parts he hath he will learn to shew to the full and use them dexterously, but not much to increase them: the faults he hath he will learn how to hide and colour them, but not much to amend them; like an ill mower, that mows on still and never whets his scythe: whereas with the learned man it fares otherwise, that he doth ever intermix the correction and amendment of his

20 mind with the use and employment thereof. Nay further, in general and in sum, certain it is that *veritas* and *bonitas* differ but as the seal and the print; for truth prints goodness, and they be the clouds of error which descend in the storms of passions and perturbations.

From moral virtue let us pass on to matter of power and commandment, and consider whether in right reason there be any comparable with that wherewith knowledge investeth and crowneth man's nature. We see the dignity of the commandment is according to the dignity of the commanded: to have

30 commandment over beasts, as herdsmen have, is a thing contemptible; to have commandment over children, as schoolmasters have, is a matter of small honour; to have commandment over galley-slaves is a disparagement rather than an honour. Neither is the commandment of tyrants much better, over people which have put off the generosity of their minds: and therefore it was ever holden that honours in free monarchies and commonwealths had a sweetness more than in tyrannies; because the commandment extendeth more over the wills of men, and not only over their deeds and services. And therefore

40 when Virgil putteth himself forth to attribute to Augustus Cæsar the best of human honours, he doth it in these words:

victorque volentes
Per populos dat jura, viamque affectat Olympo:
[Moving in conquest onward, at his will
To willing peoples he gives laws, and shapes
Through worthiest deeds on earth his course to Heaven.]

But yet the commandment of knowledge is yet higher than the commandment over the will; for it is a commandment over the reason, belief, and understanding of man, which is the highest part of the mind, and giveth law to the will itself. For there is no power on earth which setteth up a throne or chair of estate in the spirits and souls of men, and in their cogitations, imaginations, opinions, and beliefs, but knowledge and learning. And therefore we see the detestable and extreme pleasure that archheretics and false prophets and impostors are transported with, when they once find in themselves that they have a superiority in the faith and conscience of men; so great, that if they have once tasted of it, it is seldom seen that any torture or persecution can make them relinquish or abandon it. But as this is that which the author of the Revelation calleth the depth or profoundness of Satan; so by argument of contraries, the just and lawful sovereignty over men's understanding, by force of truth rightly interpreted, is that which approacheth nearest to the similitude of the divine rule.

As for fortune and advancement, the beneficence of learning is not so confined to give fortune only to states and commonwealths, as it doth not likewise give fortune to particular persons. For it was well noted long ago, that Homer hath given more men their livings than either Sylla or Caesar or Augustus ever did, notwithstanding their great largesses and donatives and distributions of lands to so many legions. And no doubt it is hard to say whether arms or learning have advanced greater numbers. And in case of sovereignty, we see that if arms or descent have carried away the kingdom, yet learning hath carried the priesthood, which ever hath been in some competition with empire.

Again, for the pleasure and delight of knowledge and learning, it far surpasseth all other in nature: for shall the pleasures of the affections so exceed the senses, as much as the obtaining of desire or victory exceedeth a song or a dinner; and must not of consequence the pleasures of the intellect or understanding

exceed the pleasures of the affections? We see in all other pleasures there is satiety, and after they be used, their verdure departeth; which sheweth well they be but deceits of pleasure, and not pleasures; and that it was the novelty which pleased, and not the quality. And therefore we see that voluptuous men turn friars, and ambitious princes turn melancholy. But of knowledge there is no satiety, but satisfaction and appetite are perpetually interchangeable; and therefore [it] appeareth to be good in itself simply, without fallacy or accident. Neither is
10 that pleasure of small efficacy and contentment to the mind of man, which the poet Lucretius describeth elegantly,

Suave mari magno, turbantibus æquora ventis, &c.

It is a view of delight (saith he) *to stand or walk upon the shore side, and to see a ship tossed with tempest upon the sea; or to be in a fortified tower, and to see two battles join upon a plain. But it is a pleasure incomparable, for the mind of man to be settled, landed, and fortified in the certainty of truth; and from thence to descry and behold the errors, perturbations, labours, and wanderings up and down of other men.*

Lastly, leaving the vulgar arguments, that by learning man
20 excelleth man in that wherein man excelleth beasts; that by learning man ascendeth to the heavens and their motions, where in body he cannot come; and the like; let us conclude with the dignity and excellency of knowledge and learning in that whereunto man's nature doth most aspire; which is immortality or continuance; for to this tendeth generation, and raising of houses and families; to this buildings, foundations, and monuments; to this tendeth the desire of memory, fame, and celebration; and in effect, the strength of all other human desires. We see then how far the monuments of wit and learning
30 are more durable than the monuments of power or of the hands. For have not the verses of Homer continued twenty-five hundred years or more, without the loss of a syllable or letter; during which time infinite palaces, temples, castles, cities, have been decayed and demolished? It is not possible to have the true pictures or statuaes of Cyrus, Alexander, Cæsar, no nor of the kings or great personages of much later years; for the originals cannot last, and the copies cannot but leese of the life and truth. But the images of men's wits and knowledges remain in books, exempted from the wrong of time and capable of perpetual
40 renovation. Neither are they fitly to be called images, because

they generate still, and cast their seeds in the minds of others, provoking and causing infinite actions and opinions in succeeding ages. So that if the invention of the ship was thought so noble, which carrieth riches and commodities from place to place, and consociateth the most remote regions in participation of their fruits, how much more are letters to be magnified, which as ships pass through the vast seas of time, and make ages so distant to participate of the wisdom, illuminations, and inventions, the one of the other? Nay further, we see some of
10 the philosophers which were least divine and most immersed in the senses and denied generally the immortality of the soul, yet came to this point, that whatsoever motions the spirit of man could act and perform without the organs of the body they thought might remain after death; which were only those of the understanding, and not of the affection; so immortal and incorruptible a thing did knowledge seem unto them to be. But we, that know by divine revelation that not only the understanding but the affections purified, not only the spirit but the body changed, shall be advanced to immortality, do disclaim
20 in these rudiments of the senses. But it must be remembered both in this last point, and so it may likewise be needful in other places, that in probation of the dignity of knowledge or learning I did in the beginning separate divine testimony from human; which method I have pursued, and so handled them both apart.

   Nevertheless I do not pretend, and I know it will be impossible for me by any pleading of mine, to reverse the judgment, either of Æsop's cock, that preferred the barleycorn before the gem; or of Midas, that being chosen judge between Apollo
30 president of the Muses, and Pan god of the flocks, judged for plenty; or of Paris, that judged for beauty and love against wisdom and power; or of Agrippina, *occidat matrem, modo imperet*, [let him kill his mother so he be emperor], that preferred empire with condition never so detestable; or of Ulysses, *qui vetulam prætulit immortalitati*, [that preferred an old woman to an immortality,] being a figure of those which prefer custom and habit before all excellency; or of a number of the like popular judgments. For these things continue as they have been: but so will that also continue whereupon learning hath ever
40 relied, and which faileth not: *Justificata est sapientia a filiis suis:* [wisdom is justified of her children].

[*Fallacies in the Human Mind*] Now we pass unto the arts of Judgment, which handle the natures of Proofs and Demonstrations; which as to Induction hath a coincidence with Invention; *for in all inductions, whether in good or vicious form, the same action of the mind which inventeth, judgeth; all one as in the sense;* but otherwise it is in proof by syllogism; for the proof being not immediate but by mean, *the invention of the mean* is one thing, and the *judgment of the consequence* is another; the one exciting only, the other examining. Therefore for the real and exact form of judgment
10 we refer ourselves to that which we have spoken of *Interpretation of Nature*.

For the other judgment by Syllogism, as it is a thing most agreeable to the mind of man, so it hath been vehemently and excellently laboured. For the nature of man doth extremely covet to have somewhat in his understanding fixed and immoveable, and as a rest and support of the mind. And therefore as Aristotle endeavoureth to prove that in all motion there is some point quiescent; and as he elegantly expoundeth the ancient fable of Atlas (that stood fixed and bare up the heaven
20 from falling) to be meant of the poles or axle-tree of heaven, whereupon the conversion is accomplished; so assuredly men have a desire to have an Atlas or axle-tree within to keep them from fluctuation, which is like to a perpetual peril of falling; therefore men did hasten to set down some Principles about which the variety of their disputations might turn.

So then this art of Judgment is but *the reduction of propositions to principles in a middle term:* the Principles to be agreed by all and exempted from argument; the Middle Term to be elected at the liberty of every man's invention; the Reduction to be of
30 two kinds, direct and inverted; the one when the proposition is reduced to the principle, which they term a *Probation ostensive*; the other when the contradictory of the proposition is reduced to the contradictory of the principle, which is that which they call *per incommodum*, or *pressing an absurdity*; the number of middle terms to be as the proposition standeth degrees more or less removed from the principle.

But this art hath two several methods of doctrine; the one by way of direction, the other by way of caution: the former
40 frameth and setteth down a true form of consequence, by the variations and deflexions from which errors and inconsequences

may be exactly judged; toward the composition and structure of which form, it is incident to handle the parts thereof, which are propositions, and the parts of propositions, which are simple words; and this is that part of logic which is comprehended in the Analytics.

The second method of doctrine was introduced for expedite use and assurance sake; discovering the more subtile forms of sophisms and illaqueations with their redargutions, which is that which is termed *Elenches*. For although in the more gross
10 sorts of fallacies it happeneth (as Seneca maketh the comparison well) as in juggling feats, which though we know not how they are done, yet we know well it is not as it seemeth to be; yet the more subtile sort of them doth not only put a man besides his answer, but doth many times abuse his judgment.

This part concerning *Elenches* is excellently handled by Aristotle in precept, but more excellently by Plato in example, not only in the persons of the Sophists, but even in Socrates himself; who professing to affirm nothing, but to infirm that which was affirmed by another, hath exactly expressed all the forms
20 of objection, fallace, and redargution. And although we have said that the use of this doctrine is for redargution, yet it is manifest the degenerate and corrupt use is for caption and contradiction; which passeth for a great faculty, and no doubt is of very great advantage: though the difference be good which was made between orators and sophisters, that the one is as the greyhound, which hath his advantage in the race, and the other as the hare, which hath her advantage in the turn, so as it is the advantage of the weaker creature.

But yet further, this doctrine of *Elenches* hath a more ample
30 latitude and extent than is perceived; namely, unto divers parts of knowledge; whereof some are laboured and other omitted. For first, I conceive (though it may seem at first somewhat strange) that that part which is variably referred sometimes to Logic sometimes to Metaphysic, touching the *common adjuncts of essences*, is but an elenche; for the great sophism of all sophisms being equivocation or ambiguity of words and phrase, specially of such words as are most general and intervene in every inquiry, it seemeth to me that the true and fruitful use (leaving vain subtilties and speculations) of the inquiry of
40 majority, minority, priority, posteriority, identity, diversity, possibility, act, totality, parts, existence, privation, and the

like, are but wise cautions against ambiguities of speech. So again the distribution of things into certain tribes, which we call categories or predicaments, are but cautions against the confusion of definitions and divisions.

Secondly, there is a seducement that worketh by the strength of the impression and not by the subtilty of the illaqueation; not so much perplexing the reason as overruling it by power of the imagination. But this part I think more proper to handle when I shall speak of Rhetoric.

10 But lastly, there is yet a much more important and profound kind of fallacies in the mind of man, which I find not observed or enquired at all, and think good to place here, as that which of all others appertaineth most to rectify judgment: the force whereof is such, as it doth not dazzle or snare the understanding in some particulars, but doth more generally and inwardly infect and corrupt the state thereof. For the mind of man is far from the nature of a clear and equal glass, wherein the beams of things should reflect according to their true incidence; nay, it is rather like an enchanted glass, full of superstition and
20 imposture, if it be not delivered and reduced. For this purpose, let us consider the false appearances that are imposed upon us by the general nature of the mind, beholding them in an example or two; as first, in that instance which is the root of all superstition, namely, *That to the nature of the mind of all men it is consonant for the affirmative or active to affect more than the negative or privative:* so that a few times hitting or presence, countervails oft-times failing or absence; as was well answered by Diagoras to him that shewed him in Neptune's temple the great number of pictures of such as had scaped shipwrack and had paid their
30 vows to Neptune, saying, *Advise now, you that think it folly to invocate Neptune in tempest: Yea but* (saith Diagoras) *where are they painted that are drowned?* Let us behold it in another instance, namely, *That the spirit of man, being of an equal and uniform substance, doth usually suppose and feign in nature a greater equality and uniformity than is in truth.* Hence it cometh that the mathematicians cannot satisfy themselves, except they reduce the motions of the celestial bodies to perfect circles, rejecting spiral lines, and labouring to be discharged of eccentrics. Hence it cometh, that whereas there are many things in nature as it were *monodica*,
40 *sui juris*, [singular, and like nothing but themselves;] yet the cogitations of man do feign unto them relatives, parallels, and

conjugates, whereas no such thing is; as they have feigned an
element of Fire, to keep square with Earth, Water, and Air,
and the like: nay, it is not credible, till it be opened, what a
number of fictions and fancies the similitude of human actions
and arts, together with the making of man *communis mensura*,
have brought into Natural Philosophy; not much better than
the heresy of the Anthropomorphites, bred in the cells of gross
and solitary monks, and the opinion of Epicurus, answerable
to the same in heathenism, who supposed the gods to be of
10 human shape. And therefore Velleius the Epicurian needed not
to have asked, why God should have adorned the heavens with
stars, as if he had been an Ædilis, one that should have set forth
some magnificent shews or plays. For if that great work-master
had been of an human disposition, he would have cast the stars
into some pleasant and beautiful works and orders, like the
frets in the roofs of houses; whereas one can scarce find a posture in square or triangle or straight line amongst such an
infinite number; so differing an harmony there is between the
spirit of Man and the spirit of Nature.
20 Let us consider again the false appearances imposed upon us
by every man's own individual nature and custom, in that
feigned supposition that Plato maketh of the cave: for certainly
if a child were continued in a grot or cave under the earth
until maturity of age, and came suddenly abroad, he would
have strange and absurd imaginations; so in like manner, although our persons live in the view of heaven, yet our spirits
are included in the caves of our own complexions and customs;
which minister unto us infinite errors and vain opinions, if they
be not recalled to examination. But hereof we have given
30 many examples in one of the errors, or peccant humours, which
we ran briefly over in our first book.
And lastly, let us consider the false appearances that are imposed upon us by words, which are framed and applied according to the conceit and capacities of the vulgar sort: and although
we think we govern our words, and prescribe it well, *Loquendum
ut vulgus, sentiendum ut sapientes*, [a man should speak like the
vulgar, and think like the wise]; yet certain it is that words,
as a Tartar's bow, do shoot back upon the understanding of the
wisest, and mightily entangle and pervert the judgment; so as
40 it is almost necessary in all controversies and disputations to
imitate the wisdom of the Mathematicians, in setting down in

the very beginning the definitions of our words and terms, that others may know how we accept and understand them, and whether they concur with us or no. For it cometh to pass for want of this, that we are sure to end there where we ought to have begun, which is in questions and differences about words. To conclude therefore, it must be confessed that it is not possible to divorce ourselves from these fallacies and false appearances, because they are inseparable from our nature and condition of life; so yet nevertheless the caution of them (for all
10 elenches, as was said, are but cautions) doth extremely import the true conduct of human judgment.

From The *Essays* (1625)
Of Truth

What is Truth? said jesting Pilate; and would not stay for an answer. Certainly there be that delight in giddiness, and count it a bondage to fix a belief; affecting free-will in thinking, as well as in acting. And though the sects of philosophers of that kind be gone, yet there remain certain discoursing wits which are of the same veins, though there be not so much blood in them as was in those of the ancients. But it is not only the difficulty and labour which men take in finding out of truth;
20 nor again that when it is found it imposeth upon men's thoughts, that doth bring lies in favour; but a natural though corrupt love of the lie itself. One of the later school of the Grecians examineth the matter, and is at a stand to think what should be in it, that men should love lies, where neither they make for pleasure, as with poets, nor for advantage, as with the merchant; but for the lie's sake. But I cannot tell: this same truth is a naked and open day-light, that doth not shew the masks and mummeries and triumphs of the world, half so stately and daintily as candle-lights. Truth may perhaps come to the
30 price of a pearl, that sheweth best by day; but it will not rise to the price of a diamond or carbuncle, that sheweth best in varied lights. A mixture of a lie doth ever add pleasure. Doth any man doubt, that if there were taken out of men's minds vain opinions, flattering hopes, false valuations, imaginations as one would, and the like, but it would leave the minds of a number of men poor shrunken things, full of melancholy and indisposition, and unpleasing to themselves? One of the

Fathers, in great severity, called poesy *vinum dæmonum* [devil's-wine], because it filleth the imagination; and yet it is but with the shadow of a lie. But it is not the lie that passeth through the mind, but the lie that sinketh in and settleth in it, that doth the hurt; such as we spake of before. But howsoever these things are thus in men's depraved judgments and affections, yet truth, which only doth judge itself, teacheth that the inquiry of truth, which is the love-making or wooing of it, the knowledge of truth, which is the presence of it, and the belief of truth, which
10 is the enjoying of it, is the sovereign good of human nature. The first creature of God, in the works of the days, was the light of the sense; the last was the light of reason; and his sabbath work ever since, is the illumination of his Spirit. First he breathed light upon the face of the matter or chaos; then he breathed light into the face of man; and still he breatheth and inspireth light into the face of his chosen. The poet that beautified the sect that was otherwise inferior to the rest, saith yet excellently well: *It is a pleasure to stand upon the shore, and to see ships tossed upon the sea; a pleasure to stand in the window of a castle,*
20 *and to see a battle and the adventures thereof below: but no pleasure is comparable to the standing upon the vantage ground of Truth,* (a hill not to be commanded, and where the air is always clear and serene,) *and to see the errors, and wanderings, and mists, and tempests, in the vale below;* so always that this prospect be with pity, and not with swelling or pride. Certainly, it is heaven upon earth, to have a man's mind move in charity, rest in providence, and turn upon the poles of truth.

To pass from theological and philosophical truth, to the truth of civil business; it will be acknowledged even by those
30 that practise it not, that clear and round dealing is the honour of man's nature; and that mixture of falsehood is like allay in coin of gold and silver, which may make the metal work the better, but it embaseth it. For these winding and crooked courses are the goings of the serpent; which goeth basely upon the belly, and not upon the feet. There is no vice that doth so cover a man with shame as to be found false and perfidious. And therefore Montaigne saith prettily, when he inquired the reason, why the word of the lie should be such a disgrace and such an odious charge? Saith he, *If it be well weighted, to say that*
40 *a man lieth, is as much to say, as that he is brave towards God and a coward towards men.* For a lie faces God, and shrinks from man.

Surely the wickedness of falsehood and breach of faith cannot possibly be so highly expressed, as in that it shall be the last peal to call the judgments of God upon the generations of men; it being foretold, that when Christ cometh, *he shall not find faith upon the earth*.

Of Adversity

It was a high speech of Seneca (after the manner of the Stoics), *that the good things which belong to prosperity are to be wished; but the good things that belong to adversity are to be admired. Bona rerum secundarum optabilia; adversarum mirabilia.* Certainly if miracles
10 be the command over nature, they appear most in adversity. It is yet a higher speech of his than the other (much too high for a heathen), *It is true greatness to have in one the frailty of a man, and the security of a God. Vere magnum habere fragilitatem hominis, securitatem Dei.* This would have done better in poesy, where transcendences are more allowed. And the poets indeed have been busy with it; for it is in effect the thing which is figured in that strange fiction of the ancient poets, which seemeth not to be without mystery; nay, and to have some approach to the state of a Christian; that *Hercules, when he went to unbind Prome-*
20 *theus* (by whom human nature is represented), *sailed the length of the great ocean in an earthen pot or pitcher;* lively describing Christian resolution, that saileth in the frail bark of the flesh through the waves of the world. But to speak in a mean. The virtue of Prosperity is temperance, the virtue of Adversity is fortitude; which in morals is the more heroical virtue. Prosperity is the blessing of the Old Testament; Adversity is the blessing of the New; which carrieth the greater benediction, and the clearer revelation of God's favour. Yet even in the Old Testa-
30 ment, if you listen to David's harp, you shall hear as many hearse-like airs as carols; and the pencil of the Holy Ghost hath laboured more in describing the afflictions of Job than the felicities of Salomon. Prosperity is not without many fears and distastes; and Adversity is not without comforts and hopes. We see in needle-works and embroideries, it is more pleasing to have a lively work upon a sad and solemn ground, than to have a dark and melancholy work upon a lightsome ground: judge therefore of the pleasure of the heart by the pleasure of the eye. Certainly virtue is like precious odours, most fragrant when
40 they are incensed or crushed: for Prosperity doth best discover vice, but Adversity doth best discover virtue.

Of Goodness and Goodness of Nature

I take Goodness in this sense, the affecting of the weal of men, which is that the Grecians call *Philanthropia*; and the word *humanity* (as it is used) is a little too light to express it. Goodness I call the habit, and Goodness of Nature the inclination. This of all virtues and dignities of the mind is the greatest; being the character of the Deity: and without it man is a busy, mischievous, wretched thing; no better than a kind of vermin. Goodness answers to the theological virtue Charity, and admits no excess, but error. The desire of power in excess
10 caused the angels to fall; the desire of knowledge in excess caused man to fall: but in charity there is no excess; neither can angel or man come in danger by it. The inclination to goodness is imprinted deeply in the nature of man, insomuch that if it issue not towards men, it will take unto other living creatures; as it is seen in the Turks, a cruel people, who nevertheless are kind to beasts, and give alms to dogs and birds; insomuch as Busbechius reporteth, a Christian boy in Constantinople had like to have been stoned for gagging in a waggishness a long-billed fowl. Errors indeed in this virtue of goodness or charity
20 may be committed. The Italians have an ungracious proverb, *Tanto buon che val niente; So good, that he is good for nothing.* And one of the doctors of Italy, Nicholas Machiavel, had the confidence to put in writing, almost in plain terms, *That the Christian faith had given up good men in prey to those that are tyrannical and unjust.* Which he spake, because indeed there was never law, or sect, did so much magnify goodness, as the Christian religion doth. Therefore, to avoid the scandal and the danger both, it is good to take knowledge of the errors of an habit so excellent. Seek the good of other men, but be not in bondage to their faces or
30 fancies; for that is but facility or softness; which taketh an honest mind prisoner. Neither give thou Æsop's cock a gem, who would be better pleased and happier if he had a barley-corn. The example of God teacheth the lesson truly; *He sendeth his rain, and maketh his sun to shine, upon the just and unjust;* but he doth not rain wealth, nor shine honour and virtues, upon men equally. Common benefits are to be communicate with all; but peculiar benefits with choice. And beware how in making the portraiture thou breakest the pattern. For divinity maketh the love of ourselves the pattern; the love of our neighbours but

the portraiture. *Sell all thou hast, and give it to the poor, and follow me:* but sell not all thou hast, except thou come and follow me; that is, except thou have a vocation wherein thou mayest do as much good with little means as with great; for otherwise in feeding the streams thou driest the fountain. Neither is there only a habit of goodness, directed by right reason; but there is in some men, even in nature, a disposition towards it; as on the other side there is a natural malignity. For there be that in their nature do not affect the good of others. The lighter sort

10 of malignity turneth but to a crossness, or frowardness, or aptness to oppose, or difficilness, or the like; but the deeper sort to envy and mere mischief. Such men in other men's calamities are, as it were, in season, and are ever on the loading part: not so good as the dogs that licked Lazarus' sores; but like flies that are still buzzing upon any thing that is raw; *misanthropi*, that make it their practice to bring men to the bough, and yet have never a tree for the purpose in their gardens, as Timon had. Such dispositions are the very errours of human nature; and yet they are the fittest timber to make great politiques of; like to

20 knee timber, that is good for ships, that are ordained to be tossed; but not for building houses, that shall stand firm. The parts and signs of goodness are many. If a man be gracious and courteous to strangers, it shews he is a citizen of the world, and that his heart is no island cut off from other lands, but a continent that joins to them. If he be compassionate towards the afflictions of others, it shews that his heart is like the noble tree that is wounded itself when it gives the balm. If he easily pardons and remits offences, it shews that his mind is planted above injuries; so that he cannot be shot. If he be thankful for

30 small benefits, it shews that he weighs men's minds, and not their trash. But above all, if he have St. Paul's perfection, that he would wish to be an *anathema* from Christ for the salvation of his brethren, it shews much of a divine nature, and a kind of conformity with Christ himself.

Of Wisdom for a Man's Self

An ant is a wise creature for itself, but it is a shrewd thing in an orchard or garden. And certainly men that are great lovers of themselves waste the public. Divide with reason between self-love and society; and be so true to thyself, as thou be not false to others; specially to thy king and country. It is a poor centre

of a man's actions, *himself*. It is right earth. For that only stands
fast upon his own centre; whereas all things that have affinity
with the heavens, move upon the centre of another, which
they benefit. The referring of all to a man's self is more tolerable
in a sovereign prince; because themselves are not only themselves, but their good and evil is at the peril of the public fortune.
But it is a desperate evil in a servant to a prince, or a citizen in
a republic. For whatsoever affairs pass such a man's hands, he
crooketh them to his own ends; which must needs be often
10 eccentric to the ends of his master or state. Therefore let princes,
or states, choose such servants as have not this mark; except
they mean their service should be made but the accessary. That
which maketh the effect more pernicious is that all proportion is
lost. It were disproportion enough for the servant's good to be
preferred before the master's; but yet it is a greater extreme,
when a little good of the servant shall carry things against a
great good of the master's. And yet that is the case of bad
officers, treasurers, ambassadors, generals, and other false and
corrupt servants; which set a bias upon their bowl, of their own
20 petty ends and envies, to the overthrow of their master's great
and important affairs. And for the most part, the good such
servants receive is after the model of their own fortune; but
the hurt they sell for that good is after the model of their
master's fortune. And certainly it is the nature of extreme self-
lovers, as they will set an house on fire, and it were but to
roast their eggs; and yet these men many times hold credit
with their masters, because their study is but to please them and
profit themselves; and for either respect they will abandon the
good of their affairs.
30 Wisdom for man's self is, in many branches thereof, a depraved thing. It is the wisdom of rats, that will be sure to leave
a house somewhat before it fall. It is the wisdom of the fox,
that thrusts out the badger, who digged and made room for
him. It is the wisdom of crocodiles, that shed tears when they
would devour. But that which is specially to be noted is, that
those which (as Cicero says of Pompey) are *sui amantes, sine
rivali*, [lovers of themselves without rival,] are many times
unfortunate. And whereas they have all their times sacrificed
to themselves, they become in the end themselves sacrifices to
40 the inconstancy of fortune; whose wings they thought by their
self-wisdom to have pinioned.

35

II
Sir Walter Ralegh
1552?–1618

Ralegh's *History of the World* is one of the many unread books of the English Renaissance. Who now wants to read a history which begins with the Creation, is as third as long again as the complete works of Shakespeare, and yet which only gets up to the Roman conquest of Greece in the second century B.C.? Modern ignorance of this great enterprise is partly justified in that most of the work is derivative, drawing on the multitude of commentators on Genesis for Book One and thereafter on Greek, Roman, and contemporary historians (Ben Jonson claimed that he was responsible for one section, the account of the Punic War in Book Two). But Ralegh's own temperament infuses much of the writing, and in many places (especially the *Preface*) his prose is of a power and resonance outstanding even in this period. The extraordinary nature of the work is explained by its circumstances, degrading though they are: Ralegh, the courtier who under Elizabeth had existed precariously on the razor's edge between general admiration of his energy and boldness and hatred of his arrogance and ruthlessness, had not succeeded in charming James I, and in 1603 his enemies managed to get him imprisoned in the Tower for supposed plots against the King. He was under attainder for high treason, and although exempted from further proceedings he was not pardoned, and was therefore in that state which was legally known as 'civil death' (being dead in law although left alive). With the exception of his brief and fatal expedition to Orinoco in 1616 he stayed in the Tower until he was executed as a sop to the Spanish Ambassador in 1618. Of all the acts of political expediency committed by James I none continues to rankle as deeply as this.

As a slight compensation for this outrageous punishment Ralegh was allowed to lead a scholarly life in the Tower, including the pursuit of scientific experiments, and was granted books, paper, and contact with his friends. His single reference to this enforced occupation is the sardonic end to the *Preface*: 'For conclusion, all the hope I have lies in this, that I have already found more ungentle and uncourteous readers of my love towards them, and well-deserving of them, than ever I shall do again. For had it been otherwise, I should hardly have had this leisure to have made myself a fool in print.' He did not merely kill time, for his intellectual eminence brought some of the leading scientists of the day to his circle, and Ralegh shared in one of the movements in the new experimental science which resulted in the Royal Society. His cast of mind has been well analysed in two recent books,[1] E. A. Strathmann placing him in the particular current of scepticism growing in England and H. Haydn setting him in the wider European movement which he has called 'the Counter-Renaissance'. Ralegh belongs to a tradition which does not accept received authority on trust and without inquiry, and he joins Bacon and many other forward-looking minds in rejecting the authority of Aristotle:

> But for myself, I shall never be persuaded that God hath shut up all the light of learning within the lantern of Aristotle's brains. . . . That these and these be the causes of these and these effects, Time hath taught us, and not reason, and so hath experience without art. The cheese-wife knoweth it as well as the philosopher, that sour rennet doth coagulate her milk into a curd. But if we ask a reason of this cause, why the sourness doth it, whereby it doth it, and the manner how, I think that there is nothing to be found in vulgar philosophy to satisfy this and many other like vulgar questions.

By 'vulgar' Ralegh seems to mean not only 'popular' but also 'secular' for the burden of his complaint is that without divine Revelation man 'cannot give a true reason for the grass under his feet, why it should be green rather than red, or, of any other colour', and that man should therefore abandon the pride of trying to probe into God's mysteries. If on this last point he seems like Bacon, who also urged a separation of science from religion, in fact he differs: Bacon intended the separation to be complete. He thought that science could achieve its domination of the physical world without the aid of religion (he was right, of course, although many critics have not forgiven him for it) where Ralegh retained an orthodox Christian belief in Revelation as an explanation which God will offer to all problems in His own good time. So although one can find many traces of

---

[1] Details are given in 'Further Reading', below, p. 266.

rationalism and scepticism in Ralegh it will not do to label him as a New Scientist.

Ralegh differs from Bacon in several other ways, of which the two most important for the understanding of the *History* are his general estimate of the state of the world and his concept of the function of history. Bacon was an optimist and a visionary who prophesied man's eventual mastery of nature and the improvement of all human activities; Ralegh as a Christian sees man as a fallen, wretched creature who is getting worse every day. He takes over the medieval *contemptu mundi* tradition[1] which persisted in the Renaissance, and passes on the Christian pessimism of models such as St Augustine or St Chrysostom, whom he quotes at one point as support for the ultimate mortification of human glory: 'Look into the sepulchres and monuments of thy ancestors, and they shall easily persuade thee by their own example, that thou art dust and dirt.'

In complete accordance with this view of man is Ralegh's view of history. Whereas for Bacon, with his deep interest in the empirical basis of the Italian historians Machiavelli and Guicciardini (see the study by H. Haydn mentioned above), history existed as an almost neutral source for the analysis of human behaviour and for the establishment of general laws and principles of politics and statecraft, Ralegh shared the traditional moral idea of history as a series of object lessons demonstrating God's judgments on wicked men: 'In a word, we may gather out of history a policy no less wise than eternal; by the comparison and application of other men's fore-passed miseries with our own like errors and ill deservings.' Nothing is said about good examples, nor about our own potential to good: man was and is a fallen worm. Ralegh's own contribution to this tradition is to show how 'ill-doing hath always been attended with ill success', and if in the body of the work he did not get beyond the Greeks and Romans he makes up for this in the *Preface* by drawing on modern history to demonstrate 'what labour, practice, peril, bloodshed and cruelty, the Kings and Princes of the world have undergone'. What follows is the most devastating potted history of England imaginable, an account of English kings from Henry I to James I selecting only the evil, treachery, and murder which they were involved in, all of

[1] The Christian tradition which encouraged a contempt for the world and all its vanity as an essential stage in preparing the soul for Heaven.

which brought not happiness but endless misery. The account concludes, ironically enough, with a panegyric of James I for not having 'any drop of the innocent blood on the sword of his justice, with which the most that forewent him have stained both their hands and fame': Ralegh himself was to prove that idle praise.

The picture of man presented by history here is a bleak one, but Ralegh's use of the Christian tactic of mortifying human pride and vanity means that he is constantly widening his attack to include not only kings but all men, human nature itself. The emotional tone of the work is therefore dark, plangent, pessimistic, and Ralegh's peculiar brand of sad eloquence (seen often in his poetry, best of all in that great work *The Ocean's Love to Cynthia*) makes the reading of it a potentially depressing experience. It is saved from being merely bleak by the firm moral basis from which Ralegh discriminates: evil and vice are attacked and 'only those few black swans' who have maintained honour and truth are spared. He does not really use satire, but the *Preface* is effective in alienating us from human monstrosities in the same way that *Gulliver's Travels* is. The force of Ralegh's eloquence, however, is never indirect but proceeds in a straight uncompromising line using all the resources of structure and imagery. In structure, as one might expect from the poetry, Ralegh uses slow, repetitive patterns, but always adjusted to the meaning, such as the significant echoing of the words 'brake faith' in the first sentence describing Henry IV, or the indignant outburst on Henry VIII, where the parallel structure of the sentences points up the mechanical yet unpredictable nature of that ruler's love and hate. These are effective uses of symmetry, but Ralegh can achieve much more complex imaginative exploitations of the principles of expected and unexpected recurrence within a fixed frame, such as this despairing analysis of that terrible paradox (or rather, oxymoron), a 'holy war':

> there is nothing more to be admired,
>   and more to be lamented,
>   than the private contention,
>   the passionate dispute,
>   the personal hatred,
>   and the perpetual war, massacres, and murders,
>   for religion among Christians;

> the discourse whereof hath so occupied the world,
>   as it hath well-near driven
> the practice thereof   out of the world.

In addition to the enormous stress given directly to the sense by the parallel structure and sound there, Ralegh surprises us by the tripling of terms at 'wars, massacres, and murders', and effectively juxtaposes those horrifying words with the almost contradictory ones 'for religion among Christians', especially as these form the main point of the sentence and have been held back till now; again, the recurrence of the ending 'the world' shifts the stress back to the preceding words 'out of', with all the sad implications of that. Many fine examples of syntactical symmetry can be found, not least in the last few paragraphs of the work where the address to Death falls into an almost exact antithetical balance as if to suggest the smooth and inevitable nature of its victory.

Ralegh's imagery is so poetic and so densely scattered that it is hardly necessary to draw attention to it. Not only does he use metaphor very powerfully in particular contexts but he reapplies with great force a traditional image until it becomes almost thematic, that of life as a play and man as an actor—and, from Ralegh's viewpoint, inevitably an actor in a series of humiliating or destructive roles. Richard III was the 'greatest master of mischief' and 'although, for the necessity of his tragedy, he had more parts to play, and more to perform in his own person, than all the rest; yet he so well fitted every affection that played with him, as if each of them had but acted his own interest'. Man's hypocrisy in pretending to have faith is so great that 'We are all (in effect) become comedians in religion . . .', but retribution will follow, and Ralegh takes up the theatrical metaphor later on in the *Preface* to construct a characteristically prolonged extension of metaphor through all its appropriate parts in order to put several more nails into the coffin of human pride:

> For, seeing God, who is the author of all our tragedies, hath written out for us and appointed all the parts we are to play, and hath not, in their distribution, been partial to the most mighty Princes of the world; that gave unto Darius the part of the greatest Emperor, and the part of the most miserable beggar—a beggar, begging water of an enemy to quench

the great drought of death; that appointed Bajazet to play the Grand Seignior of the Turks in the morning, and in the same day, the footstool of Tamerlane (both which parts Valerian had also played, being taken by Sapores); that made Bellisarius play the most victorious captain and lastly the part of a blind beggar; of which, examples of many thousands may be produced: why should other men, who are but as the least worms, complain of wrongs? Certainly, there is no other account to be made of this ridiculous World, than to resolve, that the change of Fortune on the great theatre, is but as the change of garments on the less. For, when on the one and the other, every man wears but his own skin, the players are all alike. . . . For, seeing Death, in the end of the play takes form all whatsoever fortune or force takes from any one, it were a foolish madness in the shipwreck of wordly things, where all sinks but the sorrow, to save it.

Of all the many Renaissance versions of the *Theatrum Mundi*[1] image, only one or two exceed Ralegh's in power or realization: it ranks with Macbeth's vision of the meaninglessness of existence.

> Life's but a walking shadow, a poor player,
> That struts and frets his hour upon the stage,
> And then is heard no more.

The characteristics of Ralegh's imagery shown there—a vivid, almost three-dimensional projection of the metaphor, preferably a long development of all the analogies inherent within it—can be seen in several places in the excerpts given here. Ralegh is particularly good at bringing out meaningful connections within the image in a fully realized way, as, in the passage just quoted, the detail pinning down the connection between the futility of display on both stages: 'Every man wears but his own skin, the players are all alike'; or in this concrete development of the *memento mori* idea: Death 'holds a glass before the eyes of the most beautiful, and makes them see therein their deformity and rottenness, and they acknowledge it'; or in the degrading metaphor for the sycophancy of lovers

[1] On the traditional metaphor of the world as a stage see E. R. Curtius, *European Literature*, (especially pp. 134–44) and Anne Righter, *Shakespeare and the Idea of the Play*, Chatto, 1962; Penguin, 1967.

of the world: 'They dive under water, like ducks, at every
pebble-stone that is but thrown towards them by a powerful
hand.' It is idle to dispute that in images such as these
Ralegh gives prose the imaginative explosion which we think
of as being the prerogative of poetry: his images illuminate the
topic, strengthen the argument, and move the reader emotionally. One last example must be that sentence which moves from
a superbly condensed image for the rarity of human goodness
through sober balanced clauses to the only point which gives
Ralegh or his readers any peace of mind:

> Only those few black swans I must except, who,
> having had the grace to value wordly vanities at
> no more than their own price, do, by retaining the
> comfortable memory of a well-acted life,
> > behold death without dread,
> > > and the grave without fear;
> and embrace both, as necessary guides to endless glory.

From *The History of the World* (1614)

THE PREFACE

[*The Uses of History*] To me it belongs in the first part of this
preface, following the common and approved custom of those
who have left the memories of time past to after-ages, to give,
as near as I can, the same right to history which they have done.
Yet seeing therein I should but borrow other men's words, I
will not trouble the reader with the repetition. True it is, that
among many other benefits, for which it hath been honoured,
in this one it triumpheth over all human knowledge, that it
hath given us life in our understanding, since the world itself
had life and beginning, even to this day: yea it hath triumphed
over time, which, besides it, nothing but eternity hath triumphed
over: for it hath carried our knowledge over the vast and de-
vouring space of so many thousands of years, and given so fair
and piercing eyes to our mind, that we plainly behold living
now, as if we had lived then, that great world, *magni Dei
sapiens opus*, 'the wise work,' saith Hermes, 'of a great God,' as it
was then, when but new to itself. By it, I say, it is, that we live
in the very time when it was created; we behold how it was governed; how it was covered with waters, and again repeopled;

how kings and kingdoms have flourished and fallen; and for what virtue and piety God made prosperous, and for what vice and deformity he made wretched, both the one and the other. And it is not the least debt which we owe unto history, that it hath made us acquainted with our dead ancestors; and, out of the depth and darkness of the earth, delivered us their memory and fame. In a word, we may gather out of history a policy no less wise than eternal; by the comparison and application of other men's fore-passed miseries with our own like
10 errors and ill deservings.

[*The Evil Lives of English Kings*] To pass over the rest, till we come to Edward the Second. It is certain that after the murder of that king, the issue of blood then made, though it had some times of stay and stopping, did again break out; and that so often, and in such abundance, as all our princes of the masculine race (very few excepted) died of the same disease. And although the young years of Edward the Third made his knowledge of that horrible fact no more than suspicious; yet in that he after-wards caused his own uncle the earl of Kent to die, for no other
20 offence than the desire of his brother's redemption, whom the earl as then supposed to be living, (the king making that to be treason in his uncle, which was indeed treason in himself, had his uncle's intelligence been true;) this, I say, made it manifest, that he was not ignorant of what had passed, nor greatly desirous to have had it otherwise; though he caused Mortimer to die for the same.

This cruelty the secret and unsearchable judgment of God revenged on the grandchild of Edward the Third: and so it fell out, even to the last of that line, that in the second or third
30 descent they were all buried under the ruins of those buildings, of which the mortar had been tempered with innocent blood. For Richard the Second, who saw both his treasurers, his chancellor, and his steward, with divers others of his counsellors, some of them slaughtered by the people, others in his absence executed by his enemies; yet he always took himself for over-wise to be taught by examples. The earls of Huntington and Kent, Montague and Spencer, who thought themselves as great politicians in those days as others have done in these, hoping to please the king and to secure themselves by the murder of
40 Gloucester, died soon after, with many other their adherents,

by the like violent hands; and far more shamefully than did
that duke. And as for the king himself, (who, in regard of many
deeds, unworthy of his greatness, cannot be excused, as the
disavowing himself by breach of faith, charters, pardons, and
patents,) he was in the prime of his youth deposed, and murdered by his cousin-german and vassal, Henry of Lancaster,
afterwards Henry the Fourth.

This king, whose title was weak, and his obtaining the crown
traitorous; who brake faith with the lords at his landing, pro-
10 testing to intend only the recovery of his proper inheritance;
brake faith with Richard himself, and brake faith with all the
kingdom in parliament, to whom he swore that the deposed
king should live. After that he had enjoyed this realm some few
years, and in that time had been set upon on all sides by his
subjects, and never free from conspiracies and rebellions; he
saw (if souls immortal see and discern any things after the body's
death) his grandchild Henry the Sixth, and his son the prince,
suddenly, and without mercy, murdered; the possession of the
crown (for which he had caused so much blood to be poured
20 out) transferred from his race, and by the issues of his enemies
worn and enjoyed; enemies, whom by his own practice he
supposed that he had left no less powerless, than the succession
of the kingdom questionless, by entailing the same upon his
own issues by parliament. And out of doubt, human reason could
have judged no otherwise, but that these cautious provisions
of the father, seconded by the valour and signal victories of his
son Henry the Fifth, had buried the hopes of every competitor
under the despair of all reconquest and recovery. I say, that
human reason might so have judged, were not this passage of
30 Casaubon also true: *Dies, hora, momentum, evertendis dominationi-
bus sufficit, quæ adamantinis credebantur radicibus esse fundata*: 'A
day, an hour, a moment is enough to overturn the things that
seemed to have been founded and rooted in adamant.'

Now for Henry the Sixth, upon whom the great storm of his
grandfather's grievous faults fell, as it formerly had done upon
Richard the grandchild of Edward. Although he was generally
esteemed for a gentle and innocent prince, yet as he refused
the daughter of Armagnac, of the house of Navarre, the greatest
of the princes of France, to whom he was affianced, (by which
40 match he might have defended his inheritance in France,) and
married the daughter of Anjou, (by which he lost all that he

had in France,) so as in condescending to the unworthy death
of his uncle of Gloucester, the main and strong pillar of the
house of Lancaster, he drew on himself and this kingdom the
greatest joint-loss and dishonour that ever it sustained since
the Norman Conquest. Of whom it may truly be said, which a
counsellor of his own spake of Henry the Third of France,
*Qu'il estoit un fort gentil prince; mais son reigne est advenu en un fort
mauvais temps:* 'That he was a very gentle prince, but his reign
happened in a very unfortunate season.'

10   It is true, that Buckingham and Suffolk were the practisers
and contrivers of the duke's death: Buckingham and Suffolk,
because the duke gave instructions to their authority, which
otherwise under the queen had been absolute; the queen, in
respect of her personal wound, *spretæque injuria formæ*, because
Gloucester dissuaded her marriage. But the fruit was answerable
to the seed, the success to the counsel. For after the cutting
down of Gloucester, York grew up so fast, as he dared to dispute his right, both by arguments and arms; in which quarrel,
Suffolk and Buckingham, with the greatest number of their
20 adherents, were dissolved. And although, for his breach of
oath by sacrament, it pleased God to strike down York; yet his
son the earl of March, following the plain path which his father
had trodden out, despoiled Henry the father and Edward the
son both of their lives and kingdoms. And what was the end
now of that politic lady the queen, other than this, that she
lived to behold the wretched ends of all her partakers; that she
lived to look on while her husband the king, and her only son
the prince, were hewn in sunder, while the crown was set on
his head that did it. She lived to see herself despoiled of her
30 estate and of her moveables: and lastly, her father, by rendering
up to the crown of France the earldom of Provence and other
places, for the payment of fifty thousand crowns for her ran-
som, to become a stark beggar. And this was the end of that
subtilty which Siracides calleth *fine*, but *unrighteous:* for other
fruit hath it never yielded since the world was.

And now came it to Edward the Fourth's turn (though after
many difficulties) to triumph. For all the plants of Lancaster
were rooted up, one only earl of Richmond excepted, whom
also he had once bought of the duke of Britain, but could not
40 hold him. And yet was not this of Edward such a plantation as
could any way promise itself stability. For this Edward the

45

king (to omit more than many of his other cruelties) beheld and allowed the slaughter which Gloucester, Dorset, Hastings, and others, made of Edward the prince in his own presence: of which tragical actors there was not one that escaped the judgment of God in the same kind. And he which (besides the execution of his brother of Clarence, for none other offence than he himself had formed in his own imagination) instructed Gloucester to kill Henry the Sixth, his predecessor, taught him also by the same art to kill his own sons and successors, Edward
10 and Richard. *For those kings which have sold the blood of others at a low rate, have but made the market for their own enemies, to buy of theirs at the same price.*

To Edward the Fourth succeeded Richard the Third, the greatest master in mischief of all that forewent him: who although, for the necessity of his tragedy, he had more parts to play, and more to perform in his own person, than all the rest; yet he so well fitted every affection that played with him, as if each of them had but acted his own interest. For he wrought so cunningly upon the affections of Hastings and Buckingham,
20 enemies to the queen and to all her kindred, as he easily allured them to condescend, that Rivers and Grey, the king's maternal uncle and half-brother, should (for the first) be severed from him; secondly, he wrought their consent to have them imprisoned; and lastly, (for the avoiding of future inconvenience,) to have their heads severed from their bodies. And having now brought those his chief instruments to exercise that common precept which the Devil hath written on every post, namely, to depress those whom they had grieved, and to destroy those whom they had depressed; he urged that argument so far and
30 so forcibly, as nothing but the death of the young king himself and of his brother could fashion the conclusion. For he caused it to be hammered into Buckingham's head, that whensoever the king, or his brother, should have able years to exercise their power, they would take a most severe revenge of that cureless wrong, offered to their uncle and brother, Rivers and Grey.

But this was not his manner of reasoning with Hastings, whose fidelity to his master's sons was without suspect: and yet the Devil, who never dissuades by impossibility, taught him to try him; and so he did. But when he found by Catesby, who
40 sounded him, that he was not fordable, he first resolved to kill him sitting in council; wherein having failed with his sword,

he set the hangman upon him with a weapon of more weight. And because nothing else could move his appetite, he caused his head to be stricken off before he eat his dinner. A greater judgement of God than this upon Hastings I have never observed in any story. For the self-same day that the earl Rivers, Grey, and others, were (without trial of law, or offence given) by Hastings's advice executed at Pomfret; I say, Hastings himself, in the same day, and (as I take it) in the same hour, in the same lawless manner, had his head stricken off in the Tower of
10 London. But Buckingham lived a while longer; and with an eloquent oration persuaded the Londoners to elect Richard for their king. And having received the earldom of Hereford for reward, besides the high hope of marrying his daughter to the king's only son; after many grievous vexations of mind and unfortunate attempts, being in the end betrayed and delivered up by his trustiest servant, he had his head severed from his body at Salisbury, without the trouble of any of his peers. And what success had Richard himself, after all these mischiefs and murders, policies and counterpolicies to Christian religion; and
20 after such time as with a most merciless hand he had pressed out the breath of his nephews and natural lords, other than the prosperity of so short a life, as it took end ere himself could well look over and discern it? The great outcry of innocent blood obtaining at God's hands the effusion of his, who became a spectacle of shame and dishonour both to his friends and enemies.

This cruel king Henry the Seventh cut off; and was therein (no doubt) the immediate instrument of God's justice. A politic prince he was, if ever there were any; and who by the engine of
30 his wisdom beat down and overturned as many strong oppositions, both before and after he wore the crown, as ever king of England did: I say by his wisdom, because, as he ever left the reins of his affections in the hands of his profit, so he always weighed his undertakings by his abilities, leaving nothing more to hazard than so much as cannot be denied it in all human actions. He had well observed the proceedings of Louis the Eleventh, whom he followed in all that was royal or royal-like, but he was far more just, and begun not their processes whom he hated or feared by the execution, as Louis did.
40 He could never endure any mediation in rewarding his servants; and therein exceeding wise: for whatsoever himself gave,

47

he himself received back the thanks and the love, knowing it
well that the affections of men (purchased by nothing so readily
as by benefits) were trains that better became great kings than
great subjects. On the contrary, in whatsoever he grieved his
subjects, he wisely put it off on those that he found fit ministers
for such actions. Howsoever, the taking off of Stanley's head,
who set the crown on his, and the death of the young earl of
Warwick, son to George duke of Clarence, shews, as the success
also did, that he held somewhat of the errors of his ancestors;
10 for his possession in the first line ended in his grandchildren, as
that of Edward the Third and Henry the Fourth had done.

Now for king Henry the Eighth. If all the pictures and patterns of a merciless prince were lost in the world, they might all
again be painted to the life out of the story of this king. For how
many servants did he advance in haste, (but for what virtue no
man could suspect,) and with the change of his fancy ruined
again; no man knowing for what offence! To how many others
of more desert gave he abundant flowers from whence to gather
honey, and in the end of harvest burnt them in the hive! How
20 many wives did he cut off and cast off, as his fancy and affection
changed! How many princes of the blood, (whereof some of
them for age could hardly crawl towards the block,) with a
world of others of all degrees, (of whom our common chronicles
have kept the account,) did he execute! Yea, in his very death-
bed, and when he was at the point to have given his account to
God for the abundance of blood already spilt, he imprisoned
the duke of Norfolk the father, and executed the earl of Surrey
the son: the one, whose deservings he knew not how to value,
having never omitted any thing that concerned his own honour
30 and the king's service; the other, never having committed any
thing worthy of his least displeasure: the one exceeding valiant
and advised; the other no less valiant than learned, and of excellent hope. But besides the sorrows which he heaped upon the
fatherless and widows at home, and besides the vain enterprises
abroad, wherein it is thought that he consumed more treasure
than all our victorious kings did in their several conquests;
what causeless and cruel wars did he make upon his own nephew
king James the Fifth! What laws and wills did he devise, to
establish this kingdom in his own issues! using his sharpest wea-
40 pons to cut off and cut down those branches, which sprang
from the same root that himself did. And in the end (notwith-

standing these his so many irreligious provisions) it pleased
God to take away all his own, without increase; though, for
themselves in their several kinds, all princes of eminent virtue.
For these words of Samuel to Agag, king of the Amalekites, have
been verified upon many others; *As thy sword hath made other
women childless, so shall thy mother be childless among other women....*

Oh, by what plots, by what forswearings, betrayings, op-
pressions, imprisonments, tortures, poisonings, and under what
reasons of state and politic subtilty, have these forenamed kings,
10 both strangers and of our own nation, pulled the vengeance of
God upon themselves, upon theirs, and upon their prudent
ministers! and in the end have brought those things to pass for
their enemies, and seen an effect so directly contrary to all their
own counsels and cruelties; as the one could never have hoped
for themselves, and the other never have succeeded, if no such
opposition had ever been made. God hath said it, and performed
it ever; *Perdam sapientiam sapientum*, 'I will destroy the wisdom
of the wise.'

[*Man's Corrupted Nature*] But what of all this? and to what end
20 do we lay before the eyes of the living the fall and fortures of
the dead: seeing the world is the same that it hath been; and
the children of the present time will still obey their parents? It
is in the present time that all the wits of the world are exercised.
To hold the times we have, we hold all things lawful; and either
we hope to hold them for ever, or at least we hope that there is
nothing after them to be hoped for. For, as we are content to
forget our own experience, and to counterfeit the ignorance of
our own knowledge, in all things that concern ourselves; or
persuade ourselves that God hath given us letters patents to
30 pursue all our irreligious affections with a *non obstante:* so we
neither look behind us what hath been, nor before us what
shall be. It is true, that the quantity which we have is of the
body: we are by it joined to the earth; we are compounded of
earth; and we inhabit it. The heavens are high, far off, and unsearchable; we have sense and feeling of corporal things, and of
eternal grace but by revelation. No marvel then that our
thoughts are also earthly: and it is less to be wondered at, that
the words of worthless men cannot cleanse them; seeing their
doctrine and instruction, whose understanding the Holy Ghost
40 vouchsafed to inhabit, have not performed it. For as the

prophet Isaiah cried out long agone, *Lord, who hath believed our reports?* And out of doubt, as Isaiah complained then for himself and others, so are they less believed every day after other. For although religion, and the truth thereof, be in every man's mouth, yea, in the discourse of every woman, who, for the greatest number, are but *idols of vanity*; what is it other than an universal dissimulation? We profess that we know God, but by works we deny him. *Beatitudo non est divinorum cognitio, sed vita divina.* For 'beatitude doth not consist in the knowledge of divine
10 things, but in a divine life;' for the devils know them better than men. And certainly there is nothing more to be admired, and more to be lamented, than the private contention, the passionate dispute, the personal hatred, and the perpetual war, massacres, and murders, for religion among Christians; the discourse whereof hath so occupied the world, as it hath well-near driven the practice thereof out of the world. Who would not soon resolve, that took knowledge but of the religious disputations among men, and not of their lives which dispute, that there were no other thing in their desires, than the purchase of
20 heaven; and that the world itself were but used as it ought, and as an inn or place wherein to repose ourselves in passing on towards our celestial habitation? When, on the contrary, besides the discourse and outward profession, the soul hath nothing but hypocrisy. We are all (in effect) become comedians in religion; and while we act in gesture and voice divine virtues, in all the course of our lives we renounce our persons and the parts we play. ...

And if we could afford ourselves but so much leisure as to consider, that he which hath most in the world, hath, in respect
30 of the world, nothing in it; and that he, which hath the longest time lent him to live in it, hath yet no proportion at all therein, setting it either by that which is past when we were not, or by that time which is to come in which we shall abide for ever: I say, if both, to wit, our proportion in the world and our time in the world, differ not much from that which is nothing; it is not out of any excellency of understanding that we so much prize the one, which hath (in effect) no being; and so much neglect the other, which hath no ending: coverting those mortal things of the world, as if our souls were therein immortal, and
40 neglecting those things which are immortal, as if ourselves after the world were but mortal.

But let every man value his own wisdom as he pleaseth. Let the rich man think all fools, that cannot equal his abundance; the revenger esteem all negligent, that have not trodden down their opposites; the politician, all gross, that cannot merchandise their faith: yet, when we once come in sight of the port of death, to which all winds drive us; and when, by letting fall that fatal anchor which can never be weighed again, the navigation of this life takes end; then it is, I say, that our own cogitations (those sad and severe cogitations, formerly beaten from us by our health and felicity) return again, and pay us to the uttermost for all the pleasing passages of our lives past. It is then that we cry out to God for mercy; then, when ourselves can no longer exercise cruelty towards others: and it is only then that we are strucken through the soul with this terrible sentence, *that God will not be mocked.* . . .

Certainly, these wise worldlings have either found out a new God, or have made one; and in all likelihood such a leaden one as Lewis the Eleventh wore in his cap; which, when he had caused any that he feared or hated, to be killed, he would take it from his head and kiss it; beseeching it to pardon him this one evil act more, and it should be the last; which (as at other times) he did, when, by the practice of a cardinal and a falsified sacrament, he caused the earl of Armagnac to be stabbed to death; mockeries indeed fit to be used towards a leaden, but not towards the ever-living God. But of this composition are all the devout lovers of the world, that they fear all that is dureless and ridiculous: they fear the plots and practices of their opposites, and their very whisperings: they fear the opinions of men, which beat but upon shadows: they flatter and forsake the prosperous and unprosperous, be they friends or kings: yea, they dive under water, like ducks, at every pebble-stone that is but thrown towards them by a powerful hand; and, on the contrary, they shew an obstinate and giant-like valour against the terrible judgments of the all-powerful God: yea, they shew themselves gods against God, and slaves towards men; towards men whose bodies and consciences are alike rotten.

Now for the rest: if we truly examine the difference of both conditions; to wit, of the rich and mighty, whom we call fortunate; and of the poor and oppressed, whom we account wretched; we shall find the happiness of the one, and the miserable estate of the other, so tied by God to the very instant, and

both so subject to interchange, (witness the sudden downfall
of the greatest princes, and the speedy uprising of the meanest
persons,) as the one hath nothing so certain, whereof to boast;
nor the other so uncertain, whereof to bewail itself. For there
is no man so assured of his honour, of his riches, health, or life,
but that he may be deprived of either or all the very next hour
or day to come. *Quid vesper vehat, incertum est;* 'What the evening
will bring with it, it is uncertain.' *And yet ye cannot tell* (saith
St. James) *what shall be to-morrow. To-day he is set up, and to-*
10 *morrow he shall not be found; for he is turned into dust, and his purpose*
perisheth. And although the air which compasseth adversity be
very obscure, yet therein we better discern God, than in that
shining light which environeth worldly glory; through which,
for the clearness thereof, there is no vanity which escapeth our
sight. And let adversity seem what it will; to happy men, ridiculous, who make themselves merry at other men's misfortunes;
and to those under the cross, grievous: yet this is true, that for
all that is past, to the very instant, the portions remaining are
equal to either. For be it that we have lived many years, *and*
20 (according to Solomon) *in them all we have rejoiced;* or be it that
we have measured the same length of days, and therein have
evermore sorrowed: yet, looking back from our present being,
we find both the one and the other, to wit, the joy and the woe,
sailed out of sight; and death, which doth pursue us and hold
us in chase from our infancy, hath gathered it. *Quicquid ætatis*
retro est, mors tenet: 'Whatsoever of our age is past, death holds
it.' So as whosoever he be, to whom fortune hath been a servant, and the time a friend; let him but take the account of his
memory, (for we have no other keeper of our pleasures past,)
30 and truly examine what it hath reserved, either of beauty and
youth, or foregone delights; what it hath saved, that it might
last, of his dearest affections, or of whatever else the amorous
spring-time gave his thoughts of contentment, then unvaluable;
and he shall find, that all the art which his elder years have, can
draw no other vapour out of these dissolutions, than heavy,
secret, and sad sighs. He shall find nothing remaining but those
sorrows which grow up after our fast springing youth; overtake it, when it is at a stand; and overtop it utterly, when it
begins to wither: insomuch, as looking back from the very
40 instant time, and from our now being, the poor, diseased, and
captive creature hath as little sense of all his former miseries

and pains, as he that is most blessed in common opinion hath of his forepast pleasures and delights. For whatsoever is cast behind us is just nothing; and what is to come, deceitful hope hath it. *Omnia quæ ventura sunt, in incerto jacent.* Only those few black swans I must except, who, having had the grace to value worldly vanities at no more than their own price, do, by retaining the comfortable memory of a well-acted life, behold death without dread, and the grave without fear; and embrace both, as necessary guides to endless glory.

The Conclusion to the Work

10   By this which we have already set down is seen the beginning and end of the three first monarchies of the world, whereof the founders and erectors thought that they could never have ended. That of Rome, which made the fourth, was also at this time almost at the highest. We have left it flourishing in the middle of the field, having rooted up or cut down all that kept it from the eyes and admiration of the world: but after some continuance, it shall begin to lose the beauty it had; the storms of ambition shall beat her great boughs and branches one against another, her leaves shall fall off, her limbs wither, and a rabble

20   of barbarous nations enter the field, and cut her down.

Now these great kings and conquering nations have been the subject of those ancient histories which have been preserved, and yet remain among us; and withal of so many tragical poets, as in the persons of powerful princes and other mighty men have complained against infidelity, time, destiny, and most of all against the variable success of worldly things, and instability of fortune. To these undertakings the greatest lords of the world have been stirred up rather by the desire of fame, which plougheth up the air, and soweth in the wind, than by the affection of

30   bearing rule, which draweth after it so much vexation and so many cares. And that this is true, the good advice of Cineas to Pyrrhus proves. And certainly, as fame hath often been dangerous to the living, so is it to the dead of no use at all, because separate from knowledge. Which were it otherwise, and the extreme ill bargain of buying this lasting discourse understood by them which are dissolved, they themselves would then rather have wished to have stolen out of the world without noise, than to be put in mind that they have purchased the report of

their actions in the world by rapine, oppression, and cruelty; by giving in spoil the innocent and labouring soul to the idle and insolent, and by having emptied the cities of the world of their ancient inhabitants, and filled them again with so many and so variable sorts of sorrows.

Since the fall of the Roman empire (omitting that of the Germans, which had neither greatness nor continuance) there hath been no state fearful in the east, but that of the Turk; nor in the west any prince that hath spread his wings far over his
10 nest, but the Spaniard; who, since the time that Ferdinand expelled the Moors out of Granado, have made many attempts to make themselves masters of all Europe. And it is true, that by the treasures of both Indies, and by the many kingdoms which they possess in Europe, they are at this day the most powerful. But as the Turk is now counterpoised by the Persian, so instead of so many millions as have been spent by the English, French, and Netherlands in a defensive war, and in diversions against them, it is easy to demonstrate, that with the charge of two hundred thousand pound continued but for two
20 years, or three at the most, they may not only be persuaded to live in peace, but all their swelling and overflowing streams may be brought back into their natural channels and old banks. These two nations, I say, are at this day the most eminent, and to be regarded; the one seeking to root out the Christian religion altogether, the other the truth and sincere profession thereof; the one to join all Europe to Asia, the other the rest of all Europe to Spain.

For the rest, if we seek a reason of the succession and continuance of this boundless ambition in mortal men, we may
30 add to that which hath been already said, that the kings and princes of the world have always laid before them the actions, but not the ends, of those great ones which preceded them. They are always transported with the glory of the one, but they never mind the misery of the other, till they find the experience in themselves. They neglect the advice of God, while they enjoy life, or hope it; but they follow the counsel of Death upon his first approach. It is he that puts into man all the wisdom of the world, without speaking a word, which God, with all the words of his law, promises, or threats, doth not infuse.
40 Death, which hateth and destroyeth man, is believed; God, which hath made him and loves him, is always deferred: *I have*

considered, saith Solomon, *all the works that are under the sun, and, behold, all is vanity and vexation of spirit;* but who believes it, till Death tells it us? It was Death, which opening the conscience of Charles the Fifth, made him enjoin his son Philip to restore Navarre; and king Francis the First of France, to command that justice should be done upon the murderers of the protestants in Merindol and Cabrieres, which till then he neglected. It is therefore Death alone that can suddenly make man to know himself. He tells the proud and insolent, that they are but ab-
10 jects, and humbles them at the instant, makes them cry, complain, and repent, yea, even to hate their forepast happiness. He takes the account of the rich, and proves him a ·beggar, a naked beggar, which hath interest in nothing but in the gravel that fills his mouth. He holds a glass before the eyes of the most beautiful, and makes them see therein their deformity and rottenness, and they acknowledge it.

O eloquent, just, and mighty Death! whom none could advise, thou hast persuaded; what none hath dared, thou hast done; and whom all the world hath flattered, thou only hast
20 cast out of the world and despised; thou hast drawn together all the far-stretched greatness, all the pride, cruelty, and ambition of man, and covered it all over with these two narrow words, *Hic jacet!*

III
The Character Writers

It is a sharp contrast to move from the eloquent plangency of Ralegh to the short-breathed wit and snap of the Jacobean character writers. If the distance seems great, then that is one more sign of the vitality of Renaissance prose, and the way it achieved excellence in so many different spheres. The emergence of the Character is part of that extraordinary surge of invention at the turn of the century which produced so many new forms and modes of writing—the sonnet, the epigram, the essay, satire in verse, prose and drama. Such a creative growth cannot be explained, but the twin influences which combined to bless this form come from both literature and life. Elizabethan and Jacobean society produced, by its very exuberance, a fair proportion of ostentation and eccentricity in behaviour as in dress, and the vogue for satire in the 1590s seized upon these quirks as invaluable subject-matter. The scurrilous poems of Marston and Hall, the prose pamphlets of Nashe and Greene, the early 'humour' comedies of Ben Jonson are all full of portraits (no doubt exaggerated) of vain, parading, modish pretenders to the latest fashion, whether it be tobacco, toothpicks, or an infinite number of variations in dress. The type of wit and surface brilliance shown here was taken over by the conventions of the separate series of prose portraits which came to be known as Characters, and although the Jacobean practitioners of this form were undoubtedly drawing from life they were given a model by the publication in England in 1592 of a Latin translation of the *Ethical Characters* of Theophrastus.

The Greek philosopher Theophrastus was a pupil of Aristotle, and designed his *Characters* as a semi-serious analysis of man in society: they consist of a number of sketches in an objective manner of moral and psychological types, rather than social or professional ones—such types as *The Flatterer, The Surly Man, The Coward, The Avaricious Man,* and so on. The sketches generally begin with a definition, and describe the type with humour rather than wit, as the opening of *The Stupid Man* will show:

Stupidity may be defined as sluggishness of mind in word and deed. The Stupid Man is the sort of person who reckons with counters, finds the total and then asks someone: "How much does that come to?" The day he is defendant in a law-case, he forgets all about it and goes into the country. If he goes to the theatre he falls asleep and is left there alone. When he has eaten too much and gets up at night to go to the privy he is bitten by the neighbour's dog.

Clearly Theophrastus is trying to accumulate the defining actions of such types, and therefore does not focus on an individual. Nor does he condemn immorality. The English character writers were to differ from him on these last two points, and indeed the experimentation which went on in England was so great that by 1665 Ralph Johnson could write a retrospective account[1] of 'How to write a Character' which shows just how many conventions the form had acquired. He defines the Character as 'a witty and facetious description of the nature and qualities of some person, or sort of people', and the element of wit is defined more strongly in his 'Rules for making it':

1. Choose a subject, *viz*. such a sort of men as will admit variety of observation; such be drunkards, usurers, liars, tailors, excise-men, travellers, pedlars, merchants, tapsters, lawyers, an upstart gentleman, a young Justice, a constable, an alderman, and the like.

2. Express their natures, qualities, conditions, practices, tools, desires, aims, or ends by witty allegories, or allusions to things or terms in nature or art of like resemblance, still striving for wit and pleasantness, together with tart nipping jerks about their vices or miscarriages.

3. Conclude with some witty and neat passage, leaving them to the effect of their follies and studies.

It is a very accurate analysis both of the subject-matter and of the method of many of the Characters, especially in its insistence on a concentrated sustained pressure of wit—'still striving for wit and pleasantness', and in its advice to be detailed, allusive in terms of the tools of each trade.

The first English example was JOSEPH HALL's *Characters of Virtues and Vices* (1608), recognizably near Theophrastus in

[1] Quoted by F. P. Wilson, *Seventeenth-Century Prose*, C.U.P., 1960, p. 14.

using representative actions and humour rather than wit. Hall takes the 'Ethical' of Theophrastus' title seriously, and also handles virtues, but in an abstract and rather pallid way. *The Humble Man* here is better than average but however admirable his intentions the result lacks precisely the virtue of the Character, its control of exact detail. Hall is more successful with the vices, and shows the wit typical of the genre both in surprise openings, as this to *The Unconstant*: 'The Inconstant man treads upon a moving earth and keeps no pace', and in concentrated epigrammatic conclusions, as this to *The Hypocrite*: 'In brief, he is the stranger's saint; the neighbour's disease; the blot of goodness; a rotten stick in a dark night; a poppy in a corn field; an ill tempered candle with a great snuff that in going out smells ill; an angel abroad, a devil at home; and worse when an angel than when a devil.' That intense piece of wit ('still striving for wit and pleasantness') displays one aspect of the Character which the modern reader has to adjust to, its use of wit almost as an obstacle race: you cannot read a Character at your normal reading-rate; you must use the semicolons as breathing spaces; while you work out the joke before moving on. One of the best of Hall's attempts is *The Vain-Glorious*, reprinted here, which achieves the genre's authentic distorting mirror-image of Jacobean society in a kind of monologue for the man 'who seemed busier than he was'.

Hall was a pioneer and suffered from the usual fate of pioneers in that his discovery was taken over and vastly improved by his successors. Perhaps the most brilliant volume was that produced under the name of SIR THOMAS OVERBURY, which included work by Webster (the 'Character of a Whore' written for *The White Devil* seems to me one of the least happy of these inventions). The circumstances in which this volume was produced are obscure, but if there was no active cooperation between the writers then the similarity of structure throughout demonstrates how quickly the genre developed its own conventions. The surprise opening is vastly improved on:

An Hypocrite. Is a gilded pill composed of two virtuous ingredients, natural dishonesty and artificial dissimulation.

That example depended for its effect on the image of the pill; others derive their wit from puns, such as the opening to 'An

Ordinary Widow' (a professional widow—rather like the Wife of Bath): 'is like the herald's hearse-cloth; she serves to many funerals, with a very little altering the colour. The end of her husband begins in tears, and the end of her tears begins in a husband.' A very witty use of rhetoric (the figure *chiasmus* or *antimetabole*[1]). Two of the pieces presented here (I deliberately refrain from discussing them in advance so as to preserve the reader's surprise and pleasure), *A Fine Gentleman* and *A Puritan*, have extremely ingenious openings, while *A Courtier* makes an inventive exploitation of the expected return of syntactical symmetry. The endings are just as densely witty, especially that of *A Sergeant* (a policeman) where the last sentence achieves a syntactical slowing-down in perfect accord with the image: 'He is a citizen's birdlime, and where he holds, he hangs.'

The last character writer to be considered here, JOHN EARLE (there were at least half a dozen others) is the most rewarding, for he succeeded in extending the form beyond its purely witty frame. In *Microcosmography* we still find wit, from the surprise opening:

> *A Plodding Student.* Is a kind of Alchemist or persecutor of nature, that would change the dull lead of his brain into finer metal, with success many times as unprosperous, or at least not quitting the cost, to wit, of his own oil and candles.

to the surprise close, as in his final analogy for *The Carrier*: 'He is like the prodigal child, still packing away, and still returning again. But let him pass.'

Earle is as ingenious as any one in punning, as we see from *A Bowl-Alley*, and (to break my rule of not discussing the Characters selected here) he too can exploit the expectations set up by syntax as in his record of the hypocritical female Puritan returning from church: 'When she comes home, she commends the sermon for the scripture, and two hours'—that is, 'for lasting two hours', and the incongruity of joining this with 'scripture' points up the superficiality of that type of religious enthusiasm which measured spirituality by length.

But what is different in Earle is that he can take a sympathetic attitude to the subject, as in his gentle exposure of the innocent

---

[1] By which words are repeated in inverse order, *ab* : *ba*, as: 'Eat to live, not live to eat.'

follies of the *Antiquary*, or in his serious analysis of the fixed inferiority of *A Younger Brother*. In addition to sympathy he shows considerable psychological insight:

> *A Sceptic in Religion*. Is one that hangs in the balance with all sorts of opinions, whereof not one but stirs him and none sways him.

thus catching acutely the aimless fluctuations of such a mind. Better still he brings out the self-defeating nature of *A High-Spirited Man* (the irritable, touchy, type) who is usually a comic figure but is here given some tragic overtones (as with Shakespeare's Hotspur, or Don John in *Much Ado*):

> A man quickly fired, and quickly laid down with satisfaction, but remits any injury sooner than words. Only to himself he is irreconcileable, whom he never forgives a disgrace, but is still stabbing himself with the thought of it, and no disease that he dies of sooner. He is one had rather perish than be beholden for his life, and strives more to be quit with his friend than his enemy. . . . One that will do nothing upon command, though he would do it otherwise: and if he ever does evil, it is when he is dared to it.

That is an extremely perceptive account of this sort of quarrelsome, proud, petty, unforgiving man—they are still about, as the similar type of *A Suspicious or Jealous Man* presented here will confirm. Indeed the success of Earle's psychology is that many of his characters are as recognizable today as they were then, and the degree of insight into life which he possesses ranks him with some of the dramatists. The Character is a form which obviously could not embrace many areas of human existence, but in a short time it developed faster than any one could have predicted, and did so essentially through its imaginative use of prose.

JOSEPH HALL (1574–1656)
The Humble Man

He is a friendly enemy to himself: for, though he be not out of his own favour, no man sets so low a value of his worth as himself; not out of ignorance or carelessness, but of a voluntary and meek dejectedness. He admires every thing in another,

while the same or better in himself he thinks not unworthily
contemned: his eyes are full of his own wants, and other's
perfections. He loves rather to give, than take honour; not in a
fashion of complimental courtesy, but in simplicity of his judgment: neither doth he fret at those, on whom he forceth prece-
dency, as one that hoped their modesty would have refused:
but holds his mind unfeignedly below his place, and is ready
to go lower, if need be, without discontentment. When he hath
but his due, he magnifieth courtesy, and disclaims his deserts.
10 He can be more ashamed of honour, than grieved with contempt; because he thinks that causeless, this deserved. His face,
his carriage, his habit, savour of lowliness, without affectation;
and yet he is much under that he seemeth. His words are few
and soft; never either peremptory or censorious: because he
thinks both each man more wise, and none more faulty than
himself: and, when he approacheth to the Throne of God, he is
so taken up with the divine greatness, that in his own eye she is
either vile or nothing. Places of public charge are fain to sue to
him, and hale him out of his chosen obscurity: which he holds
20 off; not cunningly to cause importunity, but sincerely in the
conscience of his defects. He frequenteth not the stages of
resorts; and then alone thinks himself in his natural element,
when he is shrouded within his own walls. He is ever jealous
over himself; and still suspecteth that which others applaud.
There is no better object of beneficence: for, what he receives,
he ascribes merely to the bounty of the giver: nothing, to merit.
He emulates no man, in any thing but goodness; and that, with
more desire, than hope, to overtake. No man is so contented
with his little, and so patient under miseries; because he knows
30 the greatest evils are below his sins, and the least favours above
his deservings. He walks ever in awe, and dare not but subject
every word and action to a high and just censure. He is a lowly
valley, sweetly planted and well watered: the proud man's earth,
whereon he trampleth: but secretly full of wealthy mines, more
worth than he that walks over them: a rich stone, set in lead:
and, lastly, a true Temple of God, built with a low roof.

The Vain-Glorious

All his humour rises up into the froth of ostentation: which, if
it once settle, falls down into a narrow room. If the excess be

in the understanding part, all his wit is in print: the press hath left his head empty; yea, not only what he had, but what he could borrow without leave. If his glory be in his devotion, he gives not an alms but on record; and, if he have once done well, God hears of it often: for, upon every unkindness, he is ready to upbraid him with his merits. Over and above his own discharge, he hath some satisfactions to spare for the common treasure. He can fulfill the law with ease, and earn God with superfluity. If he have bestowed but a little sum in the glazing,
10 paving, parieting of God's house, you shall find it in the church-window. Or, if a more gallant humour possess him, he wears all his land on his back; and, walking high, looks over his left shoulder, to see if the point of his rapier follow him with a grace. He is proud of another man's horse; and, well mounted, thinks every man wrongs him that looks not at him. A bare head in the street doth him more good than a meal's meat. He swears big at an ordinary; and talks of the court with a sharp accent: neither vouchsafes to name any not honourable nor those without some term of familiarity; and likes well to see the hearer
20 look upon him amazedly; as if he said, 'How happy is this man, that is so great with great ones!' Under pretence of seeking for a scroll of news, he draws out a handful of letters, endorsed with his own style, to the height, half reading every title; passes over the latter part, with a murmur; not without signifying, what lord sent this, what great lady the other, and for what suits: the last paper, as it happens, is his news from his honourable friend in the French Court. In the midst of dinner his lacquey comes sweating in, with a sealed note from his creditor, who now threatens a speedy arrest; and whispers the ill news in his
30 master's ear: when he aloud names a Counsellor of State, and professes to know the employment. The same messenger he calls, with an imperious nod; and, after expostulation, where he hath left his fellows, in his ear sends him for some new spur-leathers, or stockings by this time footed; and, when he is gone half the room, recalls him, and saith aloud 'It is no matter: let the greater bag alone till I come': and, yet again calling him closer, whispers, so that all the table may hear, that if his crimson suit be ready against the day, the rest need no haste. He picks his teeth when his stomach is empty; and calls for pheas-
40 ants at a common inn. You shall find him pricing the richest jewels and fairest horses, when his purse yields not money

enough for earnest. He thrusts himself into the press before some
great ladies; and loves to be seen near the head of a great train.
His talk is, how many mourners he furnished with gowns at
his father's funerals, how many messes; how rich his coat is and
how ancient; how great his alliance; what challenges he hath
made and answered; what exploits he did at Calais or Nieuport;
and, when he hath commended others' buildings, furnitures,
suits, compared them with his own. When he hath undertaken
to be the broker for some rich diamond, he wears it; and, pull-
10 ing off his gloye to stroke up his hair, thinks no eye should
have any other object. Entertaining his friend, he chides his
cook for no better cheer; and names the dishes he meant and
wants. To conclude, he is ever on the stage and acts a still
glorious part abroad; when no man carries a baser heart, no man
is more sòrdid and careless at home: he is a Spanish soldier on
an Italian theatre, a bladder full of wind, a skin full of words; a
fool's wonder, and a wise man's fool.

SIR THOMAS OVERBURY (1581-1613)
A Courtier

To all men's thinking is a man, and to most men the finest:
all things else are defined by the understanding, but this by the
20 senses; but his surest mark is, that he is to be found only about
princes. He smells; and putteth away much of his judgment
about the situation of his clothes. He knows no man that is not
generally known. His wit, like the marigold, openeth with the
sun, and therefore he riseth not before ten of the clock. He puts
more confidence in his words than meaning, and more in his
pronounciation than his words. Occasion is his Cupid, and he
hath but one receipt of making love. He follows nothing but
inconstancy, admires nothing but beauty, honours nothing
but fortune, loves nothing. The sustenance of his discourse is
30 news, and his censure like a shot depends upon the charging. He
is not, if he be out of court, but fish-like breathes destruction, if
out of his own element. Neither his motion, or aspect are
regular, but he moves by the upper spheres, and is the reflection
of higher substances.

    If you find him not here, you shall in Paul's, with a pick-
tooth in his hat, a cape-cloak, and a long stocking.

A Fine Gentleman

Is the Cinnamon tree, whose bark is more worth than his body.
He hath read the Book of good manners, and by this time each
of his limbs may read it. He alloweth of no judge, but the eye;
painting, bolstering and bombasting are his orators: by these
also he proves his industry: for he hath purchased legs, hair,
beauty, and straightness, more than nature left him. He unlocks
maiden-heads with his language, and speaks Euphues, not so
gracefully as heartily. His discourse makes not his behaviour,
but he buys it at Court, as countrymen their clothes in Birchin
10 Lane. He is somewhat like a Salamander, and lives in the flame
of love, which pains he expresses comically: and nothing grieves
him so much, as the want of a poet to make an issue in his love;
yet he sighs sweetly and speaks lamentably: for his breath is
perfumed and his words are wind. He is best in season at
Christmas; for the boar's head and reveller come together; his
hopes are laden in his quality; and lest fiddlers should take him
unprovided, he whistles his own galliard. He is a calendar of
ten years, and marriage rusts him. Afterwards he maintains himself an implement of household, by carving and ushering. For
20 all this, he is judicial only in tailors and barbers, but his opinion
is ever ready, and ever idle. If you will know more of his acts,
the broker's shop is the witness of his valour, where lies
wounded, dead, rent, and out of fashion, many a spruce suit,
overthrown by his fantasticness.

A Puritan

Is a diseased piece of Apocrypha: bind him to the Bible, and
he corrupts the whole text. Ignorance and fat feed are his
founders; his nurses, railing, rabies, and round breeches: his
life is but a borrowed blast of wind; for between two religions,
as between two doors, he is ever whistling. Truly whose child
30 he is is yet unknown; for willingly his faith allows no father:
only thus far his pedigree is found, Bragger and he flourished
about a time first; his fiery zeal keeps him continually costive,
which withers him into his own translation, and till he eat a
schoolman, he is hide-bound; he ever prays against non residents,
but is himself the greatest discontinuer, for he never keeps near
his text. Anything that the law allows, but marriage, and March

64

beer, he murmurs at; what it disallows and holds dangerous, makes him a discipline: where the gate stands open, he is ever seeking a stile: and where his learning ought to climb, he creeps through. Give him advice, you run into traditions, and urge a modest course, he cries out councils. His greatest care is to condemn obedience, his last care to serve God handsomely and cleanly. He is now become so cross a kind of teaching, that should the Church enjoin clean shirts, he were lousy. More sense than single prayers is not his; nor more in those, than still

10 the same Petitions: from which he either fears a learned faith, or doubts God understands not at first hearing. Shew him a ring, he runs back like a bear; and hates square dealing as allied to caps: a pair of organs blow him out o' th' parish, and are the only clyster-pipes to cool him. Where the meat is best there he confutes most, for his arguing is but the efficacy of his eating: good bits he holds breed good positions, and the Pope he best concludes against, in plum-broth. He is often drunk, but not as we are, temporally, nor can his sleep then cure him, for the fumes of his ambition make his very soul reel, and the

20 small beer that should allay him (silence) keeps him more surfeited, and makes his heat break out in private houses: women and lawyers are his best disciples, the one next fruit, longs for forbidden doctrine, the other to maintain forbidden titles, both which he sows amongst them. Honest he dare not be, for that loves order: yet if he can be brought to ceremony, and made but master of it, he is converted.

JOHN EARLE (1601 ?–65)
A Bowl-Alley

Is the place where there are three things thrown away beside bowls, to wit, time, money, and curses, and the last ten for one. The best sport in it is the gamester's, and he enjoys it that looks

30 on and bets not. It is the school of wrangling, and worse than the Schools, for men will cavil here for a hair's breadth, and make a stir when a straw would end the controversy. No antic screws the body into such strange flexures, and you would think them here senseless, to speak sense to their bowl, and put their trust into entreaties for a good cast. The betters are the factious noise of the alley, or the gamester's beadsmen that pray for them. They are somewhat like those that are cheated by

great men, for they lose their money and must say nothing. It is the best discovery of humours, especially in the losers, where you have fine variety of impatience, whilst some fret, some rail, some swear, and others more ridiculously comfort themselves with philosophy. To give you the moral of it: it is the emblem of the world, or the world's ambition: where most are short, or over, or wide or wrong-biassed, and some few justle into the mistress Fortune. And it is here as in the court, where the nearest are most spited, and all blows aimed at the toucher.

An Antiquary

10 He is a man strangely thrifty of time past, and an enemy indeed to his maw, whence he fetches out many things when they are now all rotten and stinking. He is one that hath that unnatural disease to be enamoured of old age and wrinkles, and loves all things, (as Dutchmen do cheese), the better for being mouldy and worm-eaten. He is of our religion, because we say it is the most ancient; and yet a broken statue would almost make him an idolater. A great admirer he is of the rust of old monuments, and reads only those characters where time hath eaten out the letters. He will go you forty miles to see a saint's well or a
20 ruined abbey; and there be but a cross or stone foot-stool in the way, he'll be considering it so long, till he forget his journey. His estate consists much in shekels, and Roman coins; and he hath more pictures of Cæsar, than James or Elizabeth. Beggars cozen him with musty things which they have raked from dung-hills, and he preserves their rags for precious relics. He loves no library, but where there are more spider's volumes than author's, and looks with great admiration on the antique work of cobwebs. Printed books he condemns, as a novelty of this latter age, but a manuscript he pores on everlastingly,
30 especially if the cover be all moth-eaten, and the dust make a parenthesis between every syllable. He would give all the books in his study (which are rarities all), for one of the old Roman binding, or six lines of Tully in his own hand. His chamber is hung commonly with strange beast's skins, and is a kind of charnel-house of bones extraordinary; and his discourse upon them, if you will hear him, shall last longer. His very attire is that which is the eldest out of fashion, and you may pick a criticism out of his breeches. He never looks upon himself

until he is grey-haired, and then he is pleased with his own antiquity. His grave does not fright him, for he has been used to sepulchres, and he likes death the better, because it gathers him to his fathers.

A She Precise Hypocrite

Is one in whom good women suffer, and have their truth misinterpreted by her folly. She is one, she knows not what herself if you ask her, but she is indeed one that has taken a toy at the fashion of religion, and is enamoured at the new fangle. She is a nonconformist in a close stomacher and ruff of Geneva print,
10 and her purity consists much in her linen. She has heard of the Rag of Rome, and thinks it a very sluttish religion, and rails at the Whore of Babylon for a very naughty woman. She has left her virginity as a relic of Popery, and marries in her tribe without a ring. Her devotion at the church is much in the turning up of her eye; and turning down the leaf in her book, when she hears named chapter and verse. When she comes home, she commends the sermon for the scripture, and two hours. She loves preaching better than praying, and of preachers, lecturers; and thinks the week-day's exercise far more edifying
20 than the Sunday's. Her oftest gossipings are Sabbath-day's journeys, where, (though an enemy to superstition), she will go in pilgrimage five mile to a silenced minister, when there is a better sermon in her own parish. She doubts of the Virgin Mary's salvation, and dares not saint her, but knows her own place in heaven as perfectly as the pew she has a key to. She is so taken up with faith she has no room for charity, and understands no good works but what are wrought on the sampler. She accounts nothing vices but superstition and an oath, and thinks adultery a less sin than to swear *by my truly*. She rails at
30 other women by the names of Jezebel and Dalilah; and calls her own daughters Rebecca and Abigail, and not Ann but Hannah. She suffers them not to learn on the virginals, because of their affinity with organs, but is reconciled to the bells for the chime's sake, since they were reformed to the tune of a psalm. She overflows so with the Bible, that she spills it upon every occasion, and will not cudgel her maids without scripture. It is a question whether she is more troubled with the Devil or the Devil with her. She is always challenging and daring him,

and her weapon is *The Practice of Piety*. Nothing angers her so
much as that women cannot preach, and in this point thinks
the Brownist erroneous; but what she cannot at the church she
does at the table, where she prattles more than any against sense
and Antichrist, till a capon's wing silence her. She expounds the
priests of Baal, reading ministers, and thinks the salvation of
of that parish as desperate as the Turks. She is a main derider
to her capacity of these that are not her preachers, and censures
all sermons but bad ones. If her husband be a tradesman, she
10 helps him to customers, howsoever to good cheer, and they
are a most faithful couple at these meetings, for they never fail.
Her conscience is like others' lust, never satisfied, and you might
better answer Scotus than her scruples. She is one that thinks
she performs all her duties to God in hearing, and shows the
fruits of it in talking. She is more fiery against the maypole than
her husband, and thinks she might do a Phineas' act to break
the pate of the fiddler. She is an everlasting argument, but I am
weary of her.

A Suspicious or Jealous Man

Is one that watches himself a mischief, and keeps a leer eye still,
20 for fear it should escape him. A man that sees a great deal more
in everything than is to be seen, and yet he thinks he sees
nothing: his own eye stands in his light. He is a fellow commonly guilty of some weaknesses, which he might conceal if
he were careless: now his over-diligence to hide them makes
men pry the more. Howsoever he imagines you have found him,
and it shall go hard but you must abuse him whether you will or
no. Not a word can be spoke, but nips him somewhere; not a jest
thrown out, but he will make it hit him. You shall have him go
fretting out of company with some twenty quarrels to every
30 man, stung and galled, and no man knows less the occasion
than they that have given it. To laugh before him is a dangerous
matter, for it cannot be at any thing but at him, and to whisper
in his company plain conspiracy. He bids you speak out, and
he will answer you, when you thought not of him. He expostu-
lates with you in passion, why you should abuse him, and explains to your ignorance wherein, and gives you very good
reason at last to laugh at him hereafter. He is one still accusing
others when they are not guilty, and defending himself when he
is not accused: and no man is undone more with apologies,

wherein he is so elaborately excessive, that none will believe him; and he is never thought worse of, than when he has given satisfaction. Such men can never have friends, because they cannot trust so far; and this humour hath this infection with it, it makes all men to them suspicious. In conclusion, they are men always in offence and vexation with themselves and their neighbours, wronging others in thinking they would wrong them, and themselves most of all in thinking they deserve it.

IV
Lancelot Andrewes
1555–1626

Of all the books published in England up to 1640 by far the fullest single group was that of religion, and among these sermons bulk largest. There were not only more sermons published than plays then, but more than drama, poetry, and fiction put together. Modern attitudes to the past have reversed the preferences, and from a literary viewpoint it cannot be doubted that this is right, for very few preachers could make great art out of good doctrine. The two who did so more than anyone else were Lancelot Andrewes and John Donne, and a greater contrast could hardly be imagined, but it is not enough to praise one and damn the other: each is great in his own way.

The revival of interest in Andrewes is largely due to an influential essay by T. S. Eliot, and although Eliot made the sad mistake of elevating Andrewes and debasing Donne (not on literary grounds but rather for being too 'personal'), he did produce some valuable criticism, most of all his famous metaphor for Andrewes's chief technique as a preacher: he 'takes a word and derives the world from it; squeezing and squeezing the word until it yields a full juice of meaning which we should never have supposed any word to possess'. This is an admirable description both of the general way in which Andrewes discovers a world within a word and of his particular method of concentration and extraction. It is a type of preaching which is not concerned with large emotional states or spiritual autobiography, but focuses entirely on the written word of the biblical text. Andrewes chooses a text appropriate to the occasion (most of the extant sermons are designed for the great Church festivals: Christmas, Easter, Whitsun), and in the opening section of the sermon announces the divisions or sections which he intends to make within it, the rest of his time being devoted to the explication of the words and all the weight of doctrine that lies behind them. It is a tough, rigorous procedure, not conducive to relaxed musing or elevated generalities—but then Andrewes did not want to write like this, and scorned factitious rhetorical displays, those 'blazes' which, he said, 'make us a

70

little sermon-warm for the while', but later 'flit and vanish', asserting that 'it is the evidence of the spirit, in the soundness of the sense, that leaves the true impression'. To apply Dryden's dictum: 'A man is to be cheated into passion, but reasoned into truth.'

But although this method sounds severe and forbidding, such is not the case. For Andrewes *logos* (The Word) is the centre and the circumference of the preacher's world, and the word exerts for him a magnetic field: although he may occasionally digress he is always brought back to the word and we with him. This constant focus on the text demands an equally intense dedication from the reader, but if he is willing to give it he will achieve much spiritual and intellectual illumination, and at the same time the energy produced, the tension and release of a strong mind in control of its powers, is also satisfying. There are other more literary consolations, too. The corollary of Andrewes's tight hold of the text is that his own language is tightly controlled, sharply structured, close-packed with meaning (a kind of micro-syntax). It is a condensed style which makes little use of the traditional symmetries of syntax, has indeed not enough room for them, but it is well suited to conveying the many sharp distinctions in the sense. Consider the recurrent antithetical contrast between what Christ endured for us and what our benefit will be—as, to give a simple example, if we consider 'what this day the Son of God did and suffered for us; and all for this end, that what he was then, we might not be; and what he is now, we might be for ever'.

There are many larger and more complex patterns, but all as tightly structured as this. It is, properly speaking, an analytical syntax, almost mathematical in the way it resolves idea and experience into their constituent parts. At the same time that the shape of language on the page is creating a series of worlds out of words, at the level of the imagination metaphor is creating a series of responses to those worlds. If Andrewes's method still seems too 'objective' we should remember that in preaching at the great Church festivals he is preaching on the great events in Christian experience—the nativity, the crucifixion, the resurrection—and on the emotions proper to each— joy, despair, hope—and his images constantly express his (and our) reactions to these. And always the great contrast is between the potential of faith and men's actual practice of it: so the prophecy of Christ's coming 'brought forth a Benedictus and a Magnificat from the true seed of Abraham; if it do not the like from us, certainly it but floats in our brains; we but warble about it'; the human brain is superficial, like something floating on liquid, or like a tame bird.

The sermon presented here is one of Andrewes's greatest (matched only by those for Good Friday 1604, Christmas 1605, and Easter 1620), and has many of his characteristics, including a thematic use of imagery which is found in the most inspired work. In the introduction we find his sensitivity to the congregation's response: 'I have before I was aware disclosed who this party is—it was not amiss I so should; not to hold you long in suspense, but to give you a little light at the first, whom it would fall on.' After the division into two parts we soon see one of Andrewes's most attractive qualities, the way that his response to the situation in his text is so strong that it produces a full imaginative reconstruction of the scene (as in the famous passage about the winter landscape which inspired Eliot's *Journey of the Magi*). Here he analyses the things that the prophet Isaiah sees first about the man coming from Bozrah: his dress ('richly arrayed') and his gait ('stoutly marching'), and comments: 'Two good familiar notes, to descry a stranger by. His apparel, whether rich or mean, by which the world most commonly takes notice of men by. His gait; for weak men have but a feeble gait. Valiant strong men tread upon the ground so, as by it you may discern their strength.' We expect the moral reaction to dress, but we are surely surprised at the perceptive comment on how a man walks—it draws on a quiet power of observation which ranks with Shakespeare's invention for Ulysses picking out Diomedes from the crowd:

> 'Tis he, I ken the manner of his gait;
> He rises on the toe. That spirit of his
> In aspiration lifts him from the earth.
>
> (*Troilus and Cressida*, IV, v.)

Again, Andrewes's power to reconstruct a scene extends to the imagined reactions of the prophet—doubtful, inquiring—where the hesitant syntax catches exactly this to-and-fro: 'Sees Him; but knows him not: thinks Him worthy the knowing; so thinking, and not knowing, is desirous to be instructed concerning Him.' Indeed, one of the triumphs of this sermon is how

Andrewes, almost like a modern novelist, controls the point of view of the prophet, only gradually allowing it to expand, and matching the slow controlled movement of thought and emotion to it.

The first part of the sermon explores the text and its scene (Bozrah surrounded with 'huge high rocks on all sides', like the threatening landscape in Giovanni di Paolo's *Christ in the Wilderness*), and the advantages are those of slow but sure illumination, as with the fresh light Andrewes casts on the familiar words 'O grave where is thy sting? O hell where is thy victory?', reminding us that Christ's 'victory' is 'his standard, alluding to the Roman standard that had in it the image of the goddess Victory'. But it is not a philological progression, dedicated to restoring the letter, for Andrewes rejects this approach scornfully:

> Go we then to the kernel and let the husk lie; let go the dead letter, and take we to us the spiritual meaning that hath some life in it. For what care we for the literal Edom or Bozrah, what became of them; what are they to us? Let us compare spiritual things with spiritual things, that is it must do us good.

The fulfilment of this insistence on spiritual, metaphorical, typological meaning comes in the second part of the sermon, with its explanation of the meaning of 'winepress'. Christ's garments are stained red, 'as if He had newly come out of some winepress', had been 'treading grapes, and pressing out wine there', but Andrewes wants to control the movement of meaning here. As ever with him, we are patient, receptive, in the power of the interpreter of Scripture, as he challenges the word 'wine', arguing that it must be a metaphor for 'blood', backing his case with a characteristic grasp of the actuality of the scene: 'We know well, our reason leads us, there could be no vintage at this time of the year, the season serves not; blood it was.'

From this point he builds up a wonderfully flexible sequence of imagery where all the metaphors fuse into one another: Christ has trodden a winepress and destroyed his enemies, but also 'He was Himself trodden and pressed; He was the grapes and clusters Himself', and this reference to the crucifixion is developed with an eloquent account of its three stages and the physical suffering of Christ, which is then carried further by returning to the metaphorical plane and expressing it in the sharpest possible syntactical sequence (the rhetorical figure *climax* or *gradatio*[1]): Christ's blood fills the 'cup of salvation' for man, 'But to make this wine, His clusters were to be cut; cut, and cast in; cast in, and trodden on; trodden and pressed out; all these before He came to be wine in the cup.'

From the cup filled by Christ's blood Andrewes turns at once to the devil's cup, sipped by Adam and poisoning all mankind; Adam himself 'degenerated into a wild strange vine', bringing forth 'bitter clusters', and these images are fused into others—the liquid is tears, myrrh, vinegar, poison—the winepress runs with the sweat of Christ's suffering, the cup becomes the redeeming power of the New Testament. It is impossible to predict how much meaning and interrelation Andrewes will discover in his images. The only other work I know in English to compare it with is Langland's *Piers Plowman*, especially the wonderful sequence in Passus XVIII that moves from the Crucifixion to the Harrowing of Hell (Bozrah), and has a comparably rich modulation of the Christian images of the cup and of thirst, as in Christ's great speech:

> For I, that am lorde of lyf· love is my drynke,
> And for that drynke to-day· I deyde vpon erthe.
> I faughte so, me threstes [thirsts] yet· for mannes soule sake;
> May no drynke me moiste· ne my thruste slake,
> Tyl the vendage falle· in the vale of Iosephath,
> That I drynke righte ripe must· *resurreccio mortuorum*.

And so here: Christ's 'coming here from Edom, will fall out to be His rising from the dead; His return from Bozrah, nothing but His vanquishing of Hell.' Within this enormously inventive sequence there are many incidental flashes of the imagination, as the reader must be left to discover. Take this translation of the whole process back into the life of the devout Christian and the preacher: 'For when we read, what do we but gather grapes here and there; and when we study what we have gathered, then are we even *in torculari*, ["in the winepress"] and press them we do, and press out of them that which daily you taste of.' Or consider the reference back to the immediate situation of the congregation in church on Easter day with an apt and vivid metaphor: the addition of a third press 'may serve as sour herbs

[1] By which the last word of one clause becomes the first word of the next.

to eat our Paschal lamb with', and when this is explained it comes as an equally unpredictable surprise. What Andrewes says elsewhere of the function of preaching seems to apply here—'the soul's cure is by words', or, one would add, words controlled by imagination.

A Sermon Preached Before The King's Majesty at Whitehall on the Thirteenth of April 1623 Being Easter-Day

Isaiah lxiii 1–3

Who is this That cometh from Edom, with red garments from Bosrah? He is glorious in His apparel, and walketh in great strength; I speak in righteousness, and am mighty to save.

Wherefore is Thine apparel red, and Thy garments like him that treadeth in the winepress?

I have trodden the winepress alone, and of all the people there was none with Me; for I will tread them in Mine anger, and tread them under foot in My wrath, and their blood shall be sprinkled upon My garments, and I will stain all My raiment.

Quis est iste Qui venit de Edom, tinctis vestibus de Bosra? Iste formosus in stola Sua, gradiens in multitudine fortitudinis Suæ. Ego, Qui loquor justitiam, et propugnator sum ad salvandum.

Quare ergo rebrum est indumentum Tuum, et vestimenta Tua sicut calcantium in torculari?

Torcular calcavi solus, et de gentibus non est vir Mecum; calcavi eos in furore Meo, et conculcavi eos in ira Mea; et apersus est sanguis eorum super vestimenta Mea, et omnia indumenta Mea inquinavi.
[*Latin Vulgate*]

Ever when we read or hear read any text or passage out of this Prophet, the Prophet Isaiah, it brings to our mind the nobleman that sitting in his chariot, read another like passage out of this same Prophet. Brings him to mind, and with him his question, 'Of whom doth the Prophet speak this? of himself or of some other?' Not of himself, that's once; it cannot be himself. It is he that asks the question. Some other then it must needs be of whom it is, and we to ask who that other was.

The tenor of Scripture that nobleman then read was out of the fifty-third chapter, and this of ours out of the sixty-third, ten chapters between. But if St. Philip had found him reading of this here, as he did of that, he would likewise have began at this same Scripture as at that he did, and preached to him Christ—

only with this difference; out of that, Christ's Passion; out of this, His Resurrection. For He That was led 'as a sheep to be slain,' and so was slain there, He it is and no other That rises and comes here back like a lion 'from Bozrah,' imbrued with blood, the blood of His enemies.

I have before I was aware disclosed who this party is—it was not amiss I so should; not to hold you long in suspense, but to give you a little light at the first, whom it would fall on. Christ it is. Two things there are that make it can be no other but He. 1. One is without the text, in the end of the chapter next before. There is a proclamation, 'Behold, here comes your Saviour;' and immediately, He That comes is this party here from Edom. He is our Saviour, and besides Him there is none, even Christ the Lord. 2. The other is in the text itself, in these words: *Torcular calcavi solus*, 'I have trod the winepress alone.' Words so proper to Christ, so every where ascribed to Him, and to Him only, as you shall not read them any where applied to any other; no, not by the Jews themselves. So as if there were no more but these two, they shew it plainly enough it is, it can be, none but Christ.

And Christ when? Even this day of all days. His coming here from Edom, will fall out to be His rising from the dead; His return from Bozrah, nothing but His vanquishing of hell. We may use His words in applying it, 'Thou hast not left My soul in hell,' 'but brought Me back from the deep of the earth again;' nothing but the act of His rising again. So that this very morning was this Scripture fulfilled in our ears.

The whole text entire is a dialogue between two, 1. the Prophet, and 2. Christ. There are in it two questions, and to the two questions two answers. 1. The Prophet's first question is touching the party Himself, who He is, in these words, 'Who is this?' to which the party Himself answers in the same verse these words, 'That am I, one That,' &c.

The Prophet's second question is about His colours, why He was all in red, in the second verse; 'Wherefore then is Thy apparel,' &c. The answer to that is in the third verse in these; 'I have trodden,' &c. 'For I will tread them down.'

Of Christ; of His rising or coming back, of His colours, of the winepress that gave Him this tincture, or rather of the two winepresses; 1. the winepress of redemption first, 2. and then of the other winepress of vengeance.

76

I

The Prophets use to speak of things to come as if they saw them present before their eyes. That makes their prophecies be called visions. In his vision here, the Prophet being taken up in Spirit sees one coming. Coming whence? From the land or country of Idumæa or Edom. From what place there? From Bozrah, the chief city in the land, the place of greatest strength. 'Who will lead me into the strong city?' that is, Bozrah. 'Who will bring me into Edom?' He that can do the first, can do the latter. Win Bozrah, and Edom is won.

10 There was a cry in the end of the chapter before: 'Behold, here comes your Saviour.' He looked, and saw one coming. Two things he descries in this party: 1. One, His habit, that He was *formosus in stola*, 'very richly arrayed;' 2. The other, His gait, that He 'came stoutly marching,' or pacing the ground very strongly. Two good familiar notes, to descry a stranger by. His apparel, whether rich or mean, which the world most commonly takes notice of men by. His gait; for weak men have but a feeble gait. Valiant strong men tread upon the ground so, as by it you may discern their strength.

20 Now this party, He came so goodly in His apparel, so stately in His march, as if by all likelihood He had made some conquest in Edom, the place He came from; had had a victory in Bozrah, the city where He had been. And the truth is, so He had. He saith it in the third verse, 'He had trodden down His enemies,' had trampled upon them, made the blood even start out of them; which blood of theirs had all to stained His garments. This was no evil news for Isaiah's countrymen, the people of God; Edom was the worst enemy they had.

With joy then, but not without admiration, such a party sees 30 the Prophet come toward him. Sees Him; but knows Him not; thinks Him worthy the knowing; so thinking, and not knowing, is desirous to be instructed concerning Him. Out of this desire asks, *Quis est?* Not of Himself, he durst not be so bold, Who are you? but of some stander by, Whom have we here? Can you tell who this might be? The first question.

But before we come to the question, a word or two of the place where He had been, and whence He came. 'Edom' and 'Bozrah,' what is meant by them? For if this party be Christ, Christ was in Egypt a child, but never in Edom that we read,

77

never at Bozrah in all His life; so as here we are to leave the letter. Some other it might be the letter might mean; we will not much stand to look after Him. For however possibly some such there was, yet it will plainly appear by the sequel, that 'the testimony of Jesus,' as it is of each other, so it 'is the spirit of this prophecy.'

Go we then to the kernel and let the husk lie; let go the dead letter, and take we to us the spiritual meaning that hath some life in it. For what care we for the literal Edom or Bozrah,
10 what became of them; what are they to us? Let us compare spiritual things with spiritual things, that is it must do us good.

I will give you a key to this, and such like Scriptures. Familiar it is with the Prophets, nothing more, than to speak to their people in their own language; than to express their ghostly enemies, the both mortal and immortal enemies of their souls, under the titles and terms of those nations and cities as were the known sworn enemies of the commonwealth of Israel. As of Egypt where they were in bondage; as of Babylon, where in captivity; elsewhere, as of Edom here, who maliced them more
20 than both those. If the Angel tell us right, Revelation the eleventh, there is 'a spiritual Sodom and Egypt where our Lord was crucified;' and if they, why not a spiritual Edom too whence our Lord rose again? Put all three together, Egypt, Babel, Edom, all their enmities, all are nothing to the hatred that hell bears us. But yet if you ask, of the three which was the worst? That was Edom. To shew, the Prophet here made good choice of his place, Edom upon earth comes nearest to the kingdom of darkness in hell, of all the rest. And that, in these respects:

First, they were the wickedest people under the sun. If there
30 were any devils upon earth, it was they; if the devil of any country, he would choose to be an Edomite. No place on earth that resembled hell nearer; next to hell on earth was Edom for all that naught was. Malachi calls Edom, 'the border of all wickedness,' 'a people with whom God was angry for ever.' In which very points, no enemies so fitly express the enemies of our souls, against whom the anger of God is eternal, and 'the smoke of whose torments shall ascend for ever.' Hell, for all that naught is. That if the power of darkness, and hell itself, if they be to be expressed by any place on earth, they cannot be
40 better expressed than in these, 'Edom' and 'Bozrah.'

I will give you another. The Edomites were the posterity of

Esau; 'the same is Edom.' So they were nearest of kin to the Jews, of all nations; so should have been their best friends. The Jews and they came of two brethren. Edom was the elder, and that was the grief, that the people of Israel coming of Jacob the younger brother, had enlarged their border; got them a better seat and country by far than they, the Edomites had. Hence grew envy, and an enemy out of envy is ever the worst. So were they, the most cankered enemies that Israel had. The case is so between us and the evil spirits. Angels they were we
10 know, and so in a sort elder brethren to us. Of the two intellectual natures, they the first created. Our case now, Christ be thanked! is much better than theirs; which is that enraged them against us, as much and more than ever any Edomite against Israel. Hell, for rancour and envy.

Yet one more. They were ready to do God's people all the mischief they were able, and when they were not able of themselves, they shewed their good-wills though, set on others. And when they had won Jerusalem, cried 'Down with it, down with it, even to the ground;' no less would serve. And when it
20 was on the ground, insulted and rejoiced above measure: 'Remember the children of Edom.' This is right the devil's property, *quarto modo*. He that hath but the heart of a man, will even rue to see his enemy lying in extreme misery. None but very devils, or devils incarnate, will do so; corrupt their compassion, cast off all pity; rejoice, insult, take delight at one's destruction. Hell for their ἐπέχαιρε κακίᾳ, 'insulting over men in misery.'

But will ye go even to the letter? none did ever so much mischief to David, as did Doeg; he was an Edomite. Nor none
30 so much to the Son of David, Christ, none bore more malice to Him first and last than did Herod; and he was an Edomite. So, which way soever we take it, next the kingdom of darkness was Edom upon earth. And Christ coming from thence, may well be said to come from Edom.

But what say you to Bozrah? This; that if the country of Edom do well set before us the whole kingdom of darkness or region of death, Bozrah may well stand for hell itself. Bozrah was the strongest hold of that kingdom, hell is so of this. The whole country of Idumea was called and known by the name
40 of Uz, that is, of strength; and what of such strength as death? all the sons of men stoop to him. Bozrah was called 'the strong

city;' hell is strong as it every way. They write, it was environed
with huge high rocks on all sides, one only cleft to come to it
by. And when you were in, there must you perish; no getting
out again. For all the world like to hell, as Abraham describes
it to him that was in it, 'they that would go from this place to
you cannot possibly, neither can they come from thence to us;'
the gulf is so great, no getting out. No *habeas corpus* from death,
no *habeas animam* out of hell; you must 'let that alone for
ever.'

10   Now then we have the Prophet's true Edom, his very
Bozrah indeed. By this we understand what they mean. 'Edom,'
the kingdom of darkness and death; 'Bozrah,' the seat of the
prince of darkness, that is, hell itself. From both which Christ
this day returned. 'His soul was not left in hell, His flesh saw
not,' but rose from, 'corruption.'

For 'over Edom,' strong as it was, yet David 'cast his shoe;'
'over' it, that is, after the Hebrew phrase, set his foot upon it
and trod it down. And Bozrah, as impregnable a hold as it was
holden, yet David won it; was led 'into the strong city,' led into
20 it, and came thence again. So did the Son of David this day
from His Edom, death, how strong soever, yet 'swallowed up
in victory' this day. And from hell His Bozrah, how hard soever
it held, as he that was in it found there was no getting thence,
Christ is got forth we see. How many souls soever were there
left, His was not left there.

And when did He this? when *solutus doloribus inferni*, 'He
loosed the pains of hell,' trod upon the serpent's head, and all
to bruised it, took from death his 'sting,' from hell his 'victory,'
that is his standard, alluding to the Roman standard that had
30 in it the image of the goddess Victory. Seized upon the *chirographum contra nos*, the ragman roll that made so strong against
us; took it, rent it, and so rent 'nailed it to His Cross;' made His
banner of it, of the law cancelled, hanging at it banner-wise.
And having thus 'spoiled principalities and powers, He made
an open show of them, triumphed over them' in *Semetipso*, 'in
His own person,'—all three are in Colossians the second,—and
triumphantly came thence with the keys of Edom and Bozrah
both, 'of hell and of death' both, at His girdle, as He shews
Himself. And when was this? if ever, on this very day. On
40 which, having made a full and perfect conquest of death, 'and
of him that hath the power of death, that is, the devil,' He rose

and returned thence this morning as a mighty Conqueror, saying as Deborah did in her song, 'O my soul, thou hast trodden down strength,' thou hast marched valiantly!

And coming back thus, from the debellation of the spiritual Edom, and the breaking up of the true Bozrah indeed, it is wondered who it should be. Note this; that nobody knew Christ at His rising, neither Mary Magdalene, nor they that went to Emmaus. No more doth the Prophet here.

Now there was reason to ask this question, for none would
10 ever think it to be Christ. There is great odds it cannot be He.
1. Not He; He was put to death, and put into His grave, and a great stone upon Him, not three days since. This party is alive and alives-like. His ghost it cannot be; He glides not as ghosts they say do, but paces the ground very strongly.

Not He; He had His apparel shared amongst the soldiers, was left all naked. This party hath gotten Him on 'glorious apparel,' rich scarlet.

Not He; for if He come, He must come in white, in the linen He was lapped in, and laid in His grave. This party comes in
20 quite another colour, all in red. So the colours suit not.

To be short, not He, for He was put to a foil, to a foul foil as ever was any; they did to Him even what they listed; scorned, insulted upon Him. It was then 'the hour and power of darkness.' This Party, whatsoever He is, hath gotten the upper hand, won the field; marches stately, Conqueror-like. His, the day sure.

Well, yet Christ it is. His answer gives Him for no other. To His answer then. The Party, it seems, overheard the Prophet's asking, and is pleased to give an answer to it Himself;
30 we are much bound to Him for it. No man can tell so well as He Himself, who He is. Some other might mistake Him, and misinform us of Him; now we are sure we are right. No *error personæ*.

His name indeed He tells not, but describes Himself by two such notes as can agree to none properly but to Christ. Of none can these two be so affirmed, as of Him they may. That by these two we know this is Christ, as plainly as if His name had been spelled to us. 1. 'Speaking righteousness;' and righteousness referred to speech, signifieth truth ever. 'No guile to be
40 found in His mouth;' and *omnis homo* is—you know what. 2. 'Mighty to save;' and *vana salus hominis*, 'vain is the help of

man.' Who ever spake so right as He spake? Or who ever was
so 'mighty to save' as He? And this is His answer to *quis est
iste.*

'That am I.' One 'that speak righteousness, and am mighty
to save.' Righteous in speaking, mighty in saving, Whose word
is truth, Whose work is salvation. Just and true of My word
and promise; powerful and mighty in performance of both.
The best description, say I, that can be of any man; by His word
and deed both.

10 And see how well they fit. Speaking is most proper; that
refers to Him, as the Word—'in the beginning was the Word'—
to His Divine nature. Saving, that refers to His very name
Jesus, given Him by the Angel as man, for that 'He should
save His people from their sins,' from which none had ever
power to save but He. There have you His two natures.

Speaking refers to His office of Priest: 'the Priest's lips to
preserve knowledge;'—the law of righteousness to be required
at his mouth. Saving, and that mightily, pertains to Him as a
King, is the office, as Daniel calls Him, of 'Messias the Captain.'
20 Righteousness He spake, by His preaching. Saving, that belongs
first to His miraculous suffering, it being far a greater miracle
for the Deity to suffer any the least injury, than to create a new
world, yea many. But secondly, which is proper to the text
and time, in His mighty subduing and treading down hell and
death, and all the power of Satan. *Prophetiza nobis*, they said at
His passion, 'Speak, who hit you' there; and *Ave Rex* they said
too;—both in scorn, but most true both.

You may refer these two, if you please, to His two main
benefits redounding to us from these two. Two things there
30 are that undo us, error and sin. From His speaking we receive
knowledge of His truth, against error. From His saving we
receive the power of grace against sin, and so are saved from
sin's sequel, Edom and Bozrah both. This is His description,
and this is enough. A full description of His Person, in His
natures, offices, benefits; in word and in deed. He it is, and can
be none but He. To reflect a little on these two.

You will observe that His speaking is set down simply, but
in His saving He is said to be 'mighty,' or, as the word is,
multus ad servandum. So, mark where the *multus* is. He is not
40 *multus ad loquendum*, 'one that saith much,' and *paucus ad servandum*, 'and then does little,' as the manner of the world is. *Multus*

is not there at His speech, it is put to *servandum*; there He is much, and His might much; 'much of might to save.'

That His might is not put in treading down or destroying. No, but *multus ad ignoscendum*, in the fifty-fifth chapter before; and *multus ad servandum*, here. 'Mighty' to shew mercy, and to save. Yet 'mighty' He is too, to destroy and tread down; else had He not achieved this victory in the text. 'Mighty to save,' implieth ever mighty to subdue; to subdue them whom He saves us from. Yet of the twain He chooseth rather the term of
10 saving, though both be true, because saving is with Him *primæ intentionis*; so, of the twain, in that He would have His might appear rather. Mighty to destroy He will not have mentioned, or come in His style; but 'mighty to save,' that is His title, that the quality He takes delight in; delights to describe Himself, and to be described by.

You will yet mark also, as the coupling of these two in the description of Christ, for not either of these alone will serve, but between them both they make it up, so that they go together, these two ever. He saves not any but those He teaches.
20 And note the order of them too. For that that stands first, He doth first, first teaches. 'Mighty to save' He is, but whom to save? whom He 'speaks righteousness' to, and they hear Him, and return not again to their former folly. There is no fancying to ourselves we can dispense with one of these, never care whether we deal with the former or no, whether we hear Him speak at all, but take hold of the latter, and be saved with a good will. No; you cannot, but if you hear Him speak first. He saith so, and sets them to Himself.

And put this to it, and I have done this point. That such as is
30 Himself, such if we hear Him will He make us to be. And the more true and soothfast any of us is of His word, the more given to do good and save, the liker to Him, and the liker to have our parts in His rising. We know *quis est iste* now. This for the first part.

II

Now, the Prophet hearing Him answer so gently, takes to him a little courage to ask Him one question more, about His colours; he was a little troubled with them. If you be so 'mighty to save' as you say, how comes it then, what ails your garments to be so red? and adds, what kind of red. And he cannot tell

what to liken them better to, than as if He had newly come out
of some winepress, had been treading grapes, and pressing out
wine there. He calls it wine, but the truth is it was no wine, it
was very blood. New wine in show, blood indeed that upon
His garments. So much appeareth in the next verse following,
where He saith Himself plainly that blood it was that was
sprinkled upon His clothes, and had stained them all over.
We know well, our reason leads us, there could be no vintage
at this time of the year, the season serves not; blood it was.

10 But because the Prophet made mention of a 'winepress,'
had hit on that simile, taking occasion upon the naming it, He
shapes him an answer according; that indeed He had been in a
'winepress.' And so He had. The truth is, He had been in one;
nay, in two then. In one He had been before this here. A double
winepress—we lose nothing by this—we find; Christ was in
both. We cannot well take notice of the one, but we must needs
touch upon the other. But thus they are distinguished. In that
former it was, *In torculari calcatus sum solus;* in this latter it is,
Torcular calcavi solus. In the former, He was Himself trodden and
20 pressed; He was the grapes and clusters Himself. In this latter
here, He that was trodden on before, gets up again, and doth
here tread upon and tread down, *calcare* and *conculcare* (both
words are in the verse) upon some others, as it might be the
Edomites. The press He was trodden in, was His Cross and
Passion. This which He came out of this day, was in His descent
and resurrection, both proper to this feast; one to Good-Friday,
the other to Easter-day.

To pursue this of the winepress a little. The press, the treading in it, is to make wine; *calcatus sum* is properly of grapes, the
30 fruit of the vine. Christ is the 'true Vine,' He saith it Himself.
To make wine of Him, He and the clusters He bare must be
pressed. So He was. Three shrewd strains they gave Him. One,
in Gethsemane, that made Him sweat blood; the wine or blood,
—all is one, came forth at all parts of Him. Another, in the
Judgment hall, Gabbatha, which made the blood run forth at
His head, with the thorns; out of His whole body, with the
scourges; out of His hands and feet, with the nails. The last
strain at Golgotha, where He was so pressed that they pressed
the very soul out of His body, and out ran 'blood and water'
40 both. *Hæc sunt Ecclesiæ gemina Sacramenta*, saith St. Augustine,
out came both Sacraments, 'the twin Sacraments of the Church.'

Out of these pressures ran the blood of the grapes of the true
Vine, the fruit whereof, as it is said in Judges the ninth,
'cheereth both God and man.' God, as a *libamen* or drink-
offering to Him; man, as 'the cup of salvation' to them. But
to make this wine, His clusters were to be cut; cut, and cast in;
cast in, and trodden on; trodden and pressed out; all these,
before He came to be wine in the cup. As likewise, when He
calls Himself *granum frumenti*, 'the wheat-corn,' these four, 1.
the sickle, 2. the flail, 3. the millstone, 4. the oven, He passed
10 through; all went over Him before He was made bread; 'the
shew-bread' to God, to us 'the Bread of life.'

But to return to the winepress, to tell you the occasion or
reason why thus it behoved to be. It was not idly done; what
need then was there of it, this first pressing? We find *calix
dæmoniorum*, the devil hath a cup. Adam must needs be sipping
of it; *Eritis sicut Dii* went down sweetly, but poisoned him,
turned his nature quite. For Adam was by God planted a
natural vine, a true root, but thereby, by that cup, degenerated
into a wild strange vine, which, instead of good grapes,
20 'brought forth' *labruscas*, 'wild grapes;' 'grapes of gall,' 'bitter
clusters,' Moses calls them; *colo-cynthidas*, the Prophet, *mors in
olla*, and *mors in calice;* by which is meant the deadly fruit of
our deadly sins.

But, as it is in the fifth chapter of this prophecy, where God
planted this vine first, He made a winepress in it, so the grapes
that came of this strange vine were cut and cast into the press:
thereof came a deadly wine, of which saith the Psalmist, 'in the
hand of the Lord there is a cup, the wine is red, it is full mixed,
and He pours out of it; and the sinners of the earth are to drink
30 it, dregs and all.' Those sinners were our fathers, and we. It
came to *Bibite ex hoc omnes;* they and we were to drink of it all,
one after another, round. Good reason to drink as we had
brewed, to drink the fruit of our own inventions, our own
words and works we had brought forth.

About the cup went, all strained at it. At last, to Christ it
came; He was none of the sinners, but was found among them.
By His good will He would have had it pass; *transeat a Me calix
iste*,—you know who That was. Yet, rather than we, than any
of us should take it—it would be our bane, He knew—He took
40 it; off it went, dregs and all. Alas, the myrrh they gave Him at
the beginning, the vinegar at the ending of His Passion, were

but poor resemblances of this cup, such as they were. That, another manner draught. We see it cast Him into so unnatural a sweat of blood all over, as if He had been wrung and crushed in a 'winepress' it could not have been more. This, lo, was the first 'winepress,' and Christ in it three days ago; and what with the scourges, nails and spears, besides so pressed as forth it ran, blood or wine, call it what you will, in such so great quantity, as never ran it more plenteously out of any winepress of them all. Here is *Christus in torculari*, Christ's *calcatus sum*.

10 Of which wine so pressed then out of Him came our cup, the cup of this day, 'the cup of the New Testament in His blood,' represented by the blood of the grape. Wherein long before old Jacob foretold Shiloh should 'wash his robe,' as full well He might have done, there came enough to have washed it over and over again. So you see now how the case stands. That former, our cup due to us and no way to Him, He drank for us that it might pass from us, and we not drink it. Ours did He drink, that we might drink of His. He 'the cup of wrath,' that we 'the cup of blessing,' set first before God as a *libamen*, at the
20 sight or scent whereof He smelleth a savour of rest, and is appeased. After reached to us, as a sovereign restorative to recover us of the devil's poison, for we also have been sipping at *calix dæmoniorum* more or less, woe to us for it! and no way but this to cure us of it.

By this time you see the need of the first press, and of His being in it. Into which He was content to be thrown and there trodden on, all to satisfy His Father out of His justice requiring the drinking up of that cup by us or by some for us, and it came to His lot. And never was there lamb so meek before the shearer,
30 nor worm so easy to be trodden on; never cluster lay so quiet and still to be bruised as did Christ in the press of His passion. Ever be He blessed for it.

Now come we to the other of this day in the text. This is not that we have touched but another, wherein the style is altered; no more *calcatus sum*, but *calcavi* and *conculcavi* too. Up it seems He gat, and down went they, and upon them He trod. His enemies of Edom lay like so many clusters under His feet; and 'He cast His shoe' over them, set His foot on them, and dashed them to pieces.
40 If it had meant His passion, it had been His own blood; but this was none of His now, but the blood of His enemies. For

when the year of redemption was past, then came the day of vengeance; then came the time for that, and not before.

For after the *consummatum est* of his own pressure, *sic oportuit impleri omnem justitiam*, and that 'all the righteousness He spake had been fulfilled,' then 'rise up, rise up thou arm of the Lord,' saith the Prophet, and 'shew thyself mightily to save': He took Him to His second attribute, to be avenged of those that had been the ruin of us all, the ruin everlasting, but for Him. To Edom, the kingdom of death, He went, whither we were to be led captives; yea even to Bozrah, to hell itself, and there 'brake the gates of brass, and made the iron-bars fly in sunder.' He That was weak to suffer, became 'mighty to save.' Of *calcatus*, He became *calcator*. He That was thrown Himself, threw them now another while into the press, trod them down, trampled upon them as upon grapes in a fat, till He made the blood spring out of them, and all to sprinkle His garments, as if He had come forth of a winepress indeed. And we before, mercifully rather than mightily by His passion, now mightily also saved by His glorious resurrection.

Thus have you two several vines, the natural and the strange vine, the sweet and the wild; two presses, that in Jewry, that in Edom; two cups, the cursed cup, and the cup of blessing; of wine or blood. His own, His enemies' blood; one, *sanguis Agni*, 'the blood of the Lamb' slain; the other, *sanguis draconis*, 'the blood of the dragon,' 'the red dragon' trod upon. One of His passion, three days since; the other of His victory, as to-day. Between His burial and His rising some doing there had been, somewhat had been done; somewhere He had been, in some new winepress, in Bozrah, that had given a new tincture of red to His raiment all over.

Both these shall you find together set down in one and the same chapter, in two verses standing close one to the other;

1. Christ represented first as a Lamb, 'a Lamb slain,' dyed in His own blood: this is the first press. 2. And immediately in the very next verse, straight represented again in a new shape, as 'a Lion' all be-bloody with the blood of His prey—'a Lion of the Tribe of Judah;' which comes home to this here. For Judah, it is said, he should 'wash his robe in the blood of the grape.' And so much for *torcular calcavi*.

We must not leave out *solus* in any wise; that both these He did 'alone,' so 'alone' as not any man in the world with Him in either.

Not in the first; there pressed He was 'alone.' All forsook Him; His disciples first; 'alone' for them. Yet then He was not 'alone,' His Father was still with Him; but after, Father and all, as appeared by His cry, 'Why hast Thou forsaken Me?' Then was He all 'alone' indeed.

Not in the second neither. The very next verse, He complains how that He looked about Him round, and could not see any would once offer to help Him. Out of Bozrah He got 'alone;' from death He rose, conquered, triumphed in *Semetipso*, 'Himself alone.' The Angel indeed rolled away the stone; but He was risen first, and the stone rolled away after.

Accordingly we to reckon of Him, that since in both these presses He was for us, He and none but He; that His, and none but His, be the glory of both. That seeing neither we for ourselves, nor any for us, could bring this to pass, but He and He only; He and He only might have the whole honour of both, have no partner in that which is only His due, and no creature's else at all, either in Heaven or earth.

And is Christ come from Bozrah? then be sure of this, that He returning thus in triumph, as it is in the sixty-eighth Psalm, the Psalm of the Resurrection, He will not leave us behind for whom He did all this, but 'His own will He bring again as He did from Basan;' as from Basan, so from Bozrah; as 'from the deep pit of the sea,' so from the deep pit of hell. 'He That raised Jesus, shall by Jesus raise us up also' from the Adama of Edom, the red mould of the earth, the power of the grave; and from the Bozrah of hell too, the gulf whence there is no scaping out. Will make us in Him, saith the Apostle, 'more than conquerors,' and tread down Satan under our feet.

You see how Christ's garments came to be 'red.' Of the winepress that made them so we have spoken, but not of the colour itself. A word of that too. It was His colour at His Passion. They put Him in purple; then it was His weed in derision, and so was it in earnest. Both 'red' it was itself, and so He made it more with the dye of His own blood. And the same colour He is now in again at His rising. Not with His own now, but with the blood of the wounded Edomites, whom treading under His feet, their blood bestained Him and His apparel. So one and the same colour at both; dying and rising in red; but with difference as much as is between His own and His enemies' blood.

The spouse in the Canticles, asked of her Beloved's colours, saith of Him, 'My Beloved is white and red.' 'White,' of His own proper: so He was when He shewed Himself in kind, 'transfigured' in the Mount; His apparel then so 'white,' no fuller in the earth could come near it. 'White' of Himself; how comes He 'red' then? Not of Himself that, but for us. That is our natural colour, we are born 'polluted in our own blood.' It is sin's colour that, for shame is the colour of sin. Our sins,
10 saith Isaiah, 'are as crimson of as deep dye as any purple.' This, the true tincture of our sins, the Edomites' colour right, for Edom is red. The tincture, I say, first of our sin original, dyed in the wool; and then again of our sins actual, dyed in the cloth too. Twice dyed; so was Christ twice. Once in His own, again in His enemies', right *dibaphus*, a perfect full colour, a true purple, of a double dye His too. So was it meet for crimson sinners to have a crimson Saviour; a Saviour of such a colour it behoved us to have. Coming then to save us, off went His white, on went our red; laid by His own righteousness to be clothed
20 with our sin. He to wear our colours, that we His; He in our red, that we in His white. So we find our 'robes' are not only 'washed clean,' but dyed a pure white in the blood of the Lamb. Yea, He died and rose again both in our colours, that we might die and rise too in His. We fall now again upon the same point in the colours we did before in the cups. He to drink the sour vinegar of our wild grapes, that we might drink His sweet in the cup of blessing. O cup of blessing, may we say of this cup! O *stolam formosam*, of that colour! *Illi gloriosam, nobis fructuosam;* 'glorious to Him, no less fruitful to us.' He in Mount Gol-
30 gotha like to us, that we in Mount Tabor like to Him. This is the substance of our rejoicing in this colour.

One more; how well this colour fits Him in respect of His two titles, *loquens justitiam*, and *multus ad servandum. Loquens justitiam*, is to wear red; *potens ad servandum* is so too. The first. To whom is this colour given? Scarlet is allowed the degree of Doctors. Why? for their speaking righteousness to us, the righteousness of God, that which Christ spake. Nay, even they which speak but the righteousness of man's law, they are honoured with it too. But Christ 'spake so as never man spake,'
40 and so call ye none on earth Doctor but One; none in comparison of Him. So of all, He to wear it. This ye shall observe in the

Revelation; at the first appearing of the Lamb, there was a
book with seven seals. No man would meddle with it; the
Lamb took it, opened the seals, read it, read out of it a lecture
of righteousness to the whole world; the righteousness of God,
that shall make us so before Him. Let Him be arrayed in scarlet;
it is His due, His Doctor's weed.

This is no new thing. The heathen king propounded it for
a reward to any that could read the hand-writing on the wall.
Daniel did it, and had it. *Sed ecce major Daniele hic.* Thus was it
in the Law. This colour was the ground of the Ephod, a principal ingredient into the Priest's vesture. Why? For, 'his lips were
to preserve knowledge,' all to require the law from his mouth.
And indeed, the very lips themselves that we speak righteousness with, are of the same colour. In the Canticles it is said, 'His
lips are like a scarlet thread.' And the fruit of the lips hath God
created peace, and the fruit of peace is sown in righteousness;
and till that be sown and spoken, never any hope of true peace.

Enough for speaking. What say you to the other, *potens ad
servandum*, which of the twain seems the more proper to this
time and place? I say that way it fits Him too, this colour. Men
of war, great captains, 'mighty to save' us from the enemies,
they take it to themselves, and their colour it is of right. A
plain text for it, Nahum the second. 'Their valiant men,' or
captains, 'are in scarlet.' And I told you Christ by Daniel is
called 'Captain Messias,' and so well might. So in His late con-
flict with Edom He shewed Himself, fought for us even to
blood. Many a bloody wound it cost Him, but returned with
the spoil of His enemies, stained with their blood; and whoso
is able so to do, is worthy to wear it. So in this respect also, so
in both; His colours become Him well.

Shall I put you in mind, that there is in these two, in either
of them, a kind of winepress? In 'mighty to save,' it is evident;
trodden in one press, treading in another. Not so evident in
'the speaking of righteousness.' Yet even in that also, there is a
press going. For when we read, what do we but gather grapes
here and there; and when we study what we have gathered,
then are we even *in torculari*, and press them we do, and press
out of them that which daily you taste of. I know there is
great odds in the liquors so pressed, and that 'a cluster of
Ephraim is worth a whole vintage of Abiezer;' but for that,
every man as he may. Nay, it may be farther said, and that truly,

that even this great title, 'Mighty to save,' comes under *loquens justitiam*. There is in the word of righteousness a saving power. 'Take the word,' saith St. James, 'graft it in you, it is able to save your souls;' even that wherein we of this calling in a sort participate with Christ, while 'by attending to reading and doctrine we save both ourselves and them that hear us;' we tread down sin, and save sinners from 'seeking death in the error of their life.'

But though there be in the word a saving power, yet is not
10 all saving power in that, nor in that only; there is a press beside. For this press is going continually among us, but there is another that goes but at times. But in that, it goes at such times as it falls in fit with the winepress here. Nay, falls in most fit of all the rest. For of it comes very wine indeed, the blood of the grapes of the true Vine, which in the blessed Sacrament is reached to us, and with it is given us that for which it was given, even remission of sins. Not only represented therein, but even exhibited to us. Both which when we partake, then have we a full and perfect communion with Christ this
20 day; of His speaking righteousness in the word preached, of His power to save in the holy Eucharist ministered. Both presses run for us, and we to partake them both.

I may not end till I tell you there remaineth yet another, a third winepress; that you may take heed of it. I will but point you to it; it may serve as sour herbs to eat our Paschal lamb with. The sun, they say, danced this morning at Christ's resurrection; the earth trembled then I am sure, there was an earthquake at Christ's rising. So there is trembling to our joy; *exultate in tremore*, as the Psalmist wills us. The vintage of the
30 earth, when the time of that is come, and when the grapes be ripe and ready for it, one there is that crieth to him with the 'sharp sickle' in his hand to 'thrust it in,' cut off the clusters, 'and cast them into the great winepress of the wrath of God.' A dismal day that, a pitiful slaughter then. It is there said, 'the blood shall come up to the horse-bridles by the space of a thousand six hundred furlongs.' Keep you out, take heed of coming in that press.

We have a kind item given us of this, here in the text, in the last verse. There be two acts of Christ; one of being trodden,
40 the other of treading down. The first is for His chosen, the other against His enemies. One is called 'the year of redemption,'

the other 'the day of vengeance.' 'The year of redemption' is
already come, and is now; we are in it; during which time the
two former winepresses run, 1. of the word, and 2. Sacrament.
'The day of vengeance' is not yet come, it is but in His heart—
so the text is—that is, but in His purpose and intent yet. But
certainly come it will, that day; and with that day comes the
last winepress with the blood to the bridles: ere it come, and
during our 'year of redemption,' that year's allowance, we are
to endeavour to keep ourselves out of it; for that is 'the day of
10 vengeance,' of *ira ventura*, God's wrath for ever. So as all we
have to study is, how we may be in at the first two, out at the
last press; and the due Christian use of the first, will keep us
from the last.

While then it is with us 'the year of redemption,' and before
that day come; while it is yet time of speaking righteousness,
that is, 'to-day if ye will hear His voice;' while 'the cup of
blessing' is held out, if we will take it, lay hold on both. That
so we may be accounted worthy to escape in that day, from that
day and the vengeance of it; and may feel the fulness of His
20 saving power in 'the word engrafted, which is able to save our
souls;' and in 'the cup of salvation' which is joined with it, and
that to our endless joy. 'The year of redemption' is last in the
verse; with that the Prophet ends. With that let us end also;
and to that end, may all that hath been spoken arrive and bring
us.

V

John Donne

1573–1631

No English preacher has excited more interest, alive or dead, than John Donne. Some part of the interest can be written down to the biographical circumstances, the making of a clergyman out of the witty and learned love poet, and to such remarkable behaviour as Donne preaching his own funeral sermon (*Death's Duel*) and posing for a portrait just before his death in his own funeral shroud. Donne was fascinated by extremes, and although his 160 sermons are largely given up to sober exposition of doctrine with a professional complement of biblical and patristic learning, when he does reach extremes it is with great intensity. In these places his own personal voice breaks through—a process which critics have described[1] as giving the sermons 'their special note of anguished contrition, unrest, and ecstasy', and during which 'we do not feel in Donne, as we do in St Paul, God speaking to man, but rather man speaking to God'. The difference with Andrewes is immediately obvious: where his senior is sharp, precise, intensely dedicated to the Word on a small scale, Donne needs much more room to build up an argument or emotion, and works in large-scale effects, best of all at those extremes of joy and despair, hope and fear. Donne is more exciting, sensational, rhetorical than Andrewes, but not so thoughtful or thought-provoking, working rather on our emotions with the twin poles of Christian exhortation, rewards and punishments, heaven and hell. The potential faults of the one are a short-sighted focus on the immediate context; of the other, over-elaboration, inflated repetition.

It is not simply some psychological peculiarity that brings Donne to these extremes, but the completely valid Christian condemnation of the world—Donne joins the Augustinian tradition in chronicling 'the most inglorious and contemptible vilification, the most deadly and peremptory nullification of man' which thoughts of death and decay produce. What makes

[1] See Douglas Bush, *English Literature in the Earlier Seventeenth Century*, O.U.P., 1945, p. 306.

the attack unique and so terrifying (as it makes the complementary state of joy so inspiring) is Donne's power as a speaker, his eloquence. As one might expect of England's greatest lyric poet, his imagery in prose has imaginative power a concrete realization: he is extremely sensitive to the use of metaphor in the Bible, often commenting on the distinction between literal and metaphorical there, or on the recurrent images. But it does not have the condensation that it has in his verse. Here as in everything he needs room to move, and one characteristic of his imagery is its prolonged extension and variation of a theme, as in this account of God's mercy:

> particular mercies are feathers of his wings, and that prayer 'Lord, let thy mercy lighten upon us, as our trust is in thee' is our birdlime; particular mercies are that cloud of quails which hovered over the host of Israel, and that prayer 'Lord let thy mercy lighten upon us' is our net to catch, our Gomer [container] to fill of those quails. The air is not so full of moats, of atoms, as the Church is of mercies; and as we can suck in no part of air but we take in those moats, those atoms, so here in the congregation we cannot suck in a word from the preacher, we cannot speak, we cannot sigh a prayer to God, but that the whole breath and air is made of mercy.

Image merges into image, and although one could analyse the associations which heighten the development it is more important to respond to it as a whole. Another characteristic use of metaphor is almost opposed: instead of starting within an image and extending it he takes a separate object, an analogy which is initially distinct but which is then brought into imaginative connection with the subject.

In the sermon which I have chosen both types of imagery are used (the classification is only important in so far as it encourages us to think analytically about metaphor). Thus for the second type, which one might call 'translation' (reviving the Latin term for metaphor, *translatio*), there is, towards the end, that remarkable geographical analogy:

> If you look upon this world in a map you find two hemispheres, two half worlds. If you crush heaven into a map, you may find two hemispheres too, two half heavens: half will be Joy, and half will be Glory; for in these two, the joy

of heaven and the glory of heaven, is all heaven often represented unto us. And as of those two hemispheres of the world
the first hath been known long before, but the other (that of
America, which is the richer in treasure) God reserved for
later discoveries; so though he reserve that hemisphere of
heaven, which is the Glory thereof, to the Resurrection, yet
the other hemisphere, the Joy of heaven, God opens to our
discovery and delivers for our habitation even whilst we
dwell in the world.

There Donne started by moving outside his real interest and
then translated this other body of experience back into the life
of his argument with a great increase in meaning, and in a slow
and deliberate way which allowed us to feel the whole force
of the analogy. Examples of the first type, extension and variation, are numerous, and few better than that in the opening
paragraph, the sequence of images for the healing power of the
Psalms, or the discussion of the Bible's metaphors for God.

Donne makes equally inventive use of the other great expressive device in Renaissance prose, syntactical symmetry. Not
a page is without examples and if one has to admit that sometimes the repetitions simply reiterate a point without adding
to it, there are also sequences where Donne fully exploits
the potential of this resource to play off expected against unexpected returns of a pattern, and to adjust the syntactical
movement to that within the sense. One sufficiently complex
example is this, taken from a sermon where the central image
is of the arrows shot by God to pierce human evil, evil which
shows itself even when pretending to be good:

In our alms there are trumpets blown,
   there's an arrow of vain-glory;
in our fastings there are disfigurings,
      there's an arrow of hypocrisy;
in our purity there is contempt of others,
      there's an arrow of pride;
in our coming to church
      there is custom and formality;
in hearing sermons
      there is affection to the parts of the preacher.
In our sinful actions these arrows abound;
in our best   actions they   lie hid;

and as thy soul is in every part of thee,
body and soul,
they stick, and stick fast, in thee,
in all thee.

Fallen man cannot escape his tendency to sin, and at each stage
in that sentence the symmetry pointed up both the vice and the
accusation, until the collapse of the pattern at the end coincided
with the reduction of the sense to its focal point—'stick fast, in
thee, in all thee'.

In the sermon which follows there are many such inventive
applications of syntactical symmetry, such as the sequence
beginning 'As soon as I hear God say' with its juxtaposition
of human greatness and catastrophe, a juxtaposition which is
caught up by the symmetries—on the other side is a weight of
glory, a weight

that turns the scale;
for as it makes all worldly prosperity as dung,
so it makes all worldly adversity as feathers.

The two extremes are typical of Donne, and they account for
two of the greatest passages here or in any of the sermons: the
first is the paragraph beginning 'Let me wither and wear out
mine age in a discomfortable, in an unwholesome, in a penurious prison', and which moves from those ominous repetitions
to a blistering presentation of man's worthless and hopeless
state if deprived of God's grace. Throughout syntax and imagery combine (it is only for convenience that one separates
them), and the images have remarkable presence—the greatest
human suffering, if God's blessing still exists, 'is but a caterpillar got into one corner of my garden, but a mildew fallen
upon one acre of my corn'. Almost more intense is the syntactical movement, with Donne's characteristic acceleration towards a climax, the repetition of 'when' acting as a punctuation-
mark which sets off the stages of the increase in height, until
all collapses on those last four terrible adverbs. One may feel
that some of the detail of the repetition is factitious (for example, the doubling of 'Almighty God'), but the overall effect is
compelling. At the opposite end of the scale from this fire and
brimstone is the vision of joy in the last paragraph ('holy Joy'
is the key phrase throughout and the sermon might help us to

understand why 'joy' is so important to Blake). Again syntax and imagery unite: 'Howling is the noise of hell, singing the voice of heaven; sadness the damp of hell, rejoicing the serenity of heaven'; 'the true joy in this world shall flow into the joy of heaven, as a river flows into the sea.' The movement becomes more and more insistent, and the incantatory repetitions of 'joy' and 'heaven' in the last few sentences help in the general speeding-up as the words gradually take off and ascend into a vision of joy 'super-invested in glory'. The best comment is again one of the preacher's own, the phrase which Donne once used to describe faith in general but which can be applied both to the substance as to the style of his sermons: 'A blessed incantation.'

The Second of my Prebend Sermons Upon My Five Psalms
Preached at St Paul's, January 29, 1626
Psalm lxiii 7

Because thou hast been my help, therefore in the shadow of thy wings will I rejoice.

The Psalms are the manna of the church. As manna tasted to every man like that he liked best, so do the Psalms minister instruction, and satisfaction, to every man, in every emergency and occasion. David was not only a clear prophet of Christ himself, but a prophet of every particular Christian; he foretells what I, what any shall do, and suffer, and say. And as the whole Book of Psalms is *oleum effusum*, (as the spouse speaks of the name of Christ) an ointment poured out upon all sorts of sores, a cerecloth that supples all bruises, a balm that searches
10 all wounds; so are there some certain Psalms, that are imperial Psalms, that command over all affections, and spread themselves over all occasions, catholic, universal Psalms, that apply themselves to all necessities. This is one of those; for, of those constitutions which are called apostolical, one is, that the church should meet every day, to sing this Psalm. And accordingly, St Chrysostom testifies, That it was decreed, and ordained by the primitive fathers, that no day should pass without the public singing of this Psalm. Under both these obligations, (those ancient constitutions, called the apostle's, and those ancient
20 decrees made by the primitive fathers) belongs to me, who have

97

my part in the service of God's church, the especial meditation,
and recommendation of this Psalm. And under a third obligation too, that it is one of those five Psalms, the daily rehearsing
whereof, is enjoined to me, by the constitutions of this church,
as five other are to every other person of our body. As the
whole book is manna, so these five Psalms are my gomer,
which I am to fill and empty every day of this manna.

Now as the spirit and soul of the whole Book of Psalms is
contracted into this Psalm, so is the spirit and soul of this
10 whole Psalm contracted into this verse. The key of the Psalm,
(as St Jerome calls the titles of the Psalms) tells us, That David
uttered this Psalm, 'when he was in the wilderness of Judah';
there we see the present occasion that moved him; and we see
what was passed between God and him before, in the first
clause of our text; ('Because thou hast been my help') and
then we see what was to come, by the rest, ('Therefore in the
shadow of thy wings will I rejoice'). So that we have here the
whole compass of time, past, present, and future; and these
three parts of time, shall be at this time, the three parts of this
20 exercise; first, what David's distress put him upon for the
present; and that lies in the context; secondly, how David
built his assurance upon that which was past; ('Because thou
hast been my help'). And thirdly, what he established to himself for the future, ('Therefore in the shadow of thy wings will
I rejoice'). First, his distress in the wilderness, his present estate
carried him upon the memory of that which God had done for
him before, and the remembrance of that carried him upon that,
of which he assured himself after. Fix upon God any where,
and you shall find him a circle; he is with you now, when you
30 fix upon him; he was with you before, for he brought you out
to this fixation; and he will be with you hereafter, for 'he is
yesterday, and to-day, and the same for ever'.

For David's present condition, who was now in a banishment, in a persecution in the wilderness of Judah, (which is our
first part) we shall only insist upon that, (which is indeed spread
over all the Psalm to the text, and ratified in the text) that in all
those temporal calamities David was only sensible of his spiritual
loss; it grieved him not that he was kept from Saul's court, but
that he was kept from God's church. For when he says, by
40 way of lamentation, 'That he was in a dry and thirsty land, where
no water was,' he expresses what penury, what barrenness,

what drought and what thirst he meant; 'To see thy power, and thy glory, so as I have seen thee in the sanctuary.' For there, 'my soul shall be satisfied as with marrow, and with fatness', and there, 'my mouth shall praise thee with joyful lips'. And in some few considerations conducing to this, that spiritual losses are incomparably heavier than temporal, and that therefore, the restitution to our spiritual happiness, or the continuation of it, is rather to be made the subject of our prayers to God, in all pressures and distresses, than of temporal, we shall determine
10 that first part. And for the particular branches of both the other parts, (the remembering of God's benefits past, and the building of an assurance for the future, upon that remembrance) it may be fitter to open them to you anon, when we come to handle them, than now. Proceed we now to our first part, the comparing of temporal and spiritual afflictions.

I

In the way of this comparison, falls first the consideration of the universality of afflictions in general, and the inevitableness thereof. It is a blessed metaphor, that the Holy Ghost hath put into the mouth of the apostle, *Pondus gloriæ*, That our 'afflictions'
20 are but 'light', because there is an 'exceeding', and an 'eternal weight of glory' attending them. If it were not for that exceeding weight of glory, no other weight in this world could turn the scale, or weigh down those infinite weights of afflictions that oppress us here. There is not only *Pestis valde gravis*, ('The pestilence grows heavy upon the land') but there is *Musca valde gravis*, God calls in but the fly, to vex Egypt, and even the fly is a heavy burden unto them. It is not only Job that complains, 'That he was a burden to himself' but even Absalom's hair was a burden to him, till it was polled. It is not only Jeremy that
30 complains, *Aggravavit compedes*, That God had made their fetters and their chains heavy to them, but the workmen in harvest complain, That God had made a fair day heavy unto them, ('We have borne the heat, and the burden of the day'). 'Sand is heavy,' says Solomon; and how many suffer so? under a sand-hill of crosses, daily, hourly afflictions, that are heavy by their number, if not by their single weight? And 'a stone is heavy'; (says he in the same place) and how many suffer so? How many, without any former preparatory cross, or comminatory, or

commonitory cross, even in the midst of prosperity, or security,
fall under some one stone, some grindstone, some millstone,
some one insupportable cross that ruins them? But then, (says
Solomon there) 'A fool's anger is heavier than both'; and how
many children, and servants, and wives suffer under the anger,
and morosity, and peevishness, and jealousy of foolish masters,
and parents, and husbands, though they must not say so?
David and Solomon have cried out, That all this world is
'vanity', and 'levity'; and (God knows) all is weight, and bur-
10 den, and heaviness, and oppression; and if there were not a
weight of future glory to counterpoise it, we should all sink
into nothing.

I ask not Mary Magdalen, whether lightness were not a
burden (for sin is certainly, sensibly a burden); but I ask Susanna
whether even chaste beauty were not a burden to her; and I ask
Joseph whether personal comeliness were not a burden to him.
I ask not Dives, who perished in the next world, the question;
but I ask them who are made examples of Solomon's rule, of
that 'sore evil,' (as he calls it) 'Riches kept to the owners thereof
20 for their hurt,' whether riches be not a burden.

All our life is a continual burden, yet we must not groan; a
continual squeezing, yet we must not pant; and as in the tenderness of our childhood, we suffer, and yet are whipped if we cry,
so we are complained of, if we complain, and made delinquents
if we call the times ill. And that which adds weight to weight,
and multiplies the sadness of this consideration, is this, That
still the best men have had most laid upon them. As soon as I
hear God say, That he hath found 'an upright man, that fears
God, and eschews evil,' in the next lines I find a commission to
30 Satan, to bring in Sabeans and Chaldeans upon his cattle, and
servants, and fire and tempest upon his children, and loath-
some diseases upon himself. As soon as I hear God say, That he
hath found 'a man according to his own heart,' I see his sons
ravish his daughters, and then murder one another, and then
rebel against the father, and put him into straits for his life. As
soon as I hear God testify of Christ at his baptism, 'This is my
beloved Son in whom I am well pleased,' I find that Son of his
'led up by the Spirit to be tempted of the devil.' And after I hear
God ratify the same testimony again, at his transfiguration,
40 ('This is my beloved Son, in whom I am well pleased') I find
that beloved Son of his, deserted, abandoned, and given over

to scribes, and Pharisees, and publicans, and Herodians, and
priests, and soldiers, and people, and judges, and witnesses,
and executioners, and he that was called the beloved Son of
God, and made partaker of the glory of heaven, in this world,
in his transfiguration, is made now the sewer of all the corruption, of all the sins of this world, as no Son of God, but a mere
man, as no man, but a contemptible worm. As though the
greatest weakness in this world, were man, and the greatest
fault in man were to be good, man is more miserable than other
10 creatures, and good men more miserable than any other
men.

But then there is *Pondus gloriæ*, 'An exceeding weight of
eternal glory,' and that turns the scale; for as it makes all worldly
prosperity as dung, so it makes all worldly adversity as feathers.
And so it had need; for in the scale against it, there are not only
put temporal afflictions, but spiritual too; and to these two
kinds, we may accommodate those words, 'He that falls upon
this stone,' (upon temporal afflictions) may be bruised, broken,
'But he upon whom that stone falls,' (spiritual afflictions) 'is in
20 danger to be ground to powder.' And then, the great, and yet
ordinary danger is, that these spiritual afflictions grow out of
temporal; murmuring, and diffidence in God, and obduration,
out of worldly calamities; and so against nature, the fruit is
greater and heavier than the tree, spiritual heavier than temporal afflictions.

They who write of natural story, propose that plant for the
greatest wonder in nature, which being no firmer than a bul-
rush, or a reed, produces and bears for the fruit thereof no other
but an entire, and very hard stone. That temporal affliction
30 should produce spiritual stoniness, and obduration, is unnatural, yet ordinary. Therefore doth God propose it, as one of
those greatest blessings, which he multiplies upon his people,
'I will take away your stony hearts, and give you hearts of flesh';
and, Lord let me have a fleshly heart in any sense, rather than a
stony heart. We find mention amongst the observers of rarities
in nature, of hairy hearts, hearts of men, that have been over-
grown with hair; but of petrified hearts, hearts of men grown
into stone, we read not; for this petrifaction of the heart, this
stupefaction of a man, is the last blow of God's hand upon the
40 heart of man in this world. Those great afflictions which are
poured out of the vials of the seven angels upon the world, are

still accompanied with that heavy effect, that that affliction hardened them. 'They were scorched with heats and plagues,' by the fourth angel, and it follows, 'They blasphemed the name of God, and repented not, to give him glory.' Darkness was induced upon them by the fifth angel, and it follows, 'They blasphemed the God of heaven, and repented not of their deeds.' And from the seventh angel there fell hailstones of the weight of talents, (perchance four pound weight) upon men; and yet these men had so much life left, as to 'blaspheme God', out of

10 that respect, which alone should have brought them to glorify God, 'Because the plague thereof was exceeding great.' And when a great plague brings them to blaspheme, how great shall that second plague be, that comes upon them for blaspheming?

Let me wither and wear out mine age in a discomfortable, in an unwholesome, in a penurious prison, and so pay my debts with my bones, and recompense the wastefulness of my youth, with the beggary of mine age; let me wither in a spital under sharp, and foul, and infamous diseases, and so recompense the wantonness of my youth, with that loathsomeness in mine age:

20 yet, if God withdraw not his spiritual blessings, his grace, his patience, if I can call my suffering his doing, my passion his action, all this that is temporal, is but a caterpillar got into one corner of my garden, but a mildew fallen upon one acre of my corn; the body of all, the substance of all is safe, as long as the soul is safe. But when I shall trust to that, which we call a good spirit, and God shall deject, and impoverish, and evacuate that spirit, when I shall rely upon a moral constancy, and God shall shake, and enfeeble, and enervate, destroy and demolish that constancy; when I shall think to refresh myself in the

30 serenity and sweet air of a good conscience, and God shall call up the damps and vapours of hell itself, and spread a cloud of diffidence, and an impenetrable crust of desperation upon my conscience; when health shall fly from me, and I shall lay hold upon riches to succour me, and comfort me in my sickness, and riches shall fly from me, and I shall snatch after favour, and good opinion, to comfort me in my poverty; when even this good opinion shall leave me, and calumnies and misinformations shall prevail against me; when I shall need peace, because there is none but thou, O Lord, that should stand for me, and then shall

40 find, that all the wounds that I have, come from thy hand, all the arrows that stick in me, from thy quiver; when I shall see,

that because I have given myself to my corrupt nature, thou
hast changed thine; and because I am all evil towards thee,
therefore thou hast given over being good towards me; when
it comes to this height, that the fever is not in the humours, but
in the spirits, that mine enemy is not an imaginary enemy,
fortune, nor a transitory enemy, malice in great persons, but
a real, and an irresistible, and an inexorable, and an everlasting
enemy, the Lord of hosts himself, the Almighty God himself,
the Almighty God himself only knows the weight of this
10 affliction, and except he put in that *pondus gloriæ*, that exceeding
weight of an eternal glory, with his own hand, into the other
scale, we are weighed down, we are swallowed up, irreparably,
irrevocably, irrecoverably, irremediably.

   This is the fearful depth, this is spiritual misery, to be thus
fallen from God. But was this David's case? Was he fallen thus
far, into a diffidence in God? No. But the danger, the precipice,
the slippery sliding into that bottomless depth, is, to be excluded from the means of coming to God, or staying with
God; and this is that that David laments here, that by being
20 banished, and driven into the wilderness of Judah, he had not
access to the sanctuary of the Lord, to sacrifice his part in the
praise, and to receive his part in the prayers of the congregation; for angels pass not to ends, but by ways and means, nor
men to the glory of the triumphant church, but by participation
of the communion of the militant. To this note David sets his
harp, in many, many psalms: sometimes, that God had suffered
his enemies to possess his tabernacle, ('He forsook the tabernacle of Shiloh, he delivered his strength into captivity, and his
glory into the enemies' hands',) but most commonly he com-
30 plains, that God disabled him from coming to the sanctuary.
In which one thing he had summed up all his desires, all his
prayers, ('One thing have I desired of the Lord, that I will look
after; that I may dwell in the house of the Lord, all the days of
my life, to behold the beauty of the Lord, and to inquire in his
temple') his vehement desire of this, he expresses again, 'My
soul thirsteth for God, for the living God; when shall I come
and appear before God?' He expresses a holy jealousy, a religious envy, even to the sparrows and swallows, yea, 'the sparrow
hath found a house, and the swallow a nest for herself, and
40 where she may lay her young, even thine altars, O Lord of
hosts, my King and my God'. Thou art my King, and my God,

and yet excludest me from that, which thou affordest to sparrows, 'And are not we of more value than many sparrows?'

And as though David felt some false-ease, some half-temptation, some whispering that way, that God is 'in the wilderness of Judah,' in every place, as well as in his 'Sanctuary', there is in the original in that place, a pathetical, a vehement, a broken expressing expressed, 'O thine altars'; it is true, (says David) thou art here in the wilderness, and I may see thee here, and serve thee here, but, 'O thine altars, O Lord of hosts, my King and my God.' When David could not come in person to that place, yet he bent towards the temple, ('In thy fear will I worship towards thy holy temple.') Which was also Daniel's devotion; when he prayed, 'his chamber windows were open towards Jerusalem'; and so is Hezekiah's turning to the wall to weep, and to pray in his sick bed, understood to be to that purpose, to conform, and compose himself towards the temple. In the place consecrated for that use, God by Moses fixes the service, and fixes the reward; and towards that place, (when they could not come to it) doth Solomon direct their devotion in the consecration of the temple, ('When they are in the wars, when they are in captivity, and pray towards this house, do thou hear them.') For, as in private prayer, when (according to Christ's command) we are shut in our chamber, there is exercised *modestia fidei*, the modesty and bashfulness of our faith, not pressing upon God in his house: so in the public prayers of the congregation, there is exercised the fervour and holy courage of our faith, for *Agmine facto obsidemus Deum*, it is a mustering of our forces, and a besieging of God. Therefore does David so much magnify their blessedness, that are in this house of God; ('Blessed are they that dwell in thy house, for they will be still praising thee') those that look towards it, may praise thee sometimes, but those men who dwell in the church, and whose whole service lies in the church, have certainly an advantage of all other men (who are necessarily withdrawn by worldly businesses) in making themselves acceptable to Almighty God, if they do their duties, and observe their church services aright.

Man being therefore thus subject naturally to manifold calamities, and spiritual calamities being incomparably heavier than temporal, and the greatest danger of falling into such spiritual calamities being in our absence from God's church, where only the outward means of happiness are ministered unto us, certainly there is much tenderness and deliberation to be used, before the church doors be shut against any man. If I would not direct a prayer to God, to excommunicate any man from the triumphant church, (which were to damn him) I would not oil the key, I would not make the way too slippery for excommunications in the militant church; for that is to endanger him. I know how distasteful a sin to God, contumacy, and contempt, and disobedience to order and authority is; and I know, (and 10 all men, that choose not ignorance, may know) that our excommunications (though calumniators impute them to small things, because, many times, the first complaint is of some small matter) never issue but upon contumacies, contempts, disobediences to the church. But they are real contumacies, not interpretative, apparent contumacies, not presumptive, that excommunicate a man in heaven; and much circumspection is required, and (I am far from doubting it) exercised in those cases upon earth; for, though every excommunication upon earth be not sealed in heaven, though it damn not the man, yet it dams up that 20 man's way, by shutting him out of that church, through which he must go to the other; which being so great a danger, let every man take heed of excommunicating himself. The impersuasible recusant does so; the negligent libertine does so; the fantastic separatist does so; the half-present man, he, whose body is here, and mind away, does so; and he, whose body is but half here, his limbs are here upon a cushion, but his eyes, his ears are not here, does so: all these are self-excommunicators, and keep themselves from hence. Only he enjoys that blessing, the want whereof David deplores, that is here entirely, 30 and is glad he is here, and glad to find this kind of service here, that he does, and wishes no other.

And so we have done with our first part, David's aspect, his present condition, and his danger of falling into spiritual miseries, because his persecution, and banishment amounted to an excommunication, to an excluding of him from the service of God, in the church. And we pass, in our order proposed at first, to the second, his retrospect, the consideration, what God had done for him before, 'Because thou hast been my help.'

II

Through this second part, we shall pass by these three steps. First, that it behoves us, in all our purposes, and actions, to propose to ourselves a copy to write by, a pattern to work by, a rule, or an example to proceed by, because it hath been thus heretofore, says David, I will resolve upon this course for the future. And secondly, that the copy, the pattern, the precedent which we are to propose to ourselves, is, the observation of God's former ways and proceedings upon us, because God hath already gone this way, this way I will await his going still. And 10 then, thirdly, and lastly, in this second part, the way that God had formerly gone with David, which was, That he had been his help, ('Because thou hast been my help'.)

First then, from the meanest artificer, through the wisest philosopher, to God himself, all that is well done, or wisely undertaken, is undertaken and done according to pre-conceptions, fore-imaginations, designs, and patterns proposed to ourselves beforehand. A carpenter builds not a house, but that he first sets up a frame in his own mind, what kind of house he will build. The little great philosopher Epictetus, would under-
20 take no action, but he would first propose to himself, what Socrates, or Plato, what a wise man would do in that case, and according to that, he would proceed. Of God himself, it is safely resolved in the School, that he never did anything in any part of time, of which he had not an eternal pre-conception, an eternal Idea, in himself before. Of which Ideas, that is, pre-conceptions, pre-determinations in God, St Augustine pronounces, *Tanta vis in ideis constituitur*, There is so much truth, and so much power in these Ideas, as that without acknowledging them, no man can acknowledge God, for he does not allow
30 God counsel, and wisdom, and deliberation in his actions, but sets God on work, before he have thought what he will do. And therefore he, and others of the fathers read that place, (which we read otherwise) *Quod factum est, in ipso vita erat;* that is, In all their expositions, whatsoever is made, in time, was alive in God, before it was made, that is, in that eternal Idea, and pattern which was in him. So also do divers of those fathers read those words to the Hebrews, (which we read, 'The things that are seen, are not made of things that do appear') *Ex invisibilibus visibilia facta sunt*, 'Things formerly invisible, were made visible'; that is, we

see them not till now, till they are made, but they had an invisible being, in that Idea, in that pre-notion, in that purpose of God before, for ever before. Of all things in heaven, and earth, but of himself, God had an Idea, a pattern in himself, before he made it.

And therefore let him be our pattern for that, to work after patterns; to propose to ourselves rules and examples for all our actions; and the more, the more immediately, the more directly our actions concern the service of God. If I ask God, by what
10 Idea he made me, God produces his *Faciamus hominem ad ima-*
ginem nostram, That there was a concurrence of the whole Trinity, to make me in Adam, according to that image which they were, and according to that Idea, which they had pre-determined. If I pretend to serve God, and he ask me for my Idea, How I mean to serve him, shall I be able to produce none? If he ask me an Idea of my religion, and my opinions, shall I not be able to say, It is that which thy word, and thy catholic church hath imprinted in me? If he ask me an Idea of my prayers, shall I not be able to say, It is that which my particular necessi-
20 ties, that which the form prescribed by thy Son, that which the care and piety of the church, in conceiving fit prayers, hath imprinted in me? If he ask me an Idea of my sermons, shall I not be able to say, It is that which the analogy of faith, the edification of the congregation, the zeal of thy work, the meditations of my heart hath imprinted in me? But if I come to pray or to preach without this kind of Idea, if I come to extemporal prayer, extemporal preaching, I shall come to an extemporal faith, and extemporal religion; and then I must look for an extemporal heaven, a heaven to be made for me; for to that heaven which
30 belongs to the catholic church, I shall never come, except I go by the way of the catholic church, by former Ideas, former examples, former patterns, to believe according to ancient beliefs, to pray according to ancient forms, to preach according to former meditations. God does nothing, man does nothing well, without these Ideas, these retrospects, this recourse to pre-conceptions, pre-deliberations.

Something then I must propose to myself, to be the rule, and the reason of my present and future actions; which was our first branch in this second part: and then the second is, that I can
40 propose nothing more availably, than the contemplation of the history of God's former proceeding with me; which is David's

way here, because this was God's way before, I will look for
God in this way still. That language in which God spake to
man, the Hebrew, hath no present tense; they form not their
verbs as our Western languages do, in the present, 'I hear',
or 'I see', or 'I read', but they begin at that which is past, 'I
have seen', and 'heard', and 'read'. God carries us in his language, in his speaking, upon that which is past, upon that which
he hath done already; I cannot have better security for present,
nor future, than God's former mercies exhibited to me. *Quis*
10 *non gaudeat*, says St Augustine, Who does not triumph with joy,
when he considers what God hath done? *Quis non et ea, quæ
nondum venerunt, ventura sperat, propter illa, quæ jam tanta impleta
sunt?* Who can doubt the performance of all, that sees the
greatest part of a prophesy performed? If I have found that
true that God hath said, of the person of anti-Christ, why
should I doubt of that which he says of the ruin of anti-Christ?
Credamus modicum quod restat, says the same father, It is much
that we have seen done, and it is but little that God hath reserved
to our faith, to believe that it shall be done.

20   There is no state, no church, no man, that hath not this tie
upon God, that hath not God in these bands, that God by
having done much for them already, hath bound himself to do
more. Men proceed in their former ways, sometimes, lest they
should confess an error, and acknowledge that they had been
in a wrong way. God is obnoxious to no error, and therefore
he does still, as he did before. Every one of you can say now
to God, Lord, thou broughtest me hither, therefore enable me
to hear; Lord, thou doest that, therefore make me understand;
and that, therefore let me believe; and that too, therefore streng-
30 then me to the practice; and all that, therefore continue me to
perseverance. Carry it up to the first sense and apprehension
that ever thou hadst of God's working upon thee, either in thyself, when thou camest first to the use of reason, or in others in
thy behalf, in thy baptism, yet when thou thinkest thou art at
the first, God had done something for thee before all that;
before that, he had elected thee, in that election which St
Augustine speaks of, *Habet electos, quos creaturus est eligendos*, God
hath elected certain men, whom he intends to create, that he
may elect them; that is, that he may declare his election upon
40 them. God had thee, before he made thee; he loved thee first,
and then created thee, that thou loving him, he might continue

his love to thee. The surest way, and the nearest way to lay hold
upon God, is the consideration of that which he had done already. So David does; and that which he takes knowledge of, in
particular, in God's former proceedings towards him, is,
because God had been his help, which is our last branch in this
part, 'Because thou hast been my help.'

From this one word, that God hath been my help, I make
account that we have both these notions; first, that God hath
not left me to myself, he hath come to my succour, he hath
10 helped me; and then, that God hath not left out myself; he
hath been my help, but he hath left something for me to do with
him, and by his help. My security for the future, in this consideration of that which is past, lies not only in this, that God
hath delivered me, but in this also, that he hath delivered me by
way of a help, and help always presumes an endeavour and
co-operation in him that is helped. God did not elect me as a
helper, nor create me, nor redeem me, nor convert me, by way
of helping me; for he alone did all, and he had no use at all of
me. God infuses his first grace, the first way, merely as a giver;
20 entirely, all himself; but his subsequent graces, as a helper; therefore we call them auxiliant graces, helping graces; and we always receive them, when we endeavour to make use of his
former grace. 'Lord, I believe,' (says the man in the Gospel to
Christ) 'help mine unbelief'. If there had not been unbelief,
weakness, imperfectness, in that faith, there had needed no
help; but if there had not been a belief, a faith, it had not been
capable of help and asistance, but it must have been an entire
act, without any concurrence on the man's part.

So that if I have truly the testimony of a rectified conscience,
30 that God hath helped me, it is in both respects; first, that he
hath never forsaken me, and then, that he hath never suffered
me to forsake myself; he hath blessed me with that grace, that
I trust in no help but his, and with his grace too, that I cannot
look for his help, except I help myself also. God did not help
heaven and earth to proceed out of nothing in the creation, for
they had no possibility of any disposition towards it; for they
had no being: but God did help the earth to produce grass, and
herbs; for, for that, God had infused a seminal disposition into
the earth, which, for all that, it could not have perfected with-
40 out his further help. As in the making of woman, there is the
very word of our text, *gnazar*, God made him a helper, one that

was to do much for him, but not without him. So that then, if I
will make God's former working upon me, an argument of his
future gracious purposes, as I must acknowledge that God hath
done much for me, so I must find, that I have done what I
could, by the benefit of that grace with him; for God promises
to be but a helper. 'Lord open thou my lips,' says David; that is
God's work entirely; and then, 'My mouth, my mouth shall
show forth thy praise'; there enters David into the work with
God. And then, says God to him, *Dilata os tuum*, 'Open thy
10 mouth,' (it is now made 'thy mouth', and therefore do thou
open it) 'and I will fill it'; all inchoations and consummations,
beginnings and perfectings are of God, of God alone; but in the
way there is a concurrence on our part, (by a successive continuation of God's grace) in which God proceeds as a helper; and I
put him to more than that, if I do nothing. But if I pray for his
help, and apprehend and husband his graces well, when they
come, then he is truly, properly my helper; and upon that security, that testimony of a rectified conscience, I can proceed to
David's confidence for the future, 'Because thou hast been my
20 help, therefore in the shadow of thy wings will I rejoice'; which
is our third, and last general part.

III

In this last part, which is, (after David's aspect, and consideration of his present condition, which was, in the effect, an exclu-
sion from God's temple, and his retrospect, his consideration
of God's former mercies to him, that he had been his help) his
prospect, his confidence for the future, we shall stay a little
upon these two steps; first, that that which he promises himself,
is not an immunity from all powerful enemies, nor a sword of
revenge upon those enemies; it is not that he shall have no
30 adversary, nor that that adversary shall be able to do him no
harm, but that he should have a refreshing, a respiration, *in
velamento alarum*, under the shadow of God's wings. And then,
(in the second place) that this way which God shall be pleased
to take, this manner, this measure of refreshing, which God shall
vouchsafe to afford, (though it amount not to a full deliverance)
must produce a joy, a rejoicing in us; we must not only not
decline to a murmuring, that we have no more, no nor rest
upon a patience for that which remains, but we must ascend to

a holy joy, as if all were done and accomplished, 'In the shadow of thy wings will I rejoice.'

First then, lest any man in his dejection of spirit, or of fortune, should stray into a jealousy or suspicion of God's power to deliver him, as God hath spangled the firmament with stars, so hath he his Scriptures with names, and metaphors, and denotations of power. Sometimes he shines out in the name of a 'sword', and of a 'target', and of a 'wall', and of a 'tower', and of a 'rock', and of a 'hill'; and sometimes in that glorious and
10 manifold constellation of all together, *Dominus exercituum*, 'The Lord of hosts.' God, as God, is never represented to us, with defensive arms; he needs them not. When the poets present their great heroes and their worthies, they always insist upon their arms, they spend much of their invention upon the description of their arms; both because the greatest valour and strength needs arms, (Goliath himself was armed) and because to expose one's self to danger unarmed, is not valour, but rashness. But God is invulnerable in himself, and is never represented armed; you find no shirts of mail, no helmets, no cuir-
20 asses in God's armoury. In that one place of Isaiah, where it may seem to be otherwise, where God is said 'to have put on righteousness as a breastplate, and a helmet of salvation upon his head'; in that prophecy God is Christ, and is therefore in that place, called 'the Redeemer'. Christ needed defensive arms, God does not. God's word does; his Scriptures do; and therefore St Jerome hath armed them, and set before every book his *prologum galeatum*, that prologue that arms and defends every book from calumny. But though God need not, nor receive not defensive arms for himself, yet God is to us a helmet, a breast-
30 plate, a strong tower, a rock, everything that may give us assurance and defence; and as often as he will, he and refresh that proclamation, *Nolite tangere Christos meos*, Our enemies shall not so much as touch us.

But here, by occasion of his metaphor in this text, (*Sub umbra alarum*, 'In the shadow of thy wings') we do not so much consider an absolute immunity, that we shall not be touched, as a refreshing and consolation, when we are touched, though we be pinched and wounded. The names of God, which are most frequent in the Scriptures, are these three, Elohim, and Adonai,
40 and Jehovah; and to assure us of his power to deliver us, two of these three are names of power. Elohim is *Deus fortis*, the

mighty, the powerful God: and (which deserves a particular consideration) Elohim is a plural name; it is not *Deus fortis*, but *Dii fortes*, powerful Gods. God is all kind of gods; all kinds, which either idolators and Gentiles can imagine, (as riches, or justice, or wisdom, or valour, or such) and all kinds which God himself hath called gods, (as princes, and magistrates, and prelates, and all that assist and help one another). God is Elohim, all these gods, and all these in their height and best of their power; for Elohim, is *Dii fortes*, Gods in the plural, and those
10 plural gods in their exaltation.

The second name of God is a name of power too, Adonai. For, Adonai is *Dominus*, the Lord, such a lord as is lord and proprietary of all his creatures, and all creatures are his creatures; and then, *Dominium est potestas tum utendi, tum abutendi*, says the law; To be absolute lord of anything, gives that lord a power to do what he will with that thing. God, as he is Adonai, 'The Lord', may give and take, quicken and kill, build and throw down, where and whom he will. So then two of God's three names are names of absolute power, to imprint, and re-imprint an assur-
20 ance in us that he can absolutely deliver us, and fully revenge us, if he will. But then, his third name, and that name which he chooses to himself, and in the signification of which name he employs Moses for the relief of his people under Pharaoh, that name Jehovah, is not a name of power, but only of essence, of being, of substance, and yet in the virtue of that name, God relieved his people. And if, in my afflictions, God vouchsafe to visit me in that name, to preserve me in my being, in my subsistence in him, that I be not shaked out of him, disinherited in him, excommunicate from him, divested of him, annihilated
30 towards him, let him, at his good pleasure, reserve his Elohim, and his Adonai, the exercises and declarations of his mighty power, to those great public causes, that more concern his glory, than anything that can befall me; but if he impart his Jehovah, enlarge himself so far towards me, as that I may live, and move, and have my being in him, though I be not instantly delivered, nor mine enemies absolutely destroyed, yet this is as much as I should promise myself, this is as much as the Holy Ghost intends in this metaphor, *Sub umbra alarum*, 'Under the shadow of thy wings', that is a refreshing, a respiration, a con-
40 servation, a consolation in all afflictions that are inflicted upon me.

Yet, is not this metaphor of 'wings' without a denotation of power. As no act of God's, though it seem to imply but spiritual comfort, is without a denotation of power, (for it is the power of God that comforts me; to overcome that sadness of soul, and that dejection of spirit, which the adversary by temporal afflictions would induce upon me, is an act of his power) so this metaphor 'The shadow of his wings', (which in this place expresses no more, than consolation and refreshing in misery, and not a powerful deliverance out of it) is so often
10 in the Scriptures made a denotation of power too, as that we can doubt of no act of power, if we have this shadow of his wings. For, in this metaphor of 'wings', doth the Holy Ghost express the maritime power, the power of some nations at sea, in navies, 'Woe to the land shadowing with wings'; that is, that hovers over the world, and intimidates it with her sails and ships. In this metaphor doth God remember his people of his powerful deliverance of them, 'You have seen what I did unto the Egyptians, and how I bare you on eagles' wings, and brought you to myself.' In this metaphor doth God threaten his
20 and their enemies, what he can do, 'The noise of the wings of his cherubim are as the noise of great waters, and of an army.' So also what he will do, 'He shall spread his wings over Bozrah, and at that day shall the hearts of the mighty men of Edom, be as the heart of a woman in her pangs.' So that, if I have the shadow of his wings, I have the earnest of the power of them too; if I have refreshing, and respiration from them, I am able to say, as those three confessors did to Nebuchadnezzar, 'My God is able to deliver me', I am sure he hath power; 'And my God will deliver me,' when it conduces to his glory, I know he
30 will; 'But, if he do not, be it known unto thee, O King, we will not serve thy gods'; be it known unto thee, O Satan, how long soever God defer my deliverance, I will not seek false comforts, the miserable comforts of this world. I will not, for I need not; for I can subsist under this shadow of these wings, though I have no more.

The mercy-seat itself was covered with the cherubim's wings; and who would have more than mercy? and a mercy-seat; that is, established, resident mercy, permanent and perpetual mercy; present and familiar mercy; a mercy-seat. Our Saviour Christ
40 intends as much as would have served their turn, if they had laid hold upon it, when he says, 'That he would have gathered

Jerusalem, as a hen gathers her chickens under her wings.' And
though the other prophets do (as ye have heard) mingle the
signification of power, and actual deliverance, in this metaphor
of wings, yet our prophet, whom we have now in especial
consideration, David, never doth so; but in every place where
he uses this metaphor of wings (which are in five or six several
Psalms) still he rests and determines in that sense, which is his
meaning here; that though God do not actually deliver us, nor
actually destroy our enemies, yet if he refresh us in the shadow
10 of his wings, if he maintain our subsistence (which is a religious
constancy) in him, this should not only establish our patience,
(for that is but half the work) but it should also produce a joy,
and rise to an exultation, which is our last circumstance, 'Therefore in the shadow of thy wings I will rejoice.'

I would always raise your hearts, and dilate your hearts, to a
holy joy, to a joy in the Holy Ghost. There may be a just fear,
that men do not grieve enough for their sins; but there may be
a just jealousy, and suspicion too, that they may fall into inordinate grief, and diffidence of God's mercy; and God hath
20 reserved us to such times, as being the later times, give us even
the dregs and lees of misery to drink. For, God hath not only
let loose into the world a new spiritual disease; which is, an
equality, and an indifferency, which religion our children, or
our servants, or our companions profess; (I would not keep
company with a man that thought me a knave, or a traitor;
with him that thought I loved not my prince, or were a faith-
less man, not to be believed, I would not associate myself; and
yet I will make him my bosom companion, that thinks I do not
love God, that thinks I cannot be saved) but God hath accom-
30 panied, and complicated almost all our bodily diseases of these
times, with an extraordinary sadness, a predominant melancholy, a faintness of heart, a cheerlessness, a joylessness of spirit,
and therefore I return often to this endeavour of raising your
hearts, dilating your hearts with a holy joy, joy in the Holy
Ghost, 'for Under the shadow of his wings', you may, you
should 'rejoice'.

If you look upon this world in a map, you find two hemispheres, two half worlds. If you crush heaven into a map, you
may find two hemispheres too, two half heavens; half will be
40 joy, and half will be glory; for in these two, the joy of heaven,
and the glory of heaven, is all heaven often represented unto

us. And as of those two hemispheres of the world, the first hath
been known long before, but the other, (that of America, which
is the richer in treasure) God reserved for later discoveries; so
though he reserve that hemisphere of heaven, which is the
glory thereof, to the resurrection, yet the other hemisphere, the
joy of heaven, God opens to our discovery, and delivers for our
habitation even whilst we dwell in this world. As God hath
cast upon the unrepent sinner two deaths, a temporal, and a
spiritual death, so hath he breathed into us two lives; for so, as
10 the word for death is doubled, *Morte morieris*, 'Thou shalt die
the death', so is the word for life expressed in the plural, *Chaiim
vitarum*, 'God breathed into his nostrils the breath of lives', of
divers lives. Though our natural life were no life, but rather a
continual dying, yet we have two lives besides that, an eternal
life reserved for heaven, but yet a heavenly life too, a spiritual
life, even in this world; and as God doth thus inflict two deaths,
and infuse two lives, so doth he also pass two judgments upon
man, or rather repeats the same judgment twice. For, that which
Christ shall say to thy soul then at the last judgment, 'Enter into
20 thy Master's joy', he says to thy conscience now, 'Enter into thy
Master's joy'. The everlastingness of the joy is the blessedness
of the next life, but the entering, the inchoation is afforded here.
For that which Christ shall say then to us, *Venite benedicti*,
'Come ye blessed', are words intended to persons that are coming, that are upon the way, though not at home; here in this
world he bids us 'come', there in the next, he shall bid us
'welcome'. The angels of heaven have joy in thy conversion,
and canst thou be without that joy in thyself? If thou desire
revenge upon thine enemies, as they are God's enemies, that
30 God would be pleased to remove and root out all such as
oppose him, that affection appertains to glory; let that alone till
thou come to the hemisphere of glory; there join with those
martyrs under the altar, *Usquequo Domine*, How long O Lord,
dost thou defer judgment? and thou shalt have thine answer
there for that. Whilst thou art here, here join with David, and
the other saints of God, in that holy increpation of a dangerous
sadness, 'Why art thou cast down O my soul? why art thou
disquieted in me?'

   That soul that is dissected and anatomized to God, in a sin-
40 cere confession, washed in the tears of true contrition, embalmed
in the blood of reconciliation, the blood of Christ Jesus, can

assign no reason, can give no just answer to that interrogatory, 'Why art thou cast down O my soul? why art thou disquieted in me?' No man is so little, as that he can be lost under these wings, no man so great, as that they cannot reach to him; *Semper ille major est, quantumcumque creverimus*, To what temporal, to what spiritual greatness soever we grow, still pray we him to shadow us under his wings; for the poor need those wings against oppression, and the rich against envy. The Holy Ghost, who is a dove, shadowed the whole world under his wings; *Incubabat aquis*, he hovered over the waters, he sat upon the waters, and he hatched all that was produced, and all that was produced so, was good. Be thou a mother, where the Holy Ghost would be a father; conceive by him; and be content that he produce joy in thy heart here. First think, that as a man must have some land, or else he cannot be in wardship, so a man must have some of the love of God, or else he could not fall under God's correction; God would not give him his physic, God would not study his cure, if he cared not for him. And then think also, that if God afford thee the shadow of his wings, that is, consolation, respiration, refreshing, though not at present, and plenary deliverance, in thy afflictions, not to thank God, is a murmuring, and not to rejoice in God's ways, is an unthankfulness. Howling is the noise of hell, singing the voice of heaven; sadness the damp of hell, rejoicing the serenity of heaven. And he that hath not this joy here, lacks one of the best pieces of his evidence for the joys of heaven; and hath neglected or refused that earnest, by which God uses to bind his bargain, that true joy in this world shall flow into the joy of heaven, as a river flows into the sea; this joy shall not be put out in death, and a new joy kindled in me in heaven; but as my soul, as soon as it is out of my body, is in heaven, and does not stay for the possession of heaven, nor for the fruition of the sight of God, till it be ascended through air, and fire, and moon, and sun, and planets and firmament, to that place which we conceive to be heaven, but without the thousandth part of a minute's stop, as soon as it issues, is in a glorious light, which is heaven, (for all the way to heaven is heaven; and as those angels, which came from heaven hither, bring heaven with them, and are in heaven here, so that soul that goes to heaven, meets heaven here; and as those angels do not divest heaven by coming, so these souls invest heaven, in their going). As my soul shall not go towards

heaven, but go by heaven to heaven, to the heaven of heavens, so the true joy of a good soul in this world is the very joy of heaven; and we go thither, not that being without joy, we might have joy infused into us, but that as Christ says, 'Our joy might be full', perfected, sealed with an everlastingness; for, as he promises, 'That no man shall take our joy from us', so neither shall death itself take it away, nor so much as interrupt it, or discontinue it, but as in the face of death, when he lays hold upon me, and in the face of the devil, when he attempts
10 me, I shall see the face of God, (for every thing shall be a glass, to reflect God upon me) so in the agonies of death, in the anguish of that dissolution, in the sorrows of that valediction, in the irreversibleness of that transmigration, I shall have a joy, which shall no more evaporate, than my soul shall evaporate, a joy, that shall pass up, and put on a more glorious garment above, and be joy superinvested in glory. Amen.

VI
Thomas Hobbes
1588–1679

Hobbes's *Leviathan* has been described by its best editor, Michael Oakeshott, as 'the greatest, perhaps the sole, masterpiece of political philosophy written in the English language' (p. viii). It is one of the rare self-contained systems in world philosophy: from a few central assumptions Hobbes works by rigorous deduction and inference to create a logical, rational, watertight view of human nature and of the state. The assumptions are by now familiar: man is a rational animal but not a benevolent one—his actions are controlled entirely by self-interest; he never does anything out of love for other people, or by reference to some ideal. In fact there are no ideals, no absolutes, no fixed ethical codes—morality is in the eye of the beholder. Given man's selfish and warring instincts, he must be restrained by civil society or else he will lapse into the state of '*mere* nature' where his life would be 'nasty, brutish, and short'. Given the need for a civil society, then that state must be controlled by a sovereign with absolute power, to whom the Church is completely subordinate, and the individual, once having opted for membership of this society, must resign himself absolutely to the King and his officers. This is a severely organized system, an 'either-or' arrangement which admits of no debate: despite his attack on absolutes and his advocacy of moral relativism, Hobbes's own system is as absolutist as could be. As he sums it up himself, having in Part I considered Man, in Part II a Civil commonwealth, he goes on to discuss a Christian commonwealth but reminds us of what has been established so far:

> That the condition of mere nature, that is to say, of absolute liberty, such as is theirs, that neither are sovereigns, nor subjects, is anarchy, and the condition of war: that the precepts, by which men are guided to avoid that condition, are the laws of nature: that a commonwealth, without sovereign power, is but a word without substance, and cannot stand: that subjects owe to sovereigns, simple obedience, in all

things wherein their obedience is not repugnant to the laws of God, I have sufficiently proved, in that which I have already written. There wants only for the entire knowledge of civil duty, to know what are those laws of God. [Book 2, chapter xxxi, opening paragraph.]

No work of English philosophy has produced more controversy than this; few if any have been more original. But although the structure and method are indisputably Hobbes's own, many of his attitudes are derived from Bacon. Like him Hobbes attacked the commonplace acceptance of any conclusions without prior testing; he too poured scorn upon the worship of Aristotle as the fountain of all knowledge, and he followed Bacon in denouncing the stagnancy of medieval scholasticism. Hobbes's insistence on the necessity for clear definitions is also derived from this source, but whereas Bacon consistently distinguished between language as used for general communication and persuasion (which could therefore legitimately use all imaginative resources) and language used for the most demanding stages of scientific research (which thus had to be factual and non-ambiguous), Hobbes applied the second principle generally and, as we shall see, tried to exclude metaphor altogether. The greatest difference between these two giants among seventeenth-century English philosophy is in the structure of their works: although Bacon ultimately evolved a fairly consistent and rigorous scientific method, his own philosophical works are a piecemeal, opportunist assembly of the ideas and experiments of the moment, Hobbes, in *Leviathan* especially, succeeded in making his method the organizing principle of the work itself. The method is one of constantly expanding deduction from first principles, and could be described as a working out in linguistic terms of the processes of Euclidean geometry. The comparison is in fact literally true, for the well-known turning-point in Hobbes's life was his dramatic discovery in 1629 of the principles of geometry. In the engaging narrative of John Aubrey's *Brief Lives* the story goes as follows:

He was forty years old before he looked on Geometry; which happened accidentally. Being in a Gentleman's Library, Euclid's Elements lay open, and 'twas the *47 El. libri 1*. He read the Proposition. *By G——*, said he (he would now and then swear an emphatical Oath by way of emphasis) *this is impossible!* So he reads the Demonstration of it, which referred him back to such a Proposition; which proposition he read. That referred him back to another, which he also read. *Et sic deinceps* [and so on] that at last he was demonstratively convinced of that truth. This made him in love with Geometry.

I have heard Mr Hobbes say that he was wont to draw lines on his thigh and on the sheets, abed, and also multiply and divide.

The extraordinary appetite with which Hobbes pursued his study of geometry is clearly the sign of great, almost pure intellectual energy. Geometry also appealed to his authoritarian side, for by the process of reasoning from indisputable axioms one could reach indisputable conclusions. This method he put to good use in *Leviathan*, giving the book a wholly systematic structure, but (if a layman might be permitted this criticism) whereas geometry is a self-sufficient discipline with its own abstract conventions, the analysis of man and society is constantly open to the comparison with life itself. And it is precisely at this point that *Leviathan* looks to be a monster, for the straightforwardness of Hobbes's system of definition and deduction (it admits no discussion of contrary evidence) results in many explanations 'from first principles' which do not tally with our experience of life and give consequently a curiously naïve appearance to them, as if the author were a visitor from another planet.

The entire consistency of attitude applies to language fundamentally. Language was developed by men for the communication of thought; words represent thoughts like signs; these signs must therefore be as clear and unambiguous as possible. At first sight Hobbes's own prose style seems to fulfil his injunctions admirably: his vocabulary is simple, his sentence structure is short and simple, and he abandons the traditional syntactical symmetries in the same way that he abjures any emotional influence on our logical processes. Any syntactical balances that we find in Hobbes are either accidental or convenient for framing mere lists: without language 'there had been amongst men, neither commonwealth, nor society, nor contract, nor peace, no more than amongst lions, bears, and wolves'.

His attitude to metaphor is of one piece with his advocacy of

clarity: the second abuse of speech occurs when men 'use words
metaphorically; that is, in other sense than that they are ordained for; and thereby deceive others'; but although hazar-
dous, metaphors are less dangerous than other abuses 'because
they *profess* their inconstancy'. [My italics.] Our reaction to this
doctrine is divided, for although Hobbes is right to say that 'in
reasoning a man must take heed of words' (in our own time
linguistic philosophy has shown just how much care must be
taken), on the other hand it is naïve to think that language
could ever be free of metaphor, or even that conceptual processes could exist without using analogy. But the consequences
for literature are in any case serious, and Hobbes both shares
and strengthens that distrust of metaphor which was to change
the whole nature of prose in the seventeenth century.

Even Hobbes's system had its loopholes, and he should have
remembered the injunction of Bacon that the human mind is
not a mechanical or mathematical construct, nor an accurate
mirror, but an 'enchanted glass', full of inconsistencies and
unpredictable developments. Here indeed is one of them, for
Hobbes's conclusive, destructive attack on metaphor is itself
totally dependent on metaphor, not only for its concepts but
most of all for the emotional tone with which it is conveyed:

> To conclude, the light of human minds is perspicuous words,
> but by exact definitions first snuffed, and purged from ambi-
> guity; *reason* is the *pace*; increase of *science*, the way; and the
> benefit of mankind, the *end*. And, on the contrary, metaphors,
> and senseless and ambiguous words, are like *ignes fatui*; and
> reasoning upon them is wandering amongst innumerable ab-
> surdities; and their end, contention and sedition, or con-
> tempt.

It would be a useful exercise to chart exactly the metamor-
phosis of the basic image of knowledge as light, from a
candle to a delusive will-o'-the-wisp, but the important point
to grasp is that without metaphor Hobbes could not have communicated his distrust of metaphor. And time and again when
he is most involved in his subject he has to resort to metaphor
or simile, and invariably does so with great vigour:

> For words are wise men's counters, they do but reckon by
> them; but they are the money of fools, that value them by the

authority of an Aristotle, a Cicero, or a Thomas, or any other doctor whatsoever, if but a man. ... a man that seeketh precise truths had need to remember what every name he uses stands for, and to place it accordingly, or else he will find himself entangled in words, as a bird in lime twigs, the more he struggles the more belimed.

Those are two admirable analogies for the arbitrary value of words and for the fallacies innate in them (both ideas and images partly derived from Bacon), expressed with Hobbes's characteristic firmness and tartness—but their very presence subverts a whole section of his system.

The reader who is aware of this fundamental inconsistency in Hobbes reads *Leviathan* with a slightly mischievous intent, picking out things that ought not to be there and have somehow been smuggled through the frontier guards, but this attitude changes to one of enjoyment or even delight at Hobbes's ingenuity in formulating apt and universal analogies to damage his enemies at their weakest points. Not all of *Leviathan* exists at the imaginative level of the three chapters selected here, but the fact that the density of imagery varies according to the degree with which Hobbes is emotionally involved with his subject-matter is the best validation of the true function of metaphor, especially in prose. He even excels at longer, more carefully sustained analogies, where an element of conscious metaphorical thought must be supposed—such as the comparison (in I, 4) of men who trust books indiscriminately and only subsequently discover their weakness with birds caught in a room and deceived by 'the false light of a glass window' (the analogy holds exactly); or that (in I, 5) between a similar type of credulity in taking up 'conclusions on the trust of authors' and the accounting errors that could be made by not checking the component parts of any account; or those fine images of building and medicine in II, 29. These longer analogies (often almost allegorical) are transcended by the great central image of the book, of society as one living organism, which extends from the symbolic frontispiece of a king made up of the bodies of all his subjects through a whole series of ingenious applications of the metaphor to the details of society. To conclude, a similar type of organic imagery is shown with great ingenuity in the review of the various diseases in a commonwealth

(II, 29).[1] When he comes to 'mixed government', the to him abhorrent triple division between levying money, holding power, and making laws he finds an analogy that almost serves:

> To what disease in the natural body of man, I may exactly compare this irregularity of a commonwealth, I know not. But I have seen a man, that had another man growing out of his side, with a head, arms, breast, and stomach of his own; if he had had another man growing out of his other side, the comparison might then have been exact.

With rare restraint Hobbes did not make a clear statement of his emotional attitude, but I take it that he is not recommending such a model either in life or in politics. But at what other period outside the Renaissance could a writer have seriously compared a type of social structure to a Siamese twin? Hobbes may in one aspect be a precursor of Wittgenstein, but in many others he belongs to the same world as Hooker and Spenser.

From *Leviathan* (1651)

Part I. Of Man

Chapter IV. Of Speech

Original of Speech. The invention of *printing*, though ingenious, compared with the invention of *letters*, is no great matter. But who was the first that found the use of letters, is not known. He that first brought them into Greece, men say was Cadmus, the son of Agenor, king of Phœnicia. A profitable invention for continuing the memory of time past, and the conjunction of mankind, dispersed into so many, and distant regions of the earth; and withal difficult, as proceeding from a watchful observation of the divers motions of the tongue, palate, lips, and
10 other organs of speech; whereby to make as many differences of characters, to remember them. But the most noble and profitable invention of all other, was that of SPEECH, consisting of *names* or *appellations*, and their connexion; whereby men register their thoughts; recall them when they are past; and also declare them one to another for mutual utility and conversation; without which, there had been amongst men, neither commonwealth, nor society, nor contract, nor peace, no more than

[1] It is noteworthy that for every disease Hobbes looks for an analogy almost consciously.

amongst lions, bears, and wolves. The first author of *speech* was God himself, that instructed Adam how to name such creatures as he presented to his sight; for the Scripture goeth no further in this matter. But this was sufficient to direct him to add more names, as the experience and use of the creatures should give him occasion; and to join them in such manner by degrees, as to make himself understood; and so by succession of time, so much language might be gotten, as he had found use for; though not so copious, as an orator or philosopher has
10 need of: for I do not find any thing in the Scripture, out of which, directly or by consequence, can be gathered, that Adam was taught the names of all figures, numbers, measures, colours, sound, fancies, relations; much less the names of words and speech, as *general, special, affirmative, negative, interrogative, optative, infinitive,* all which are useful; and least of all, of *entity, intentionality, quiddity,* and other insignificant words of the school.

But all this language gotten, and augmented by Adam and his posterity, was again lost at the Tower of Babel, when, by the hand of God, every man was stricken, for his rebellion, with an
20 oblivion of his former language. And being hereby forced to disperse themselves into several parts of the world, it must needs be, that the diversity of tongues that now is, proceeded by degrees from them, in such manner, as need, the mother of all inventions, taught them; and in tract of time grew everywhere more copious.

The Use of Speech. The general use of speech, is to transfer our mental discourse, into verbal; or the train of our thoughts, into a train of words; and that for two commodities, whereof one is the registering of the consequences of our thoughts; which being
30 apt to slip out of our memory, and put us to a new labour, may again be recalled, by such words as they were marked by. So that the first use of names is to serve for *marks,* or *notes* of remembrance. Another is, when many use the same words, to signify, by their connexion and order, one to another, what they conceive, or think of each matter; and also what they desire, fear, or have any other passion for. And for this use they are called *signs.* Special uses of speech are these; first, to register, what by cogitation, we find to be the cause of any thing, present or past; and what we find things present or past
40 may produce, or effect; which in sum, is acquiring of arts.

Secondly, to show to others that knowledge which we have attained, which is, to counsel and teach one another. Thirdly, to make known to others our wills and purposes, that we may have the mutual help of one another. Fourthly, to please and delight ourselves and others, by playing with our words, for pleasure or ornament, innocently.

Abuses of speech. To these uses, there are also four correspondent abuses. First, when men register their thoughts wrong, by the inconstancy of the signification of their words; by which they
10 register for their conception, that which they never conceived, and so deceive themselves. Secondly, when they use words metaphorically; that is, in other sense than that they are ordained for; and thereby deceive others. Thirdly, by words, when they declare that to be their will, which is not. Fourthly, when they use them to grieve one another; for seeing nature hath armed living creatures, some with teeth, some with horns, and some with hands, to grieve an enemy, it is but an abuse of speech, to grieve him with the tongue, unless it be one whom we are obliged to govern; and then it is not to grieve, but to
20 correct and amend.

The manner how speech serveth to the remembrance of the consequence of causes and effects, consisteth in the imposing of *names*, and the *connexion* of them.

Names, proper, common and universal. Of names, some are *proper*, and singular to one only thing, as *Peter, John, this man, this tree*; and some are *common* to many things, *man, horse, tree*; every of which, though but one name, is nevertheless the name of divers particular things; in respect of all which together, it is called an *universal*; there being nothing in the world universal but
30 names; for the things named are every one of them individual and singular.

One universal name is imposed on many things, for their similitude in some quality, or other accident; and whereas a proper name bringeth to mind one thing only, universals recall any one of those many.

And of names universal, some are of more, and some of less extent; the larger comprehending the less large; and some again of equal extent, comprehending each other reciprocally. As for example: the name *body* is of larger signification than the word
40 *man*, and comprehendeth it; and the names *man* and *rational*, are

THOMAS HOBBES

of equal extent, comprehending mutually one another. But
here we must take notice, that by a name is not always understood, as in grammar, one only word; but sometimes, by cir-
cumlocution, many words together. For all these words, *he that
in his actions observeth the laws of his country,* make but one name,
equivalent to this one word, *just.*

By this imposition of names, some of larger, some of stricter
signification, we turn the reckoning of the consequences of
things imagined in the mind, into a reckoning of the conse-
10 quences of appellations. For example: a man that hath no use of
speech at all, such as is born and remains perfectly deaf and
dumb, if he set before his eyes a triangle, and by it two right
angles, such as are the corners of a square figure, he may, by
meditation, compare and find, that the three angles of that
triangle, are equal to those two right angles that stand by it.
But if another triangle be shown him, different in shape from
the former, he cannot know, without a new labour, whether
the three angles of that also be equal to the same. But he that
hath the use of words, when he observes, that such equality
20 was consequent, not to the length of the sides, nor to any other
particular thing in his triangle; but only to this, that the sides
were straight, and the angles three; and that that was all, for
which he named it a triangle; will boldly conclude universally,
that such equality of angles is in all triangles whatsoever; and
register his invention in these general terms, *every triangle hath
its three angles equal to two right angles.* And thus the consequence
found in one particular, comes to be registered and remembered,
as a universal rule, and discharges our mental reckoning, of
time and place, and delivers us from all labour of the mind,
30 saving the first, and makes that which was found true *here,* and
now, to be true in *all times* and *places.*

But the use of words in registering our thoughts is in nothing
so evident as in numbering. A natural fool that could never
learn by heart the order of numeral words, as *one, two,* and *three,*
may observe every stroke of the clock, and nod to it, or say *one,
one, one,* but can never know what hour it strikes. And it seems,
there was a time when those names of number were not in use;
and men were fain to apply their fingers of one or both hands,
to those things they desired to keep account of; and that thence
40 it proceeded, that now our numeral words are but ten, in any
nation, and in some but five; and then they begin again. And

he that can tell ten, if he recite them out of order, will lose himself, and not know when he has done. Much less will he be able to add, and subtract, and perform all other operations of arithmetic. So that without words there is no possibility of reckoning of numbers; much less of magnitudes, of swiftness, of force, and other things, the reckonings whereof are necessary to the being, or well-being of mankind.

When two names are joined together into a consequence, or affirmation, as thus, *a man is a living creature*; or thus, *if he be a*
10 *man, he is a living creature*; if the latter name, *living creature*, signify all that the former name *man* signifieth, then the affirmation, or consequence, is *true*; otherwise *false*. For *true* and *false* are attributes of speech, not of things. And where speech is not, there is neither *truth* nor *falsehood*; *error* there may be, as when we expect that which shall not be, or suspect what has not been; but in neither case can a man be charged with untruth.

Necessity of definitions. Seeing then that truth consisteth in the right ordering of names in our affirmations, a man that seeketh precise truth had need to remember what every name he uses
20 stands for, and to place it accordingly, or else he will find himself entangled in words, as a bird in lime twigs, the more he struggles the more belimed. And therefore in geometry, which is the only science that it hath pleased God hitherto to bestow on mankind, men begin at settling the significations of their words; which settling of significations they call *definitions*, and place them in the beginning of their reckoning.

By this it appears how necessary it is for any man that aspires to true knowledge, to examine the definitions of former authors; and either to correct them, where they are negligently set down,
30 or to make them himself. For the errors of definitions multiply themselves according as the reckoning proceeds, and lead men into absurdities, which at last they see, but cannot avoid, without reckoning anew from the beginning, in which lies the foundation of their errors. From whence it happens, that they which trust to books do as they that cast up many little sums into a greater, without considering whether those little sums were rightly cast up or not; and at last finding the error visible, and not mistrusting their first grounds, know not which way to clear themselves, but spend time in fluttering over their books;
40 as birds that entering by the chimney, and finding themselves

enclosed in a chamber, flutter at the false light of a glass window, for want of wit to consider which way they came in. So that in the right definition of names lies the first use of speech; which is the acquisition of science: and in wrong, or no definitions, lies the first abuse; from which proceed all false and senseless tenets; which make those men that take their instruction from the authority of books, and not from their own meditation, to be as much below the condition of ignorant men, as men endued with true science are above it. For between true
10 science and erroneous doctrines, ignorance is in the middle. Natural sense and imagination are not subject to absurdity. Nature itself cannot err; and as men abound in copiousness of language, so they become more wise, or more mad than ordinary. Nor it is possible without letters for any man to become either excellently wise, or, unless his memory be hurt by disease or ill constitution of organs, excellently foolish. For words are wise men's counters, they do but reckon by them; but they are the money of fools, that value them by the authority of an Aristotle, a Cicero, or a Thomas, or any other doctor whatso-
20 ever, if but a man.

Subject to names, is whatsoever can enter into or be considered in an account, and be added one to another to make a sum, or subtracted one from another and leave a remainder. The Latins called accounts of money *rationes*, and accounting *ratiocinatio*; and that which we in bills or books of account call *items*, they call *nomina*, that is *names*; and thence it seems to proceed, that they extended the word *ratio* to the faculty of reckoning in all other things. The Greeks have but one word, λόγος, for both *speech* and *reason*; not that they thought there was no speech
30 without reason, but no reasoning without speech: and the act of reasoning they called *syllogism*, which signifieth summing up of the consequences of one saying to another. And because the same thing may enter into account for divers accidents, their names are, to show that diversity, diversely wrested and diversified. This diversity of names may be reduced to four general heads.

Names. First, a thing may enter into account for *matter* or *body*; as *living, sensible, rational, hot, cold, moved, quiet*; with all which names the word *matter*, or *body*, is understood; all such being
40 names of matter.

Secondly, it may enter into account, or be considered, for some accident or quality which we conceive to be in it; as for *being moved*, for *being so long*, for *being hot*, &c.; and then, of the name of the thing itself, by a little change or wresting, we make a name for that accident, which we consider; and for *living* put into the account *life*; for *moved, motion*; for *hot, heat*; for *long, length*, and the like; and all such names are the names of the accidents and properties by which one matter and body is distinguished from another. These are called *names abstract*, because severed, not from matter, but from the account of matter.

Thirdly, we bring into account the properties of our own bodies, whereby we make such distinction; as when anything is seen by us, we reckon not the thing itself, but the sight, the colour, the idea of it in the fancy: and when anything is heard, we reckon it not, but the hearing or sound only, which is our fancy or conception of it by the ear; and such are names of fancies.

Use of names positive. Fourthly, we bring into account, consider, and give names to, *names* themselves, and to *speeches*: for *general, universal, special, equivocal,* are names of names. And *affirmation, interrogation, commandment, narration, syllogism, sermon, oration,* and many other such, are names of speeches. And this is all the variety of names *positive*; which are put to mark somewhat which is in nature, or may be feigned by the mind of man, as bodies that are, or may be conceived to be; or of bodies, the properties that are, or may be feigned to be; or words and speech.

Negative names, with their uses. There be also other names, called *negative*, which are notes to signify that a word is not the name of the thing in question; as these words, *nothing, no man, infinite, indocible, three want four,* and the like; which are nevertheless of use in reckoning, or in correcting of reckoning, and call to mind our past cogitations, though they be not names of any thing because they make us refuse to admit of names not rightly used.

Words insignificant. All other names are but insignificant sounds; and those of two sorts. One when they are new and yet their meaning not explained by definition; whereof there have been abundance coined by Schoolmen, and puzzled philosophers.

Another, when men make a name of two names, whose significations are contradictory and inconsistent; as this name, an *incorporeal body*, or, which is all one, an *incorporeal substance*, and a great number more. For whensoever any affirmation is false, the two names of which it is composed, put together and made one, signify nothing at all. For example, if it be a false affirmation to say *a quadrangle is round*, the word *round quadrangle* signifies nothing, but is a mere sound. So likewise, if it be false to say that virtue can be poured, or blown up and down, the
10 words *inpoured virtue, inblown virtue,* are as absurd and insignificant as a *round quadrangle*. And therefore you shall hardly meet with a senseless and insignificant word, that is not made up of some Latin or Greek names. A Frenchman seldom hears our Saviour called by the name of *parole*, but by the name of *verbe* often; yet *verbe* and *parole* differ no more, but that one is Latin, the other French.

Understanding. When a man, upon the hearing of any speech, hath those thoughts which the words of that speech and their connexion were ordained and constituted to signify, then he is
20 said to understand it; *understanding* being nothing else but conception caused by speech. And therefore if speech be peculiar to man, as for aught I know it is, then is understanding peculiar to him also. And therefore of absurd and false affirmations, in case they be universal, there can be no understanding; though many think they understand them, when they do but repeat the words softly, or con them in their mind.

What kinds of speeches signify the appetites, aversions, and passions of man's mind; and of their use and abuse, I shall speak when I have spoken of the passions.

30 *Inconstant names.* The names of such things as affect us, that is, which please and displease us, because all men be not alike affected with the same thing, nor the same man at all times, are in the common discourses of men of *inconstant* signification. For seeing all names are imposed to signify our conceptions, and all our affections are but conceptions, when we conceive the same things differently, we can hardly avoid different naming of them. For though the nature of that we conceive, be the same; yet the diversity of our reception of it, in respect of different constitutions of body, and prejudices of opinion, gives
40 every thing a tincture of our different passions. And therefore

in reasoning a man must take heed of words; which besides the signification of what we imagine of their nature, have a signification also of the nature, disposition, and interest of the speaker; such as are the names of virtues and vices; for one man calleth *wisdom*, what another calleth *fear*; and one *cruelty*, what another *justice*; one *prodigality*, what another *magnanimity*; and one *gravity*, what another *stupidity*, &c. And therefore such names can never be true grounds of any ratiocination. No more can metaphors, and tropes of speech: but these are less dangerous, because they
10 profess their inconstancy; which the other do not.

Chapter V. Of Reason and Science

Reason, what it is. When a man *reasoneth*, he does nothing else but conceive a sum total, from *addition* of parcels; or conceive a remainder, from *subtraction* of one sum from another; which, if it be done by words, is conceiving of the consequence of the names of all the parts, to the name of the whole; or from the names of the whole and one part, to the name of the other part. And though in some things, as in numbers, besides adding and subtracting, men name other operations, as *multiplying* and *dividing*, yet they are the same; for multiplication, is but adding
20 together of things equal; and division, but subtracting of one thing, as often as we can. These operations are not incident to numbers only, but to all manner of things that can be added together, and taken one out of another. For as arithmeticians teach to add and subtract in *numbers*; so the geometricians teach the same in *lines, figures,* solid and superficial, *angles, proportions, times,* degrees of *swiftness, force, power,* and the like; the logicians teach the same in *consequences of words*; adding together two *names* to make an *affirmation*, and two *affirmations* to make a *syllogism*; and *many syllogisms* to make a *demonstration*; and from
30 the *sum*, or *conclusion* of a *syllogism*, they subtract one *proposition* to find the other. Writers of politics add together *pactions* to find men's *duties*; and lawyers, *laws* and *facts*, to find what is *right* and *wrong* in the actions of private men. In sum, in what matter soever there is place for *addition* and *subtraction*, there also is place for *reason*; and where these have no place, there *reason* has nothing at all to do.

Reason defined. Out of all which we may define, that is to say determine, what that is, which is meant by this word *reason*, when we reckon it amongst the faculties of the mind. For REASON, in this sense, is nothing but *reckoning*, that is adding and subtracting, of the consequences of general names agreed upon for the *marking* and *signifying* of our thoughts; I say *marking* them when we reckon by ourselves, and *signifying*, when we demonstrate or approve our reckonings to other men.

Right reason, where. And, as in arithmetic, unpractised men must, and professors themselves may often, err, and cast up false; so also in any other subject of reasoning, the ablest, most atten-
10 tive, and most practised men may deceive themselves, and infer false conclusions; not but that reason itself is always right reas-on, as well as arithmetic is a certain and infallible art: but no one man's reason, nor the reason of any one number of men, makes the certainty; no more than an account is therefore well cast up, because a great many men have unanimously approved it. And therefore, as when there is a controversy in an account, the parties must by their own accord, set up, for right reason, the reason of some arbitrator, or judge, to whose sentence they will both stand, or their controversy must either come to blows,
20 or be undecided, for want of a right reason constituted by nature; so is it also in all debates of what kind soever. And when men that think themselves wiser than all others, clamour and demand right reason for judge, yet seek no more, but that things should be determined, by no other men's reason but their own, it is as intolerable in the society of men, as it is in play after trump is turned, to use for trump on every occasion, that suit whereof they have most in their hand. For they do nothing else, that will have every of their passions, as it comes to bear sway in them, to be taken for right reason, and that in their own con-
30 controversies: bewraying their want of right reason, by the claim they lay to it.

The use of reason. The use and end of reason, is not the finding of the sum and truth of one, or a few consequences, remote from the first definitions, and settled significations of names, but to begin at these, and proceed from one consequence to another. For there can be no certainty of the last conclusion, without a certainty of all those affirmations and negations, on which it was grounded and inferred. As when a master of a family, in taking an account, casteth up the sums of all the bills of expense into one sum, and not regarding how each bill is summed up,

by those that give them in account; nor what it is he pays for;
he advantages himself no more, than if he allowed the account
in gross, trusting to every of the accountants' skill and honesty:
so also in reasoning of all other things, he that takes up conclusions on the trust of authors, and doth not fetch them from
the first items in every reckoning, which are the significations
of names settled by definitions, loses his labour; and does not
know any thing, but only believeth.

Of error and absurdity. When a man reckons without the use of
words, which may be done in particular things, as when upon
the sight of any one thing, we conjecture what was likely to
have preceded, or is likely to follow upon it; if that which he
thought likely to follow, follows not, or that which he thought
likely to have preceded it, hath not preceded it, this is called
error; to which even the most prudent men are subject. But
when we reason in words of general signification, and fall upon
a general inference which is false, though it be commonly
called *error*, it is indeed an *absurdity*, or senseless speech. For
error is but a deception, in presuming that somewhat is past, or
to come; of which, though it were not past, or not to come, yet
there was no impossibility discoverable. But when we make a
general assertion, unless it be a true one, the possibility of it is
inconceivable. And words whereby we conceive nothing but
the sound, are those we call *absurd, insignificant*, and *nonsense*.
And therefore if a man should talk to me of a *round quadrangle*;
or, *accidents of bread in cheese*; or, *immaterial substances*; or of *a
free subject*; a *free will*; or any *free*, but free from being hindered
by opposition, I should not say he were in an error, but that his
words were without meaning, that is to say, absurd.

I have said before, in the second chapter, that a man did excel
all other animals in this faculty, that when he conceived any
thing whatsoever, he was apt to inquire the consequences of it,
and what effects he could do with it. And now I add this other
degree of the same excellence, that he can by words reduce the
consequences he finds to general rules, called *theorems*, or
aphorisms; that is, he can reason, or reckon, not only in number,
but in all other things, whereof one may be added unto, or
subtracted from another.

But this privilege is allayed by another; and that is, by the
privilege of absurdity; to which no living creature is subject,

but man only. And of men, those are of all most subject to it, that profess philosophy. For it is most true that Cicero saith of them somewhere; that there can be nothing so absurd, but may be found in the books of philosophers. And the reason is manifest. For there is not one of them that begins his ratiocination from the definitions, or explications of the names they are to use; which is a method that hath been used only in geometry; whose conclusions have thereby been made indisputable.

Causes of absurdity. 1. The first cause of absurd conclusions I ascribe to the want of method; in that they begin not their ratiocination from definitions; that is, from settled significations of their words: as if they could cast account, without knowing the value of the numeral words, *one, two,* and *three.*

And whereas all bodies enter into account upon divers considerations, which I have mentioned in the precedent chapter; these considerations being diversely named, divers absurdities proceed from the confusion, and unfit connexion of their names into assertions. And therefore,

2. The second cause of absurd assertions, I ascribe to the giving of names of *bodies* to *accidents*; or of *accidents* to *bodies*; as they do, that say, *faith is infused,* or *inspired*; when nothing can be *poured,* or *breathed* into anything, but body; and that, *extension* is *body*; that *phantasms* are *spirits,* &c.

3. The third I ascribe to the giving of the names of the *accidents* of *bodies without us,* to the *accidents* of our *own bodies*; as they do that say the *colour is in the body*; *the sound is in the air,* &c.

4. The fourth, to the giving of the names of *bodies* to *names,* or *speeches*; as they do that say, that *there be things universal*; that *a living creature is genus,* or *a general thing,* &c.

5. The fifth, to the giving of the names of *accidents* to *names* and *speeches*; as they do that say, *the nature of a thing is its definition*; *a man's command is his will*; and the like.

6. The sixth, to the use of metaphors, tropes, and other rhetorical figures, instead of words proper. For though it be lawful to say, for example, in common speech, *the way goeth, or leadeth hither, or thither*; *the proverb says this or that,* whereas ways cannot go, nor proverbs speak; yet in reckoning, and seeking of truth, such speeches are not to be admitted.

7. The seventh, to names that signify nothing; but are taken up, and learned by rote from the schools, as *hypostatical,*

transubstantiate, consubstantiate, eternal-now, and the like canting of Schoolmen.

To him that can avoid these things it is not easy to fall into any absurdity, unless it be by the length of an account; wherein he may perhaps forget what went before. For all men by nature reason alike, and well, when they have good principles. For who is so stupid, as both to mistake in geometry, and also to persist in it, when another detects his error to him?

Science. By this it appears that reason is not, as sense and memory,
10 born with us; nor gotten by experience only, as prudence is; but attained by industry; first in apt imposing of names; and secondly by getting a good and orderly method in proceeding from the elements, which are names, to assertions made by connexion of one of them to another; and so to syllogisms, which are the connexions of one assertion to another, till we come to a knowledge of all the consequences of names appertaining to the subject in hand; and that is it, men call SCIENCE. And whereas sense and memory are but knowledge of fact, which is a thing past and irrevocable; *Science* is the knowledge
20 of consequences, and dependence of one fact upon another: by which, out of that we can presently do, we know how to do something else when we will, or the like another time; because when we see how any thing comes about, upon what causes, and by what manner; when the like causes come into our power, we see how to make it produce the like effects.

Children therefore are not endued with reason at all, till they have attained the use of speech; but are called reasonable creatures, for the possibility apparent of having the use of reason in time to come. And the most part of men, though they have the
30 use of reasoning a little way, as in numbering to some degree; yet it serves them to little use in common life; in which they govern themselves, some better, some worse, according to their differences of experience, quickness of memory, and inclinations to several ends; but specially according to good or evil fortune, and the errors of one another. For as for *science*, or certain rules of their actions, they are so far from it, that they know not what it is. Geometry they have thought conjuring: but for other sciences, they who have not been taught the beginnings and some progress in them, that they may see how they be
40 acquired and generated, are in this point like children, that

having no thought of generation, are made believe by the women that their brothers and sisters are not born, but found in the garden.

But yet they that have no *science*, are in better, and nobler condition, with their natural prudence; than men, that by misreasoning, or by trusting them that reason wrong, fall upon false and absurd general rules. For ignorance of causes, and of rules, does not set men so far out of their way, as relying on false rules, and taking for causes of what they aspire to, those
10 that are not so, but rather causes of the contrary.

To conclude, the light of human minds is perspicuous words, but by exact definitions first snuffed, and purged from ambiguity; *reason* is the *pace*; increase of *science*, the *way*; and the benefit of mankind, the *end*. And, on the contrary, metaphors, and senseless and ambiguous words, are like *ignes fatui*; and reasoning upon them is wandering amongst innumerable absurdities; and their end, contention and sedition, or contempt.

Prudence and sapience, with their difference. As much experience, is *prudence*; so, is much science *sapience*. For though we usually
20 have one name of wisdom for them both, yet the Latins did always distinguish between *prudentia* and *sapientia*; ascribing the former to experience, the latter to science. But to make their difference appear more clearly, let us suppose one man endued with an excellent natural use and dexterity in handling his arms; and another to have added to that dexterity, an acquired science, of where he can offend, or be offended by his adversary, in every possible posture or guard: the ability of the former, would be to the ability of the latter, as prudence to sapience; both useful; but the latter infallible. But they that trusting only to the
30 authority of books, follow the blind blindly, are like him that, trusting to the false rules of a master of fence, ventures presumptuously upon an adversary, that either kills or disgraces him.

Signs of science. The signs of science are some, certain and infallible; some, uncertain. Certain, when he that pretendeth the science of any thing, can teach the same; that is to say, demonstrate the truth thereof perspicuously to another; uncertain, when only some particular events answer to his pretence, and upon many occasions prove so as he says they must. Signs of
40 prudence are all uncertain; because to observe by experience,

THOMAS HOBBES

and remember all circumstances that may alter the success, is impossible. But in any business, whereof a man has not infallible science to proceed by; to forsake his own natural judgment, and be guided by general sentences read in authors, and subject to many exceptions, is a sign of folly, and generally scorned by the name of pedantry. And even of those men themselves, that in councils of the commonwealth love to show their reading of politics and history, very few do it in their domestic affairs, where their particular interest is concerned; having prudence enough for their private affairs: but in public they study more the reputation of their own wit, than the success of another's business.

Part II. Of Commonwealth
*Chapter xxix. Of Those Things That Weaken, or Tend to the
Dissolution of a Commonwealth*

Dissolution of commonwealths proceedeth from their imperfect institution. Though nothing can be immortal, which mortals make; yet, if men had the use of reason they pretend to, their commonwealths might be secured, at least from perishing by internal diseases. For by the nature of their institution, they are designed to live, as long as mankind, or as the laws of nature, or as justice itself, which gives them life. Therefore when they come to be dissolved, not by external violence, but intestine disorder, the fault is not in men, as they are the *matter*; but as they are the *makers*, and orderers of them. For men, as they become at last weary of irregular jostling, and hewing one another, and desire with all their hearts, to conform themselves into one firm and lasting edifice: so for want, both of the art of making fit laws, to square their actions by, and also of humility, and patience, to suffer the rude and cumbersome points of their present greatness to be taken off, they cannot without the help of a very able architect, be compiled into any other than a crazy building, such as hardly lasting out their own time, must assuredly fall upon the heads of their posterity.

Amongst the *infirmities* therefore of a commonwealth, I will reckon in the first place, those that arise from an imperfect institution, and resemble the diseases of a natural body, which proceed from a defectuous procreation.

Want of absolute power. Of which, this is one, *that a man to obtain a kingdom, is sometimes content with less power, than to the peace, and defence of the commonwealth is necessarily required.* From whence it cometh to pass, that when the exercise of the power laid by, is for the public safety to be resumed, it hath the resemblance of an unjust act; which disposeth great numbers of men, when occasion is presented, to rebel; in the same manner as the bodies of children, gotten by diseased parents, are subject either to untimely death, or to purge the ill quality, derived from their
10 vicious conception, by breaking out into biles and scabs. And when kings deny themselves some such necessary power, it is not always, though sometimes, out of ignorance of what is necessary to the office they undertake; but many times out of a hope to recover the same again at their pleasure. Wherein they reason not well; because such as will hold them to their promises, shall be maintained against them by foreign commonwealths; who in order to the good of their own subjects let slip few occasions to *weaken* the estate of their neighbours. So was Thomas Becket, archbishop of Canterbury, supported against
20 Henry the Second, by the Pope; the subjection of ecclesiastics to the commonwealth, having been dispensed with by William the Conqueror at his reception, when he took an oath, not to infringe the liberty of the church. And so were the barons, whose power was by William Rufus, to have their help in transferring the succession from his elder brother to himself, increased to a degree inconsistent with the sovereign power, maintained in their rebellion against King John, by the French.

Nor does this happen in monarchy only. For whereas the style of the ancient Roman commonwealth, was, *The Senate and*
30 *People of Rome*; neither senate, nor people pretended to the whole power; which first caused the seditions, of Tiberius Gracchus, Caius Gracchus, Lucius Saturninus, and others; and afterwards the wars between the senate and the people, under Marius and Sylla; and again under Pompey and Cæsar, to the extinction of their democracy, and the setting up of monarchy.

The people of Athens bound themselves but from one only action; which was, that no man on pain of death should propound the renewing of the war for the island of Salamis; and yet thereby, if Solon had not caused to be given out he was mad,
40 and afterwards in gesture and habit of a madman, and in verse, propounded it to the people that flocked about him, they had

had an enemy perpetually in readiness, even at the gates of their city; such damage, or shifts, are all commonwealths forced to, that have their power never so little limited.

Private judgment of good and evil. In the second place, I observe the *diseases* of a commonwealth, that proceed from the poison of seditious doctrines, whereof one is, *That every private man is judge of good and evil actions*. This is true in the condition of mere nature, where there are no civil laws; and also under civil government, in such cases as are not determined by the law.
10 But otherwise, it is manifest, that the measure of good and evil actions, is the civil law; and the judge the legislator, who is always representative of the commonwealth. From this false doctrine, men are disposed to debate with themselves, and dispute the commands of the commonwealth; and afterwards to obey, or disobey them, as in their private judgments they shall think fit; whereby the commonwealth is distracted and *weakened*.

Erroneous conscience. Another doctrine repugnant to civil society, is, that *whatsoever a man does against his conscience, is sin*; and it
20 dependeth on the presumption of making himself judge of good and evil. For a man's conscience, and his judgment is the same thing, and as the judgment, so also the conscience may be erroneous. Therefore, though he that is subject to no civil law, sinneth in all he does against his conscience, because he has no other rule to follow but his own reason; yet it is not so with him that lives in a commonwealth; because the law is the public conscience, by which he hath already undertaken to be guided. Otherwise in such diversity, as there is of private consciences, which are but private opinions, the commonwealth
30 must needs be distracted, and no man dare to obey the sovereign power, further than it shall seem good in his own eyes.

Pretence of inspiration. It hath been also commonly taught, *that faith and sanctity, are not to be attained by study and reason, but by supernatural inspiration, or infusion*. Which granted, I see not why any man should render a reason of his faith; or why every Christian should not be also a prophet; or why any man should take the law of his country, rather than his own inspiration, for the rule of his action. And thus we fall again in the fault of taking upon us to judge of good and evil; or to make judges of

it, such private men as pretend to be supernaturally inspired, to the dissolution of all civil government. Faith comes by hearing, and hearing by those accidents, which guide us into the presence of them that speak to us; which accidents are all contrived by God Almighty; and yet are not supernatural, but only, for the great number of them that concur to every effect, unobservable. Faith and sanctity, are indeed not very frequent; but yet they are not miracles, but brought to pass by education, discipline, correction, and other natural ways, by which God
10 worketh them in his elect, at such times as he thinketh fit. And these three opinions, pernicious to peace and government, have in this part of the world, proceeded chiefly from the tongues, and pens of unlearned divines, who joining the words of Holy Scripture together, otherwise than is agreeable to reason, do what they can, to make men think, that sanctity and natural reason, cannot stand together.

Subjecting the sovereign power to civil laws. A fourth opinion, repugnant to the nature of a commonwealth, is this, *that he that hath the sovereign power is subject to the civil laws.* It is true, that sov-
20 ereigns are all subject to the laws of nature; because such laws be divine, and cannot by any man, or commonwealth be abrogated. But to those laws which the sovereign himself, that is, which the commonwealth maketh, he is not subject. For to be subject to laws, is to be subject to the commonwealth, that is to the sovereign representative, that is to himself; which is not subjection, but freedom from the laws. Which error, because it setteth the laws above the sovereign, setteth also a judge above him, and a power to punish him; which is to make a new sovereign; and again for the same reason a third, to punish the second; and so
30 continually without end, to the confusion, and dissolution of the commonwealth.

Attributing of absolute propriety to subjects. A fifth doctrine, that tendeth to the dissolution of a commonwealth, is, *that every private man has an absolute propriety in his goods; such, as excludeth the right of the sovereign.* Every man has indeed a propriety that excludes the right of every other subject: and he has it only from the sovereign power; without the protection whereof, every other man should have equal right to the same. But if the right of the sovereign also be excluded, he cannot perform the office
40 they have put him into; which is, to defend them both from

foreign enemies, and from the injuries of one another; and consequently there is no longer a commonwealth.

And if the propriety of subjects, exclude not the right of the sovereign representative to their goods; much less to their offices of judicature, or execution, in which they represent the sovereign himself.

Dividing of the sovereign power. There is a sixth doctrine, plainly, and directly against the essence of a commonwealth; and it is this, *that the sovereign power may be divided*. For what is it to divide
10 the power of a commonwealth, but to dissolve it; for powers divided mutually destroy each other. And for these doctrines, men are chiefly beholding to some of those, that making profession of the laws, endeavour to make them depend upon their own learning, and not upon the legislative power.

Imitation of neighbour nations. And as false doctrine, so also oftentimes the example of different government in a neighbouring nation, disposeth men to alteration of the form already settled. So the people of the Jews were stirred up to reject God, and to call upon the prophet Samuel, for a king after the manner of
20 the nations: so also the lesser cities of Greece, were continually disturbed, with seditions of the aristocratical, and democratical factions; one part of almost every commonwealth, desiring to imitate the Lacedemonians; the other, the Athenians. And I doubt not, but many men have been contented to see the late troubles in England, out of an imitation of the Low Countries; supposing there needed no more to grow rich, than to change, as they had done, the form of their government. For the constitution of man's nature, is of itself subject to desire novelty. When therefore they are provoked to the same, by the neigh-
30 bourhood also of those that have been enriched by it, it is almost impossible for them, not to be content with those that solicit them to change; and love the first beginnings, though they be grieved with the continuance of disorder; like hot bloods, that having gotten the itch, tear themselves with their own nails, till they can endure the smart no longer.

Imitation of the Greeks and Romans. And as to rebellion in particular against monarchy; one of the most frequent causes of it, is the reading of the books of policy, and histories of the ancient Greeks, and Romans; from which, young men, and all others

that are unprovided of the antidote of solid reason, receiving
a strong, and delightful impression, of the great exploits of
war, achieved by the conductors of their armies, receive withal
a pleasing idea, of all they have done besides; and imagine their
great prosperity, not to have proceeded from the emulation of
particular men, but from the virtue of their popular form of
government: not considering the frequent seditions, and civil
wars, produced by the imperfection of their policy. From the
reading, I say, of such books, men have undertaken to kill
their kings, because the Greek and Latin writers, in their
books, and discourses of policy, make it lawful, and laudable,
for any man so to do; provided, before he do it, he call him
tyrant. For they say not *regicide*, that is, killing a king, but *tyran-
nicide*, that is, killing of a tyrant is lawful. From the same books,
they that live under a monarch conceive an opinion, that the
subjects in a popular commonwealth enjoy liberty; but that in
monarchy they are all slaves. I say, they that live under a monarchy conceive such an opinion; not they that live under a
popular government: for they find no such matter. In sum, I
cannot imagine, how any thing can be more prejudicial to a
monarchy, than the allowing of such books to be publicly read,
without present applying such correctives of discreet masters, as
are fit to take away their venom: which venom I will not doubt
to compare to the biting of a mad dog, which is a disease the
physicians call *hydrophobia*, or *fear of water*. For as he that is so
bitten, has a continual torment of thirst, and yet abhorreth
water; and is in such an estate, as if the poison endeavoured to
convert him into a dog: so when a monarchy is once bitten to
the quick, by those democratical writers, that continually snarl
at that estate; it wanteth nothing more than a strong monarch,
which nevertheless out of a certain *tyrannophobia*, or fear of being
strongly governed, when they have him, they abhor.

The opinion that there be more sovereigns than one in the commonwealth.
As there have been doctors, that hold there be three souls in a
man; so there be also that think there may be more souls, that
is, more sovereigns, than one, in a commonwealth; and set up a
supremacy against the *sovereignty*; *canons* against *laws*; and a
ghostly authority against the *civil*; working on men's minds, with
words and distinctions, that of themselves signify nothing, but
bewray by their obscurity; that there walketh, as some think,

invisibly another kingdom, as it were a kingdom of fairies, in the dark. Now seeing it is manifest, that the civil power, and the power of the commonwealth is the same thing; and that supremacy, and the power of making canons, and granting faculties, implieth a commonwealth; it followeth, that where one is sovereign, another supreme; where one can make laws, and another make canons; there must needs be two commonwealths, of one and the same subjects; which is a kingdom divided in itself, and cannot stand. For notwithstanding the
10 insignificant distinction of *temporal*, and *ghostly*, they are still two kingdoms, and every subject is subject to two masters. For seeing the *ghostly* power challengeth the right to declare what is sin, it challengeth by consequence to declare what is law, sin being nothing but the transgression of the law; and again, the civil power challenging to declare what is law, every subject must obey two masters, who both will have their commands be observed as law; which is impossible. Or, if it be but one kingdom, either the *civil*, which is the power of the commonwealth, must be subordinate to the *ghostly*, and then there is no sov-
20 ereignty but the *ghostly*; of the *ghostly* must be subordinate to the *temporal*, and then there is no *supremacy* but the *temporal*. When therefore these two powers oppose one another, the commonwealth cannot but be in great danger of civil war and dissolution. For the *civil* authority being more visible, and standing in the clearer light of natural reason, cannot choose but draw to it in all times a very considerable part of the people: and the *spiritual*, though it stand in the darkness of School distinctions, and hard words, yet because the fear of darkness and ghosts, is greater than other fears, cannot want a party sufficient to
30 trouble, and sometimes to destroy a commonwealth. And this is a disease which not unfitly may be compared to the epilepsy, or falling sickness, which the Jews took to be one kind of possession by spirits, in the body natural. For as in this disease, there is an unnatural spirit, or wind in the head that obstructeth the roots of the nerves, and moving them violently, taketh away the motion which naturally they should have from the power of the soul in the brain, and thereby causeth violent, and irregular motions, which men call convulsions, in the parts; insomuch as he that is seized therewith, falleth down sometimes
40 into the water, and sometimes into the fire, as a man deprived of his senses; so also in the body politic, when the spiritual

power, moveth the members of a commonwealth, by the terror of punishments, and hope of rewards, which are the nerves of it, otherwise than by the civil power, which is the soul of the commonwealth, they ought to be moved; and by strange, and hard words suffocates their understanding, it must needs thereby distract the people, and either overwhelm the commonwealth with oppression, or cast it into the fire of a civil war.

Mixed government. Sometimes also in the merely civil government, there be more than one soul; as when the power of levy-
10 ing money, which is the nutritive faculty, has depended on a general assembly; the power of conduct and command, which is the motive faculty, on one man; and the power of making laws, which is the rational faculty, on the accidental consent, not only of those two, but also of a third; this endangereth the commonwealth, sometimes for want of consent to good laws: most often for want of such nourishment, as is necessary to life, and motion. For although few perceive, that such government, is not government, but division of the commonwealth into three factions, and call it mixed monarchy; yet the truth is, that
20 it is not one independent commonwealth, but three independent factions; nor one representative person, but three. In the kingdom of God, there may be three persons independent, without breach of unity in God that reigneth; but where men reign, that be subject to diversity of opinions, it cannot be so. And therefore if the king bear the person of the people, and the general assembly bear also the person of the people, and another assembly bear the person of a part of the people, they are not one person, nor one sovereign, but three persons, and three sovereigns.
30 To what disease in the natural body of man, I may exactly compare this irregularity of a commonwealth, I know not. But I have seen a man, that had another man growing out of his side, with a head, arms, breast, and stomach, of his own; if he had had another man growing out of his other side, the comparison might then have been exact.

Want of money. Hitherto I have named such diseases of a commonwealth, as are of the greatest, and most present danger. There be other not so great; which nevertheless are not unfit to be observed. At first, the difficulty of raising money, for the
40 necessary uses of the commonwealth; especially in the approach

of war. This difficulty ariseth from the opinion, that every subject hath a propriety in his lands and goods, exclusive of the
sovereign's right to the use of the same. From whence it cometh
to pass, that the sovereign power, which foreseeth the necessities and dangers of the commonwealth, finding the passage of
money to the public treasury obstructed, by the tenacity of the
people, whereas it ought to extend itself, to encounter, and
prevent such dangers in their beginnings, contracteth itself as
long as it can, and when it cannot longer, struggles with the
10 people by stratagems of law, to obtain little sums, which not
sufficing, he is fain at last violently to open the way for present
supply, or perish; and being put often to these extremities, at
last reduceth the people to their due temper; or else the commonwealth must perish. Insomuch as we may compare this distemper very aptly to an ague; wherein, the fleshy parts being
congealed, or by venomous matter obstructed, the veins which
by their natural course empty themselves into the heart, are not,
as they ought to be, supplied from the arteries, whereby there
succeedeth at first a cold contraction, and trembling of the
20 limbs; and afterward a hot, and strong endeavour of the heart,
to force a passage for the blood; and before it can do that, con-
tenteth itself with the small refreshments of such things as cool
for a time, till, if nature be strong enough, it break at last the
contumacy of the parts obstructed, and dissipateth the venom
into sweat; or, if nature be too weak, the patient dieth.

Monopolies, and abuses of publicans. Again, there is sometimes in a
commonwealth, a disease, which resembleth the pleurisy; and
that is, when the treasure of the commonwealth, flowing out
of its due course, is gathered together in too much abundance,
30 in one, or a few private men, by monopolies, or by farms of the
public revenues; in the same manner as the blood in a pleurisy,
getting into the membrane of the breast, breedeth there an
inflammation, accompanied with a fever, and painful stitches.

Popular men. Also, the popularity of a potent subject, unless the
commonwealth have very good caution of his fidelity, is a
dangerous disease; because the people, which should receive
their motion from the authority of the sovereign, by the flattery
and by the reputation of an ambitious man are drawn away
from their obedience to the laws, to follow a man, of whose
40 virtues, and designs they have no knowledge. And this is

commonly of more danger in a popular government, than in a monarchy; because an army is of so great force, and multitude, as it may easily be made believe, they are the people. By this means it was, that Julius Cæsar, who was set up by the people against the senate, having won to himself the affections of his army, made himself master both of senate and people. And this proceeding of popular, and ambitious men, is plain rebellion; and may be resembled to the effects of witchcraft.

Excessive greatness of a town, multitude of corporations. Another
10 infirmity of a commonwealth, is the immoderate greatness of a town, when it is able to furnish out of its own circuit, the number, and expense of a great army: as also the great number of corporations; which are as it were many lesser commonwealths in the bowels of a greater, like worms in the entrails of a natural man.

Liberty of disputing against sovereign power. To which may be added, the liberty of disputing against absolute power, by pretenders to political prudence; which though bred for the most part in the lees of the people, yet animated by false doc-
20 trines, are perpetually meddling with the fundamental laws, to the molestation of the commonwealth; like the little worms, which physicians call *ascarides*.

We may further add, the insatiable appetite, or βουλιμία, of enlarging dominion; with the incurable *wounds* thereby many times received from the enemy; and the *wens*, of ununited conquests, which are many times a burthen, and with less danger lost, than kept; as also the *lethargy* of ease, and *consumption* of riot and vain expense.

Dissolution of the commonwealth. Lastly, when in a war, foreign or
30 intestine, the enemies get a final victory; so as, the forces of the commonwealth keeping the field no longer, there is no further protection of subjects in their loyalty; then is the commonwealth DISSOLVED, and every man at liberty to protect himself by such courses as his own discretion shall suggest unto him. For the sovereign is the public soul, giving life and motion to the commonwealth; which expiring, the members are governed by it no more, than the carcase of a man, by his departed, though immortal, soul. For though the right of a sovereign monarch cannot be extinguished by the act of another; yet the

obligation of the members may. For he that wants protection, may seek it anywhere; and when he hath it, is obliged, without fraudulent pretence of having submitted himself out of fear, to protect his protection as long as he is able. But when the power of an assembly is once suppressed, the right of the same perisheth utterly; because the assembly itself is extinct; and consequently, there is no possibility for the sovereignty to re-enter.

VII
Sir Thomas Browne
1605–82

Browne used to be the most admired prose writer in English. Many a nineteenth-century critic from Lamb and Coleridge onwards waxed eloquent over his purple passages with their richness of elaboration in sound and rhythm. For C. H. Herford a Beethoven symphony was the only possible comparison to 'the magnificent discourse' of *Urn Burial*, 'with its vast undulations of rhythmic sound, its triumphal processions, its funeral pageants, its abysmal plunges into unfathomable depths, its ecstatic soarings to the heights of heaven'; for another critic the famous fifth and last chapter of that work was the most perfect piece of prose in English; and dozens of writers recorded their admiration of his 'music'. To a modern reader these raptures look suspicious: behind the hyperbolic, transcendental affirmations of his beauty there lies the assumption that Browne's gorgeous manipulation of sound and rhythm are sufficient in themselves to make his work artistic. In reply, we might quote the caveat of a modern critic[1] who is sympathetic to Browne but not dazzled:

> The danger with a man like Browne, no very clear or profound thinker yet with a style so elaborate, is when the matter is not answerable to the style, when the reader becomes aware of a discrepancy between the poverty of the thought and the pomp of language and cadence expended on it.

Further, we would want to argue that rhythm or sound may be almost as important resources as imagery or syntactical structure, but that for them as for other expressive devices their *raison d'être* is their ability to support and extend meaning: great prose is the imaginative union of form and structure, and if we feel that a writer is indulging the resources of language for their own sake then we must regard his style as specious. 'More matter with less art.'

Browne's control of sound and rhythm seem to have been overvalued, and valued for the wrong reasons. If we turn to the

---

[1] F. P. Wilson, *Seventeenth-Century Prose*, p. 85.

conclusion of *Urn-Burial* we find that a more revealing characteristic of his prose is the way that his sentences form little
worlds of their own. Each one is sharply chiselled, arranged
into a clearly-shaped whole, often with quite precise boundaries
drawn by punctuation within it, but there is seldom any flow
of movement or argument between sentences or through a
whole paragraph. Browne's style is *paratactic*, adding on members (and thoughts), not *hypotactic*, where both thought and
structure are subordinated to some unifying concern: his sentences are single, mystifying, oracular. Thus he speculates:

> If we begin to die when we live, and long life be but a pro-
> longation of death; our life is a sad composition. We live
> with death, and die not in a moment. How many pulses made
> up the life of Methuselah, were work for Archimedes: Com-
> mon Counters sum up the life of Moses his man. Our days
> become considerable like petty sums by minute accumula-
> tions; where numerous fractions make up but small round
> numbers; and our days of a span long make not one little
> finger.

There are no laws governing syntactical structure, of course,
and the paratactic mode is capable of the imaginative extension
of thought, such as sudden accelerations between cause and
effect, or surprise reversals, or all kinds of sparking effects produced by the friction between the members and the narrow
areas in which they turn. But in Browne there are few instances
where this aggregative structure is used to illuminate thought;
indeed the thought is much the same within a single section, so
that the syntax seems merely to be a mannerism. Worse still
Browne attempts to introduce finality into his arguments either
by beginning sentences with 'But', or by joining parts within
them by 'and', often to lead to a challenging but merely
rhetorical question. For the latter technique take the second
sentence here: 'The number of the dead long exceedeth all that
shall live. [*true?*] The night of time far surpasseth the day, . . .
and who knows when was the Aequinox?'; and for the first
take the third paragraph in this chapter. These sequences are
disconcerting: words like 'but' or 'and' are given a specious
importance, less than they seem at first to have, but more than
they deserve. And often they join non-sequiturs, or Browne's
favourite intellectual and stylistic device, the paradox.

Religio Medici is a gallery of paradoxes. No work better expresses the whimsical, quizzical nature of Browne, lost in speculation over mysteries, aloof from the crowd, devoted to himself:

> The world that I regard is my self; it is the Microcosm of my own frame that I cast mine eye on; for the other, I use it but like the Globe, and turn it round sometimes for my recreation. Men that look upon my outside, perusing only my condition and Fortunes, do err in my altitude; for I am above Atlas his shoulders.

Browne is, he is convinced, unique: so many sections in the work serve only to distinguish his reactions from the commonplace ones of other people ('such extravagant and irregular heads as mine'), or to record with pride his ability to accept the most impossible paradoxes: 'In Philosophy, where Truth seems double-fac'd, there is no man more Paradoxical than my self: but in Divinity I love to keep the road.' Yet in divinity most of all he finds paradoxes:

> Methinks there be not impossibilities enough in religion for an active faith. . . . I love to lose my self in a mystery, to pursue my reason to an *O altitudo!* 'Tis my solitary recreation to pose my apprehension with those involved enigmas and riddles of the Trinity: with Incarnation and Resurrection.

Although the true Christian needs to be able to accept these mysteries without dogmatic scrutiny, Browne seems to go beyond this: one suspects that he is attracted to the problem of faith just because it is contradictory, an enormous insoluble mystery, and therefore an endless source of recreation. As he says in the next paragraph: 'Where I cannot satisfy my reason, I love to humour my fancy.' If the Christian mysteries were less paradoxical, one worries, he would not be so interested in them. The results of this deep-rooted love of paradox are everywhere to be seen, contradictions are cherished and Browne constructs his own examples such as the extraordinary one included here on the idea that because flesh decays we are all cannibals—'we have devour'd ourselves' (it is Hamlet's argument of 'how a king may go a progress through the guts of a beggar' carried a stage further), or the even more remarkable one towards the end of Part One on the text 'Before Abraham was, I am', which Browne takes to the ultimate: 'Though my grave be England, my dying place was paradise: and Eve miscarried of my before she conceiv'd of Cain.' Although these paradoxes are startling, on reflection they can sometimes seem merely a succession of whimsical half-truths.

But if Browne has been overpraised, and if there are aspects of his work which make us suspect him of pride, arrogance, and a complacent satisfaction with mystification (all these things are expressed in a frank, naïve and inoffensive way, however, which almost disarms criticism), there are other sides to him which we can admire. The arguments for the existence of God in *Religio Medici*, although they are not likely to be revived today, are not contemptible, and his separation of rational inquiry from faith in that book is still the most sensible solution to a problem which vexed Renaissance men. The feature of his style which has been undervalued and which gives most pleasure is his unobtrusive but imaginative use of metaphor. Although there are some recurrent images, generally they are used for local illumination and argument—martyrs served God 'in the fire, whereas we honour him but in the sunshine'; 'There is no road or ready way to virtue: it is not an easy point of art to disentangle our selves from this riddle, or web of sin'; many men have such 'unstable judgments that cannot consist in the narrow point and centre of virtue without a reel or stagger to the circumference'; or in more sustained images such as this for the evidence of God in the universe:

> In this mass of nature there is a set of things that carry in their front (although not in capital letters, yet in stenography and short characters,) something of divinity, which to wiser reasons serve as luminaries in the abyss of knowledge, and to judicious belief as scales and roundles to mount the pinnacles and highest places of divinity.

That is an impressive modulation from what E. R. Curtius has shown to be the traditional image of the universe as a book (with the recently invented 'stenography' or shorthand system as an ingenious variation on it) to knowledge first as light and then as 'roundles' or steps of a ladder to ascend to God. In the now faded purple of *Urn-Burial* there are several images that have escaped in the adulation of sound and rhythm: the dead bones have, 'in a yard under ground, and thin walls of clay, outworn all the strong and specious buildings above it; and quietly rested under the drums and tramplings of three conquests.' Equally concrete and sensitive are metaphors such as these: eternity 'maketh pyramids pillars of snow'; 'the iniquity of oblivion blindly scattereth her poppy'; 'afflictions induce callosities, miseries are slippery, or fall like snow upon us': although one must have reservations about the self-indulgent melancholic tone here these are still evidences of a powerful imagination. Corrective, but not destructive, criticism may help to reveal which aspects of Browne's art are of lasting value.

From *Religio Medici* (1643)

I, 6. I could never divide myself from any man upon the difference of an opinion, or be angry with his judgement for not agreeing with me in that from which, perhaps within a few days, I should dissent myself. I have no genius to disputes in religion, and have often thought it wisdom to decline them; especially upon a disadvantage, or when the cause of truth might suffer in the weakness of my patronage. Where we desire to be informed 'tis good to contest with men above ourselves; but to confirm and establish our opinions 'tis best to argue with judge-
10 ments below our own, that the frequent spoils and victories over their reasons may settle in ourselves an esteem and conconfirmed opinion of our own. Every man is not a proper champion for truth, nor fit to take up the gauntlet in the case of verity. Many, from the ignorance of these maxims and an inconsiderate zeal unto truth, have too rashly charged the troops of error, and remain as trophies unto the enemies of truth. A man may be in as just possession of truth as of a city, and yet be forced to surrender. 'Tis therefore far better to enjoy her with peace than to hazard her on a battle. If, there-
20 fore, there rise any doubts in my way, I do forget them, or at least defer them till my better settled judgement and more manly reason be able to resolve them; for I perceive every man's own reason is his best Oedipus, and will, upon a reasonable truce, find a way to loose those bonds wherewith the subtleties of error have enchained our more flexible and tender judgements. In philosophy, where truth seems double-faced there is no man more paradoxical than myself; but in divinity I love to keep the road, and—though not in an implicit yet an humble faith—follow the great wheel of the Church, by which I move,

not reserving any proper poles or motion from the epicycle of
my own brain. By this means I leave no gap for heresies, schisms
or errors, of which at present I hope I shall not injure truth
to say I have no taint or tincture. I must confess my greener
studies have been polluted with two or three—not any begotten
in the latter centuries, but old and obsolete; such as could never
have been revived but by such extravagant and irregular heads
as mine; for indeed, heresies perish not with their authors, but
like the river Arethusa, though they lose their currents in one
10 place, they rise up again in another. . . .

I, 8. That heresies should arise we have the prophecy of Christ,
but that old ones should be abolished we hold no prediction.
That there must be heresies is true not only in our church, but
also in any other. Even in doctrines heretical there will be
super-heresies; and Arians not only divided from their church
but also among themselves; for heads that are disposed unto
schism, and complexionally propense to innovation, are naturally indisposed for a community, nor will ever be confined unto
the order or economy of one body. And therefore, when they
20 separate from others they knit but loosely among themselves;
nor contented with a general breach or dichotomy with their
church, do subdivide and mince themselves almost into atoms.
'Tis true that men of singular parts and humours have not been
free from singular opinions and conceits in all ages; retaining
something not only beside the opinion of his own church or
any other, but also any particular author; which notwithstanding, a sober judgement may do without offence or heresy. For
there is yet, after all the decrees of councils and the niceties of
the Schools, many things untouched, unimagined, wherein the
30 liberty of an honest reason may play and expatiate with security,
and far without the circle of an heresy.

I, 9. As for those wingy mysteries in divinity and airy subtleties
of religion, which have unhinged the brains of better heads,
they never stretch the pia mater of mine. Methinks there be not
impossibilities enough in religion for an active faith. The
deepest mysteries ours contains have not only been illustrated
but maintained by syllogism and the rule of reason. I love to
lose myself in a mystery, to pursue my reason to an *O altitudo!*
'Tis my solitary recreation to pose my apprehension with those
40 involved enigmas and riddles of the Trinity, with Incarnation

and Resurrection. I can answer all the objections of Satan and my rebellious reason with that odd resolution I learned of Tertullian, *Certum est, quia impossibile est*. I desire to exercise my faith in the difficultest points, for to credit ordinary and visible objects is not faith but persuasion. Some believe the better for seeing Christ's sepulchre, and when they have seen the Red Sea, doubt not of the miracle. Now contrary, I bless myself and am thankful that I lived not in the days of miracles, that I never saw Christ nor his disciples. I would not have been one
10 of the Israelites that passed the Red Sea, nor one of Christ's patients on whom he wrought his wonders. Then had my faith been thrust upon me, nor should I enjoy that greater blessing pronounced to all that believe and saw not. 'Tis an easy and necessary belief to credit what our eye and sense hath examined. I believe he was dead, buried, and rose again; and desire to see him in his glory rather than to contemplate him in his cenotaph or sepulchre. Nor is this much to believe. As we have reason, we owe this faith unto history: they only had the advantage of a bold and noble faith who lived before his coming, who upon
20 obscure prophecies and mystical types could raise a belief and expect apparent impossibilities.

I, 10. 'Tis true there is an edge in all firm belief, and with an easy metaphor we may say the sword of faith; but in these obscurities I rather use it in the adjunct the Apostle gives it, a buckler; under which I perceive a wary combatant may lie invulnerable. Since I was of understanding to know we know nothing, my reason hath been more pliable to the will of faith. I am now content to understand a mystery without a rigid definition, in an easy and platonic description. That allegorical
30 description of Hermes pleaseth me beyond all the metaphysical definitions of divines. Where I cannot satisfy my reason, I love to humour my fancy. . . .

I, 36. The whole creation is a mystery, and particularly that of man. At the blast of his mouth were the rest of the creatures made, and at his bare word they started out of nothing; but in frame of man—as the text describes it—he played the sensible operator, and seemed not so much to create as make him. When he had separated the materials of other creatures there consequently resulted a form and soul, but having raised the
40 walls of man he was driven to a second and harder creation, of

a substance like himself, an incorruptible and immortal soul.
For these two affections we have the philosophy and opinion
of the heathens, the flat affirmative of Plato and not a negative
from Aristotle. There is another scruple cast in by divinity
concerning its production, much disputed in the German
auditories, and with that indifferency and equality of arguments
as leave the controversy undetermined. I am not of Paracelsus'
mind, that boldly delivers a receipt to make a man without
conjunction, yet cannot but wonder at the multitude of heads
10 that do deny traduction, having no other argument to confirm
their belief than that rhetorical sentence and antimetathesis of
Augustine, *Creando infunditur, infundendo creatur*. Either opinion
will consist well enough with religion, yet I should rather incline
to this did not one objection haunt me, not wrung from speculations and subtleties, but from common sense and observation;
not picked from the leaves of any author, but bred amongst the
weeds and tares of mine own brain. And this is a conclusion
from the equivocal and monstrous productions in the copula-
tion of man with beast; for if the soul be not transmitted and
20 transfused in the seed of the parents, why are not these productions merely beasts, but have also a tincture and impression of
reason in as high a measure as it can evidence itself in those
improper organs? Nor truly can I peremptorily deny that the
soul, in this her sublunary estate, is wholly and in all acceptions
inorganical, but that for the performance of her ordinary
actions there is required not only a symmetry and proper disposition of organs, but a crasis and temper correspondent to its
operation. Yet is not this mass of flesh and visible structure the
instrument and proper corps of the soul, but rather of sense,
30 and that the hand of reason. In our study of anatomy there is a
mass of mysterious philosophy, and such as reduced the very
heathens to divinity; yet amongst all those rare discoveries and
curious pieces I find in the fabric of man I do not so much content myself as in that I find not; that is, no organ or proper
instrument for the rational soul. For in the brain, which we
term the seat of reason, there is not anything of moment more
than I can discover in the cranie of a beast: and this is a sensible
and no inconsiderable argument of the inorganity of the soul,
at least in that sense we usually so receive it. Thus are we men,
40 and we know not how; there is something in us that can be
without us, and will be after us; though it is strange that it hath

no history what it was before us, nor can tell how it entered in us.

I, 37. Now, for the walls of flesh wherein the soul doth seem to be immured before the Resurrection, it is nothing but an elemental composition and a fabric that must fall to ashes. *All flesh is grass* is not only metaphorically but literally true, for all those creatures which we behold are but the herbs of the field digested into flesh in them, or more remotely carnified in ourselves. Nay, further, we are what we all abhor, anthropophagi and cannibals, devourers not only of men but of ourselves, and
10 that not in an allegory but a positive truth. For all this mass of flesh that we behold came in at our mouths; this frame we look upon hath been upon our trenchers. In brief, we have devoured ourselves, and yet do live and remain ourselves. I cannot believe the wisdom of Pythagoras did ever positively and in a literal sense affirm his metempsychosis or impossible transmigration of the souls of men into beasts. Of all metamorphoses and transformations I believe only one; that is, of Lot's wife, for that of Nebuchadnezzar proceeded not so far. In all others I conceive no further verity than is contained in their implicit sense and
20 morality. I believe that the whole frame of a beast doth perish, and is left in the same estate after death as before it was materialled into life; that the souls of men know neither contrary nor corruption; that they subsist beyond the body, and outlive death by the privilege of their proper natures, and without a miracle; that the souls of the faithful, as they leave earth, take possession of heaven; that those apparitions and ghosts of departed persons are not the wandering souls of men but the unquiet walks of devils, prompting and suggesting us unto mischief, blood and villainy; instilling and stealing into our
30 hearts that the blessed spirits are not at rest in their graves, but wander solicitous of the affairs of the world. That these phantasms appear often, and do frequent cemeteries, charnel houses and churches, it is because these are the dormitories of the dead, where the devil, like an insolent champion, beholds with pride the spoils and trophies of his victory in Adam.

I, 38. This is that dismal conquest we all deplore, that make us so often cry, O *Adam, quid fecisti?* I thank God I have not those strait ligaments or narrow obligations unto the world as to dote on life, or be convulsed and tremble at the name of death. Not
40 that I am insensible of the dread and horror thereof, or by

raking into the bowels of the deceased, or the continual sight
of anatomies, skeletons or cadaverous relics, like vespilloes or
grave-makers, I am become stupid or have forgot the apprehension of mortality; but that marshalling all the horrors and
contemplating the extremities thereof, I find not anything therein able to daunt the courage of a man, much less a well-resolved
Christian. And therefore am not angry with the error of our
first parents or unwilling to bear a part of this common fate,
and like the best of them, to die: that is, to cease to breathe, to
10 take a farewell of the elements, to be a kind of nothing for a
moment, to be within one instant of a spirit. When I take a full
view and circle of myself without this reasonable moderator
and equal piece of justice, death, I do conceive myself the miser-
ablest person extant. Were there not another life that I hope for,
all the vanities of this world should not entreat a moment's
breath from me. Could the devil work my belief to imagine I
could never die, I would not outlive that very thought. I have
so abject a conceit of this common way of existence, this retaining to the sun and elements, I cannot think this is to be a
20 man or to live according to the dignity of humanity. In expectation of a better, I can with patience embrace this life, yet in my
best meditations do often desire death. It is a symptom of
melancholy to be afraid of death, yet sometimes to desire it.
This latter I have often discovered in myself, and think no man
ever desired life as I have sometimes death. I honour any man
that contemns it, nor can I highly love any that is afraid of it.
This makes me naturally love a soldier, and honour those
tattered and contemptible regiments that will die at the command of a sergeant. For a pagan there may be motives to be in
30 love with life; but for a Christian that is amazed at death, I see
not how he can escape this dilemma: that he is too sensible of
this life, or hopeless of the life to come.

I, 39. Some divines count Adam thirty years old at his creation,
because they suppose him created in the perfect age and stature
of man; and surely we are all out of the computation of our age,
and every man is some months older than he bethinks him. For
we live, move, have a being and are subject to the actions of
the elements and the malice of diseases in that other world, the
truest microcosm, the womb of our mother; for besides that
40 general and common existence we are conceived to hold in our

157

chaos, and whilst we sleep within the bosom of our causes, we
enjoy a being and life in three distinct worlds, wherein we
receive most manifest graduations. In that obscure world and
womb of our mother our time is short, computed by the moon;
yᵉ longer than the days of many creatures that behold the sun;
ourselves being not yet without life, sense and reason, though
for the manifestation of its actions it awaits the opportunity of
objects, and seems to live there but in its root and soul of vege-
tation. Entering afterwards upon the scene of the world, we
10 arise up and become another creature, performing the reasonable actions of man and obscurely manifesting that part of divinity in us, but not in complement and perfection till we have
once more cast our secundine—that is, this slough of flesh—
and are delivered into the last world, that ineffable place of
Paul, that proper *ubi* of spirits. The smattering I have of the
philosopher's stone—which is nothing else but the perfectest
exaltation of gold—hath taught me a great deal of divinity, and
instructed my belief how that immortal spirit and incorruptible
substance of my soul may lie obscure and sleep awhile within
20 this house of flesh. Those strange and mystical transmigrations
that I have observed in silkworms turned my philosophy into
divinity. There is in those works of nature which seem to
puzzle reason something divine, and that hath more in it than
the eye of a common spectator doth discover. I have therefore
forsaken those strict definitions of death by privation of life,
extinction of natural heat, separation etc., of soul and body, and
have framed one in an hermetical way unto mine own fancy: *Est
mutatio ultima qua perficitur nobile illud extractum microcosmi.* For to
me, that consider things in a natural and experimental way, man
30 seems to be but a digestion or a preparative way unto that last
and glorious elixir which lies imprisoned in the chains of flesh.

I, 40. I am naturally bashful, nor hath conversation, age or
travel been able to effront or enharden me, yet I have one part
of modesty which I have seldom discovered in another: that
is—to speak truly—I am not so much afraid of death as ashamed
thereof. 'Tis the very disgrace and ignominy of our natures,
that in a moment can so disfigure us that our nearest friends,
wife and children stand afraid and start at us. The birds and
beasts of the field, that before in a natural fear obeyed us, for-
40 getting all allegiance begin to prey upon us. This very conceit

hath in a tempest disposed and left me willing to be swallowed
in the abyss of waters, wherein I had perished unseen, unpitied,
without wondering eyes, tears of pity, lectures of mortality; and
none had said, *Quantum mutatus ab illo!* Not that I am ashamed
of the anatomy of my parts, or can accuse nature for playing the
bungler in any part of me, or my own vicious life for contracting any shameful disease upon me whereby I might not call
myself as wholesome a morsel for the worms as any.

I, 41. Some, upon the courage of a fruitful issue, wherein, as in
10 the truest chronicle, they seem to outlive themselves, can with
greater patience away with death. This conceit and counterfeit
subsisting in our progenies seems to me a mere fallacy, unworthy the desires of a man that can but conceive a thought of
the next world, who in a nobler ambition should desire to live
in his substance in heaven rather than in his name and shadow
on earth. And therefore at my death I mean to take a total adieu
of the world, not caring for a monument, history or epitaph;
not so much as the bare memory of my name to be found anywhere but in the universal register of God. I am not yet so
20 cynical as to approve the testament of Diogenes, nor do I altogether allow that rodomontado of Lucan,

> *Coelo tegitur, qui non habet urnam.*
> He that unburied lies wants not his hearse,
> For unto him a tomb's the universe

but commend in my calmer judgement their ingenuous intentions that desire to sleep by the urns of their fathers, and strive
to go the nearest way unto corruption. I do not envy the temper
of crows and daws, nor the numerous and weary days of our
fathers before the Flood. If there be any truth in astrology, I may
30 outlive a jubilee. As yet I have not seen one revolution of
Saturn, nor hath my pulse beat thirty years, and yet, excepting
one, have seen the ashes and left underground all the kings of
Europe; have been contemporary to three emperors, four
Grand Seigniers and as many Popes. Methinks I have out-
lived myself, and begin to be weary of the sun. I have shaken
hands with delight in my warm blood and canicular days. I
perceive I do anticipate the vices of age: the world to me is but
a dream or mock-show, and we all therein but pantaloons and
antics to my severer contemplations. The course and order of

my life would be a very death unto another. I use myself to all diets, humours, airs, hunger, thirst, cold, heat, want, plenty, necessity, dangers, hazards. When I am cold I cure not myself by heat; when sick, not by physic. Those that know how I live may justly say I regard not life, nor stand in fear of death.

I, 42. It is not, I confess, an unlawful prayer to desire to surpass the days of our Saviour, or wish to outlive that age wherein he thought fittest to die, yet if—as divinity affirms—there shall be no grey hairs in heaven, but all shall rise in the perfect state of
10 men, we do but outlive those perfections in this world to be recalled unto them by a greater miracle in the next, and run on here but to be retrograde hereafter. Were there any hopes to outlive vice, or a point to be superannuated from sin, it were worthy of our knees to implore the days of Methuselah. But age doth not rectify but incurvate our natures, turning bad dispositions into worser habits, and—like diseases—brings on incurable vices; for every day as we grow weaker in age we grow stronger in sin, and the number of our days doth but make our sins innumerable. The same vice committed at sixteen is not
20 the same, though it agree in all other circumstances, at forty, but swells and doubles from the circumstances of our ages, when besides the constant and inexcusable habit of transgressing, the maturity of our judgement cuts off pretence unto excuse or pardon. Every sin, the oftener it is committed, the more it acquireth in the quality of evil: as it succeeds in time, so it proceeds in degrees of badness; for as they proceed they ever multiply, and, like figures in arithmetic, the last stands for more than all that went before it. And though I think no man can live well once but he that could live twice, yet for my own
30 part I would not live over my hours past, or begin again the thread of my days: not upon Cicero's ground, because I have lived them well, but for fear I should live them worse. I find my growing judgement daily instruct me how to be better, but my untamed affections and confirmed vitiosity makes me daily do worse. I find in my confirmed age the same sins I discovered in my youth: I committed many then because I was a child, and because I commit them still, I am yet an infant. Therefore I perceive a man may be twice a child before the days of dotage, and stand in need of Aeson's bath before threescore.

40 *I, 43.* And truly there goes a great deal of providence to pro-

duce a man's life unto threescore. There is more required than an able temper for those years. Though the radical humour contain in it sufficient oil for seventy, yet I perceive in some it gives no light past thirty; men assign not all the causes of long life that write whole books thereof. They that found themselves on the radical balsam or vital sulphur of the parts determine not why Abel lived not so long as Adam. There is therefore a secret glome or bottom of our days; 'twas his wisdom to determine them, but his perpetual and waking providence that fulfils and
10 accomplisheth them; wherein the spirits, ourselves and all the creatures of God in a secret and disputed way do execute his will. Let them not therefore complain of immaturity that die about thirty. They fall but like the whole world, whose solid and well-composed substance must not expect the duration and period of its constitution. When all things are completed in it, its age is accomplished; and the last and general fever may as naturally destroy it before six thousand as me before forty. There is therefore some other hand that twines the thread of life than that of nature. We are not only ignorant in antipathies
20 and occult qualities; our ends are as obscure as our beginnings. The line of our days is drawn by night, and the various effects therein by a pencil that is invisible; wherein though we confess our ignorance, I am sure we do not err if we say it is the hand of God.

From *Hydriotaphia, Urn-Burial* or *A Discourse of the Sepulchral Urns Lately Found in Norfolk* (1658)

The Fifth and Last Chapter

Now since these dead bones have already outlasted the living ones of Methuselah, and in a yard under ground, and thin walls
30 of clay, out-worn all the strong and specious buildings above it; and quietly rested under the drums and tramplings of three conquests; what Prince can promise such diuturnity unto his relics, or might not gladly say,

Sic ego componi versus in ossa velim.

Time which antiquates Antiquities, and hath an art to make dust of all things, hath yet spared these *minor* Monuments. In vain we hope to be known by open and visible conservatories, when to be unknown was the means of their continuation and obscurity their protection. If they died by violent hands, and were thrust into their urns, these bones become considerable, and some old philosophers would honour them, whose souls they conceived most pure, which were thus snatched from their bodies; and to retain a stronger propension unto them: whereas they weariedly left a languishing corpse, and with faint desires of reunion. If they fell by long and aged decay, yet wrapped up in the bundle of time, they fall into indistinction, and make but one blot with infants. If we begin to die when we live, and long life be but a prolongation of death; our life is a sad composition; we live with death, and die not in a moment. How many pulses made up the life of Methuselah, were work for Archimedes: common counters sum up the life of Moses his man. Our days become considerable like petty sums by minute accumulations; where numerous fractions make up but small round numbers; and our days of a span long make not one little finger.

If the nearness of our last necessity, brought a nearer conformity unto it, there were a happiness in hoary hairs, and no calamity in half senses. But the long habit of living indisposeth us for dying: when avarice makes us the sport of death; when even David grew politicly cruel; and Solomon could hardly be said to be the wisest of men. But many are too early old, and before the date of age. Adversity stretcheth our days, misery makes Alcmena's nights, and time hath no wings unto it. But the most tedious being is that which can unwish it self, content to be nothing, or never to have been, which was beyond the mal-content of Job, who cursed not the day of his life, but his nativity; content to have so far been, as to have a title to future being; although he had lived here but in an hidden state of life, and as it were an abortion.

What song the Syrens sang, or what name Achilles assumed when he hid himself among women, though puzzling questions are not beyond all conjecture. What time the persons of these ossuaries entred the famous nations of the dead, and slept with princes and counsellors, might admit a wide solution. But who were the proprietaries of these bones, or what bodies these ashes made up, were a question above Antiquarism. Not to be resolved by man, nor easily perhaps by spirits, except we consult the provincial guardians, or tutelary observators. Had they made as good provision for their names, as they have done for their relics, they had not so grossly erred in the art of perpetua-

SIR THOMAS BROWNE

tion. But to subsist in bones, and be but pyramidally extant, is a
fallacy in duration. Vain ashes, which in the oblivion of names,
persons, times, and sexes, have found unto themselves a fruitless continuation, and only arise unto late posterity, as em-
blems of mortal vanities; antidotes against pride, vain-glory,
and madding vices. Pagan vain-glories which thought the
world might last for ever, had encouragement for ambition,
and finding no Atropos unto the immortality of their Names,
were never damped with the necessity of oblivion. Even old
10 ambitions had the advantage of ours, in the attempts of their
vain-glories, who acting early, and before the probable meridian of time, have by this time found great accomplishment of
their designs, whereby the ancient Heroes have already outlasted their monuments and mechanical preservations. But in
this latter scene of time we cannot expect such mummies unto
our memories, when ambition may fear the Prophecy of Elias,
and Charles the fifth can never hope to live within two Methu-
selas of Hector.
    And therefore restless inquietude for the diuturnity of our
20 memories unto present considerations, seems a vanity almost out
of date, and superannuated piece of folly. We cannot hope to
live so long in our names, as some have done in their persons,
one face of Janus holds no proportion to the other. 'Tis too
late to be ambitious. The great mutations of the world are acted,
or time may be too short for our designs. To extend our memories by monuments, whose death we daily pray for, and
whose duration we cannot hope, without injury to our expectations, in the advent of the last day, were a contradiction to our
beliefs. We whose generations are ordained in this setting part of
30 time, are providentially taken off from such imaginations. And
being necessitated to eye the remaining particle of futurity, are
naturally constituted unto thoughts of the next world, and cannot excusably decline the consideration of that duration, which
maketh pyramids pillars of snow, and all that's past a moment.
    Circles and right lines limit and close all bodies, and the
mortal right-lined-circle must conclude and shut up all. There
is no antidote against the Opium of time, which temporally
considereth all things; our fathers find their graves in our short
memories, and sadly tell us how we may be buried in our sur-
40 vivors. Grave-stones tell truth scarce forty years: generations
pass while some trees stand, and old families last not three

oaks. To be read by bare inscriptions like many in Gruter, to
hope for eternity by enigmatical epithets, or first letters of our
names, to be studied by antiquaries, who we were, and have
new names given us like many of the mummies, are cold consolations unto the students of perpetuity, even by everlasting
languages.

To be content that times to come should only know there
was such a man, not caring whether they knew more of him,
was a frigid ambition in Cardan: disparaging his horoscopal
10 inclination and judgement of himself, who cares to subsist like
Hippocrates' patients, or Achilles' horses in Homer, under
naked nominations, without deserts and noble acts, which are
the balsam of our memories, the entelechia and soul of our
subsistences. To be nameless in worthy deeds exceeds an infamous history. The Canaanitish woman lives more happily
without a name, then Herodias with one. And who had not
rather have been the good thief, then Pilate?

But the iniquity of oblivion blindly scattereth her poppy,
and deals with the memory of men without distinction to merit
20 or perpetuity. Who can but pity the founder of the pyramids?
Herostratus lives that burnt the temple of Diana, he is almost
lost that built it; time hath spared the epitaph of Adrian's horse,
confounded that of himself. In vain we compute our felicities
by the advantage of our good names, since bad have equal durations; and Thersites is like to live as long as Agamemnon. Who
knows whether the best of men be known? or whether there be
not more remarkable persons forgot, then any that stand re-
membred in the known account of time? Without the favour
of the everlasting register the first man had been as unknown
30 as the last, and Methuselah's long life had been his only Chronicle.

Oblivion is not to be hired: the greater part must be content
to be as though they had not been, to be found in the register
of God, not in the record of man. Twenty seven names make
up the first story, and the recorded names ever since contain
not one living century. The number of the dead long exceedeth
all that shall live. The night of time far surpasseth the day, and
who knows when was the equinox? Every hour adds unto that
current arithmetic, which scarce stands one moment. And since
death must be the Lucina of life, and even pagans could doubt
40 whether thus to live, were to die; since our longest sun sets at
right descensions, and makes but winter arches, and therefore

it cannot be long before we lie down in darkness, and have our
light in ashes; since the brother of death daily haunts us with
dying memento's, and time that grows old it self, bids us hope
no long duration: diuturnity is a dream and folly of expectation.

Darkness and light divide the course of time, and oblivion
shares with memory, a great part even of our living beings; we
slightly remember our felicities, and the smartest strokes of
affliction leave but short smart upon us. Sense endureth no
extremities, and sorrows destroy us or themselves. To weep into
10 stones are fables. Afflictions induce callosities, miseries are
slippery, or fall like snow upon us, which notwithstanding is no
stupidity. To be ignorant of evils to come, and forgetful of
evils past, is merciful provision in nature, whereby we digest
the mixture of our few and evil days, and our delivered senses
not relapsing into cutting remembrances, our sorrows are not
kept raw by the edge of repetitions. A great part of antiquity
contented their hopes of subsistency with a transmigration of
their souls. A good way to continue their memories, while
having the advantage of plural successions, they could not but
20 act something remarkable in such variety of beings, and enjoying the fame of their passed selves, make accumulation of glory
unto their last durations. Others rather than be lost in the un-
comfortable night of nothing, were content to recede into the
common being, and make one particle of the publick soul of
all things, which was no more then to return into their unknown
and divine original again. Egyptian ingenuity was more un-
satisfied, contriving their bodies in sweet consistences, to attend
the return of their souls. But all was vanity, feeding the wind,
and folly. The Egyptian Mummies, which Cambyses or time
30 hath spared, avarice now consumeth. Mummy is become merchandise, Mizraim cures wounds, and Pharaoh is sold for
balsams.

In vain do individuals hope for immortality, or any patent
from oblivion, in preservations below the moon: Men have
been deceived even in their flatteries above the sun, and studied
conceits to perpetuate their names in heaven. The various
cosmography of that part hath already varied the names of
contrived constellations; Nimrod is lost in Orion, and Osyris in
the Dog-star. While we look for incorruption in the heavens,
40 we find they are but like the earth; durable in their main bodies,
alterable in their parts: whereof beside comets and new stars,

perspectives begin to tell tales. And the spots that wander about
the Sun, with Phaetons favour, would make clear conviction.

There is nothing strictly immortal, but immortality; whatever hath no beginning may be confident of no end (all others
have a dependent being, and within the reach of destruction)
which is the peculiar of that necessary essence that cannot destroy it self; and the highest strain of omnipotency to be so
powerfully constituted, as not to suffer even from the power of
it self. But the sufficiency of Christian immortality frustrates all
10 earthly glory, and the quality of either state after death makes
a folly of posthumous memory. God who can only destroy our
souls, and hath assured our resurrection, either of our bodies or
names hath directly promised no duration. Wherein there is so
much of chance that the boldest expectants have found unhappy
frustration; and to hold long subsistence, seems but a scape
in oblivion. But man is a noble animal, splendid in ashes, and
pompous in the grave, solemnizing nativities and deaths with
equal lustre, nor omitting ceremonies of bravery, in the infamy
of his nature.

20 Life is a pure flame, and we live by an invisible Sun within us.
A small fire sufficeth for life, great flames seemed too little after
death, while men vainly affected precious pyres, and to burn
like Sardanapalus, but the wisdom of funeral laws found the
folly of prodigal blazes, and reduced undoing fires, unto the
rule of sober obsequies, wherein few could be so mean as not
to provide wood, pitch, a mourner, and an urn.

Five languages secured not the epitaph of Gordianus; the
man of God lives longer without a tomb than any by one, invisibly interred by angels, and adjudged to obscurity, though
30 not without some marks directing human discovery. Enoch and
Elias without either tomb or burial, in an anomalous state of
being, are the great examples of perpetuity, in their long and
living memory, in strict account being still on this side death,
and having a late part yet to act upon this stage of earth. If in
the decretory term of the world we shall not all die but be
changed, according to received translation; the last day will
make but few graves; at least quick resurrections will anticipate
lasting sepulchures; some graves will be opened before they be
quite closed, and Lazarus be no wonder. When many that feared
40 to die shall groan that they can die but once, the dismal state is
the second and living death, when life puts despair on the

damned; when men shall wish the coverings of mountains, not of monuments, and annihilation shall be courted.

While some have studied monuments, others have studiously declined them: and some have been so vainly boisterous, that they durst not acknowledge their graves; wherein Alaricus seems most subtle, who had a river turned to hide his bones at the bottom. Even Sylla that thought himself safe in his urn, could not prevent revenging tongues, and stones thrown at his monument. Happy are they whom privacy makes innocent, who
10 deal so with men in this world, that they are not afraid to meet them in the next, who when they die, make no commotion among the dead, and are not touched with that poetical taunt of Isaiah.

Pyramids, Arches, Obelisks, were but the irregularities of *vain-glory*, and wild enormities of ancient magnanimity. But the most magnanimous resolution rests in the Christian religion, which trampleth upon pride, and sets on the neck of ambition, humbly pursuing that infallible perpetuity, unto which all others must diminish their diameters and be poorly seen in angles of contingency.

20 Pious spirits who passed their days in raptures of futurity, made little more of this world, then the world that was before it, while they lay obscure in the chaos of preordination, and night of their fore-beings. And if any have been so happy as truly to understand Christian annihilation, extasis, exolution, liquefaction, transformation, the kiss of the Spouse, gustation of God, and ingression into the divine shadow, they have already had an handsome anticipation of heaven; the glory of the world is surely over, and the earth in ashes unto them.

To subsist in lasting Monuments, to live in their produc-
30 tions, to exist in their names, and predicament of Chymera's, was large satisfaction unto old expectations and made one part of their *Elyziums*. But all this is nothing in the metaphysics of true belief. To live indeed is to be again our selves, which being not only an hope but an evidence in noble believers; 'Tis all one to lie in St. Innocents Church-yard, as in the Sands of Egypt: ready to be any thing, in the extasie of being ever, and as content with six foot as the moles of Adrianus.

Lucan

——*Tabesne cadavera solvat
An rogus haud refert.——*

VIII
John Milton
1608–74

Towards the end of his *Apology for Smectymnuus* Milton turns to his readers, as he does so often, and gives us a plain statement of his views on the relationship between truth and eloquence:

> For me, readers, although I cannot say that I am utterly untrained in those rules which best rhetoricians have given, or unacquainted with those examples which the prime authors of eloquence have written in any learned tongue; yet true eloquence I find to be none, but the serious and hearty love of truth: and that whose mind whatsoever is fully possessed with a fervent desire to know good things, and with the dearest charity to infuse the knowledge of them into others, when such a man would speak, his words (by what I can express), like so many nimble and airy servitors, trip about him at command, and in well-ordered files, as he would wish, fall aptly into their own places.

The opening double negatives modestly conceal the fact that Milton was one of the most knowledgeable readers of logic and rhetoric in English and the argument that rhetoric must be based on truth or be completely false is a traditional defence in the eternal debate over rhetoric. Neither of these points is exceptional, but the final image of the words simply falling into position at the obedience of the good man is a well-meant but naïve evasion of the issue: they have been 'nimble and airy servitors' of bad men often, and to destructive effect. On the other hand, the exponents of good will hardly carry the day unless they can persuade these 'well-ordered files' to form positions which will impress other people by the moral rigour of the argument and by the force and persuasiveness of the expression. I quote this passage not to pick holes in it: but merely because it is revealing both of the purpose and of the style of Milton's prose.

Almost all of Milton's prose-writing is controversial: to defend general issues such as freedom from censorship, or particular ones such as the conduct of religious and political

affairs during the Commonwealth; and to attack abhorrent
practices, from the divorce laws to the rule of kings and bishops.
In taking part in controversy he is fulfilling the duty of the
humanist (in the wide Renaissance concept of the term as a
man dedicated to the study of the classics and to putting the
values of that culture into practice) to engage not in the contemplative life, that of the hermit or monk pursuing study for his
own private ends, but in the active life, where he brings all his
knowledge and character to the service of the state. This is a
very powerful movement in the English Renaissance, and can
be followed in the life as in the work of many of our greatest
writers—Sir Thomas More, Wyatt, Ascham, Sidney, Bacon,
Ralegh, Hooker, Ben Jonson, and Milton himself. This is the
tradition behind those famous words in *Areopagitica*:

> I cannot praise a fugitive and cloistered virtue, unexercised
> and unbreathed, that never sallies out and sees her adversary,
> but slinks out of the race, where that immortal garland is to
> be run for, not without dust or heat. . . . To sequester out of
> the world into Atlantic and Utopian politics which can never
> be drawn into use, will not mend our condition. . . .

The individual's duty is 'to serve', to put his gifts to use: in
Ben Jonson's words 'knowledge which sleeps is dead', or in
Bacon's, 'in this theatre of men's life it is reserved only for God
and Angels to be lookers on'. Milton embraced his duty with
energy and industry, producing many powerful controversial
works. The effect on the content and attitudes in his prose is
that whereas other seventeenth-century writers presented here
argue, analyse man and society, speculate on human depravity
or mystery, Milton is to be found in two postures: he is either
praising his own side ('truth'), or he is attacking his enemies.

The effect of this double purpose on the style of his prose is
that syntax, sentence structure, and imagery are enlisted for
clearly defined and powerful purposes, elevating at times to
visionary height and at others crushing, trampling into the
ground. But there are other factors which influence Milton's
prose, and which come as a surprise to the reader either of Milton's verse or of other Renaissance prose writers. From the
styles of his verse one might expect Milton in prose to be equally
elaborate or latinate or complex (it would be a naïve assumption, but an innocent enough one): in fact here his vocabulary

is plain, his sentence structure quite straightforward (there are
digressions and additions, but there are no involutions), and
the whole texture of his prose is English, and spoken English
at that. English by severe control of his knowledge, too: for
all his immense learning there is hardly a quotation in Greek
or Latin in his prose (that is, as a quotation; in the divorce and
political tracts he refers to classical authors but usually trans-
lates them). One has only to compare him to Bacon, Browne,
Andrewes, Donne, or even Dryden, to see that there are not
many prose writers in this period who used the learned languages less. One cause of this plainness in Milton is his love of
simplicity, and obviously he is influenced by the Puritans' distrust of ostentatious learning and by their stress on the vernacular. And perhaps it is from the same influence that the desire
for plainnness goes further, into syntax, for despite his acquaintance with the examples which 'the prime authors of eloquence
have written in any tongue', Milton does not use the syntactical
symmetries of a Cicero or a Demosthenes: he is a plain man,
using simple structures. I would not suggest that these symmetries are 'un-English', for the examples found here show that
the vitality of our prose in the Renaissance was much due to its
power to absorb and transform other influences.

   This is perhaps sufficient information to explain why Milton's
prose is as it is; now we must ask how good it is. One of its
most obvious features is sentence length, and Milton has
often been criticized for writing 'long and shapeless' periods.
But there are no laws governing sentence length, and although
we can appreciate the great artistic potential of symmetrical
syntax we can surely agree that Milton's unpatterned writing
has its own virtues. His sentence structure is, typically, paratactic, but unlike Browne's self-conscious and fragmented use
of that mode, Milton's sentences are all-embracing, developing
in unexpected directions with afterthoughts and unpredictable
energies. The *Apology* is directed against an attack on Milton's
party by Bishop Joseph Hall; Milton explains that he would
have left the authors of *Smectymnuus* to deal with Hall themselves, and does so in a sentence whose new movements are
best seen if they are numbered:

(i) But when I saw his weak arguments headed with sharp
    taunts,

(ii) and that his design was if he could not refute them, yet
at least with quips and snapping adages to vapour them
out,
(iii) which they, bent only upon the business, were minded
to let pass;
(iv) by how much I saw them taking little thought for their
own injuries, I must confess I took it as my part the less
to endure that my respected friends,
(v) through their own unnecessary patience, should thus lie
at the mercy of a coy flirting style;
(vi) to be girded with frumps and curtal gibes by one who
makes sentences by the statute, as if all above three
inches long were confiscate.

Other readers of this sentence might place the divisions
differently, but on any scheme one sees how Milton's thought
always moves off in fresh directions, taking up new ideas and
qualifications: it is not tidy, but it is alive. In his last clause
Milton rejects any attempts to standardize length or structure
where Hall had chosen the fashionable short-breathed Senecan
mode. It will not do to dismiss Milton's power here, even
though the reader must patiently 'stay with' a sentence until it
unleashes its tension.

In that mocking description of Hall's sentences ('curtal', like
a dog with a cropped tail) we see something of Milton's great
power in abuse, his ability to make opponents look ridiculous,
either by calling them pungent names or by elevating the abuse
to the status of imagery. There is a wonderful sequence in
Areopagitica where Milton draws on Puritan allegory to create
a fable worthy of Bunyan, of how 'a wealthy man', bothered
with the 'piddling' day-to-day accounts of religion, engages a
clergyman to do all his Christian trading for him so that he
himself can happily get on with his own profits. For abuse the
vernacular is well exploited, from fairly low levels of mockery,
such as on one impracticability of censorship if the writer wants
to add afterthoughts while the book is being printed: 'The
printer dares not go beyond his licensed copy; so often then
must the author trudge to his leave-giver, that those his new
insertions may be viewed; and many a jaunt will be made. . . .';
when licensed books finally appear, 'every acute reader' of
Milton's opinion will be ready 'to ding the book a quoit's dis-

tance from him'. The vigour of those colloquialisms—'trudge', 'jaunt', 'ding', 'quoit' is all the more surprising in the dignified context of *Areopagitica*; in the *Apology* there is a running stream of abuse directed against Hall, only a trickle of which is excerpted here. Even from this small dose we can see the vigour of Milton's language, as he engages in a dialogue with his opponent who had given a malicious account of how Milton spent the day: ' "in playhouses", he says, "and the bordelloes." Your intelligence, unfaithful spy of Canaan?'—as if he had got Hall by the throat! Again we feel the withering force of Milton's sarcasm in his description of the antics of young clerics acting in public, 'writhing and unboning their clergy limbs'. Hall's attack is evidently ridiculous, but it does provoke Milton to one of his splendid autobiographical passages, a dignified self-defence which is also very significant of the Renaissance ideal of the close connection between literature and life, seen both in the character of the artist (a writer 'ought himself to be a true poem') and in the way in which men can acquire ethical teaching from Romances which celebrate chastity and virtue (as in that great book, Sidney's *Arcadia*, or in *The Faerie Queene*).

But Milton is not merely destructive: at the other extreme of praise and affirmation his eloquence is remarkable, nowhere more so than in *Areopagitica*. Few prose writers in English have such a wide range of styles, and if he rivals Nashe in the liveliness of his abuse he ranks with Hooker and Bacon in the sonorous, dignified mode, and he surpasses even these in those visionary passages which are not echoed again in English until Blake. The opening arguments about the dangers of censorship show Milton's ability to create fully-formed images:

> For books are not absolutely dead things, but do contain a potency of life in them to be as active as that soul whose progeny they are; nay they do preserve as in a vial the purest efficacy and extraction of that living intellect that bred them. I know they are as lively, and as productive, as those fabulous dragon's teeth; and being sown up and down, may chance to spring up armed men. ... a good book is the precious life-blood of a master spirit, embalmed and treasured up on purpose to a life beyond life.

We have already read one inspiration for these ideas—compare Bacon's metaphors for the immortality of literature:

The images of men's wits and knowledges remain in books, exempted from the wrong of time and capable of perpetual renovation. Neither are they fitly to be called images, because they generate still, and cast their seeds in the mind of others, provoking and causing infinite actions and opinions in succeeding ages.

Milton adds his own shading to the picture, especially the wit, for in this section we find a remarkable ingenuity in argument, producing paradoxes that are more solid and more stimulating than Browne's. If you kill a good book, you kill 'reason itself', God's gift to man; and by moving on a metaphorical plane from the life of intellect as some precious liquid in a vial, Milton equates it with the life of man to produce further paradoxes. If we 'spill that seasoned life of man' in the vial of a book:

a kind of homicide may be thus committed, sometimes a martyrdom, and if it extends to the whole impression, a massacre; whereof the execution ends not in the slaying of an elemental life, but strikes at that ethereal and fifth essence, the breath of reason itself, slays an immortality rather than a life.

By an essentially metaphorical argument Milton arrives at the breathtaking result that censorship can destroy not only books, and not only reason, but the quintessence, immortality itself— a surprising development worthy of Donne, but which carries our assent if we value 'the life of intellect'. We also assent to that very different mode towards the end where Milton puts on his singing robes and moves prose up to its highest level in the great Blake-like vision of England awakening as if it were some enormous giant, and turning to truth and virtue, an affirmation which is carried as vigorously by the images as is the characteristically opposed movement of destruction, here reducing the enemy to its lowest point, a flock of starlings, fluttering timorously about with their 'envious gabble'. Truth is also eloquent.

From *Areopagitica. A Speech for the Liberty of Unlicensed Printing, to the Parliament of England* (1644)

I deny not, but that it is of greatest concernment in the church and commonwealth, to have a vigilant eye how books demean

themselves, as well as men; and thereafter to confine, imprison, and do sharpest justice on them as malefactors; for books are not absolutely dead things, but do contain a progeny of life in them to be as active as that soul was whose progeny they are; nay, they do preserve as in a vial the purest efficacy and extraction of that living intellect that bred them. I know they are as lively, and as vigorously productive, as those fabulous dragon's teeth: and being sown up and down, may chance to spring up armed men. And yet, on the other hand, unless wariness be used, as
10 good almost kill a man as kill a good book: who kills a man kills a reasonable creature, God's image; but he who destroys a good book, kills reason itself, kills the image of God, as it were, in the eye. Many a man lives a burden to the earth; but a good book is the precious life-blood of a master-spirit, embalmed and treasured up on purpose to a life beyond life. It is true, no age can restore a life, whereof, perhaps, there is no great loss; and revolutions of ages do not oft recover the loss of a rejected truth, for the want of which whole nations fare the worse. We should be wary, therefore, what persecution we
20 raise against the living labours of public men, how we spill that seasoned life of man, preserved and stored up in books; since we see a kind of homicide may be thus committed, sometimes a martyrdom; and if it extend to the whole impression, a kind of massacre, whereof the execution ends not in the slaying of an elemental life, but strikes at the ethereal and fifth essence, the breath of reason itself; slays an immortality rather than a life. But lest I should be condemned of introducing licence, while I oppose licensing, I refuse not the pains to be so much historical, as will serve to shew what hath been done by
30 ancient and famous commonwealths, against this disorder, till the very time that this project of licensing crept out of the inquisition, was catched up by our prelates, and hath caught some of our presbyters. . . .

But if it be agreed we shall be tried by visions, there is a vision recorded by Eusebius, far ancienter than this tale of Jerome, to the nun Eustochium, and besides, has nothing of a fever in it. Dionysius Alexandrinus was, about the year 240, a person of great name in the church, for piety and learning, who had wont to avail himself much against heretics, by being conversant in
40 their books; until a certain presbyter laid it scrupulously to his

174

conscience, how he durst venture himself among those defiling
volumes. The worthy man, loath to give offence, fell into a new
debate with himself, what was to be thought; when suddenly
a vision sent from God (it is his own epistle that so avers it)
confirmed him in these words: 'Read any books whatever come
to thy hands, for thou art sufficient both to judge aright, and to
examine each matter.' To this revelation he assented the sooner,
as he confesses, because it was answerable to that of the apostle
to the Thessalonians: 'Prove all things, hold fast that which is
10 good.'

And he might have added another remarkable saying of the
same author: 'To the pure, all things are pure;' not only meats
and drinks, but all kind of knowledge, whether of good or
evil: the knowledge cannot defile, nor consequently the books,
if the will and conscience be not defiled. For books are as
meats and viands are; some of good, some of evil substance;
and yet God in that unapocryphal vision said without exception, 'Rise, Peter, kill and eat;' leaving the choice to each man's
discretion. Wholesome meats to a vitiated stomach differ little
20 or nothing from unwholesome; and best books to a naughty
mind are not unapplicable to occasions of evil. Bad meats will
scarce breed good nourishment in the healthiest concoction;
but herein the difference is of bad books, that they to a discreet
and judicious reader serve in many respects to discover, to
confute, to forewarn, and to illustrate. Whereof what better
witness can ye expect I should produce, than one of your own
now sitting in parliament, the chief of learned men reputed in
this land, Mr Selden; whose volume of natural and national
laws proves, not only by great authorities brought together, but
30 by exquisite reasons and theorems almost mathematically de-
monstrative, that all opinions, yea, errors, known, read, and
collated, are of main service and assistance toward the speedy
attainment of what is truest.

I conceive, therefore, that when God did enlarge the universal diet of man's body, (saving ever the rules of temperance,) he then also, as before, left arbitrary the dieting and
repasting of our minds; as wherein every mature man might
have to exercise his own leading capacity. How great a virtue
is temperance, how much of moment through the whole life
40 of man! Yet God commits the managing so great a trust, without particular law or prescription, wholly to the demeanour of

JOHN MILTON

every grown man. And therefore when he himself tabled the
Jews from heaven, that omer, which was every man's daily
portion of manna, is computed to have been more than might
have well sufficed the heartiest feeder thrice as many meals.
For those actions which enter into a man, rather than issue out
of him, and therefore defile not, God uses not to captivate
under a perpetual childhood of prescription, but trusts him
with the gift of reason to be his own chooser; there were but
little work left for preaching, if law and compulsion should
10 grow so fast upon those things which heretofore were governed
only by exhortation. Solomon informs us, that much reading is
a weariness to the flesh, but neither he, nor other inspired
author, tells us that such or such reading is unlawful; yet certainly had God thought good to limit us herein, it had been
much more expedient to have told us what was unlawful, than
what was wearisome.

As for the burning of those Ephesian books by St Paul's
converts; it is replied, the books were magic, the Syriac so
renders them. It was a private act, a voluntary act, and leaves
20 us to a voluntary imitation: the men in remorse burnt those
books which were their own; the magistrate by this example is
not appointed; these men practised the books, another might
perhaps have read them in some sort usefully. Good and evil
we know in the field of this world grow up together almost
inseparably; and the knowledge of good is so involved and
interwoven with the knowledge of evil, and in so many cunning
resemblances hardly to be discerned, that those confused seeds
which were imposed upon Psyche as an incessant labour to cull
out, and sort asunder, were not more intermixed. It was from
30 out the rind of one apple tasted, that the knowledge of good
and evil, as two twins cleaving together, leaped forth into the
world. And perhaps this is that doom which Adam fell into of
knowing good and evil; that is to say, of knowing good by
evil.

As therefore the state of man now is; what wisdom can there
be to choose, what continence to forbear, without the knowledge of evil? He that can apprehend and consider vice with all
her baits and seeming pleasures, and yet abstain, and yet distinguish, and yet prefer that which is truly better, he is the true
40 warfaring Christian. I cannot praise a fugitive and cloistered
virtue unexercised and unbreathed, that never sallies out and

176

seeks her adversary, but slinks out of the race, where that immortal garland is to be run for, not without dust and heat.
Assuredly we bring not innocence into the world, we bring
impurity much rather; that which purifies us is trial, and trial
is by what is contrary. That virtue therefore which is but a
youngling in the contemplation of evil, and knows not the
utmost that vice promises to her followers, and rejects it, is but
a blank virtue, not a pure; her whiteness is but an excremental
whiteness; which was the reason why our sage and serious poet
10 Spenser, (whom I dare be known to think a better teacher than
Scotus or Aquinas,) describing true temperance under the
person of Guyon, brings him in with his palmer through the
cave of Mammon, and the bower of earthly bliss, that he might
see and know, and yet abstain.

Since therefore the knowledge and survey of vice is in this
world so necessary to the constituting of human virtue, and
the scanning of error to the confirmation of truth, how can we
more safely, and with less danger, scout into the regions of sin
and falsity, than by reading all manner of tractates, and hearing
20 all manner of reason? And this is the benefit which may be had
of books promiscuously read. . . .

To sequester out of the world into Atlantic and Utopian
politics, which never can be drawn into use, will not mend our
condition; but to ordain wisely as in this world of evil, in the
midst whereof God hath placed us unavoidably. Nor is it
Plato's licensing of books will do this, which necessarily pulls
along with it so many other kinds of licensing, as will make us
all both ridiculous and weary, and yet frustrate; but those un-
written, or at least unconstraining laws of virtuous education,
30 religious and civil nurture, which Plato there mentions, as the
bonds and ligaments of the commonwealth, the pillars and the
sustainers of every written statute; these they be, which will
bear chief sway in such matters as these, when all licensing will
be easily eluded. Impunity and remissness for certain are the
bane of a commonwealth; but here the great art lies, to discern
in what the law is to bid restraint and punishment, and in what
things persuasion only is to work. If every action which is good
or evil in man at ripe years were to be under pittance, prescription, and compulsion, what were virtue but a name, what praise
40 could be then due to well doing, what gramercy to be sober,
just, or continent?

Many there be that complain of divine Providence for suffering Adam to transgress. Foolish tongues! when God gave him reason, he gave him freedom to choose, for reason is but choosing; he had been else a mere artificial Adam, such an Adam as he is in the motions. We ourselves esteem not of that obedience, or love, or gift, which is of force; God therefore left him free, set before him a provoking object ever almost in his eyes; herein consisted his merit, herein the right of his reward, the praise of his abstinence. Wherefore did he create
10 passions within us, pleasures round about us, but that these rightly tempered are the very ingredients of virtue? They are not skilful considerers of human things, who imagine to remove sin, by removing the matter of sin; for, besides that it is a huge heap increasing under the very act of diminishing, though some part of it may for a time be withdrawn from some persons, it cannot from all, in such a universal thing as books are; and when this is done, yet the sin remains entire. Though ye take from a covetous man all his treasure, he has yet one jewel left, ye cannot bereave him of his covetousness. Banish all objects of
20 lust, shut up all youth into the severest discipline that can be exercised in any hermitage, ye cannot make them chaste, that came not thither so: such great care and wisdom is required to the right managing of this point.

Suppose we could expel sin by this means; look how much we thus expel of sin, so much we expel of virtue: for the matter of them both is the same: remove that, and ye remove them both alike. This justifies the high providence of God, who, though he commands us temperance, justice, continence, yet, pours out before us even to a profuseness all desirable things,
30 and gives us minds that can wander beyond all limit and satiety. Why should we then affect a rigour contrary to the manner of God and of nature, by abridging or scanting those means, which books freely permitted, are both to the trial of virtue and the exercise of truth?

It would be better done, to learn that the law must needs be frivolous, which goes to restrain things, uncertainly and yet equally working to good and to evil. And were I the chooser, a dram of well-doing should be preferred before many times as much the forcible hinderance of evil doing. For God sure
40 esteems the growth and completing of one virtuous person, more than the restraint of ten vicious. . . .

Well knows he who uses to consider, that our faith and knowledge thrives by exercise, as well as our limbs and complexion.
Truth is compared in scripture to a streaming fountain; if her
waters flow not in a perpetual progression, they sicken into a
muddy pool of conformity and tradition. A man may be a
heretic in the truth; and if he believe things only because his
pastor says so, or the assembly so determines, without knowing
other reason, though his belief be true, yet the very truth he
holds becomes his heresy. There is not any burden that some
10 would gladlier post off to another, than the charge and care of
their religion. There be, who knows not that there be? of protestants and professors, who live and die in as errant and implicit faith, as any lay papist of Loretto.

A wealthy man, addicted to his pleasure and to his profits,
finds religion to be a traffic so entangled, and of so many piddling accounts, that of all mysteries he cannot skill to keep a
stock going upon that trade. What should he do? Fain he
would have the name to be religious, fain he would bear up
with his neighbours in that. What does he therefore, but
20 resolves to give over toiling, and to find himself out some
factor, to whose care and credit he may commit the whole
managing of his religious affairs; some divine of note and
estimation that must be. To him he adheres, resigns the whole
warehouse of his religion, with all the locks and keys, into his
custody; and indeed makes the very person of that man his
religion; esteems his associating with him a sufficient evidence
and commendatory of his own piety. So that a man may say his
religion is now no more within himself, but is become a dividual
moveable, and goes and comes near him, according as that
30 good man frequents the house. He entertains him, gives him
gifts, feasts him, lodges him; his religion comes home at night,
prays, is liberally supped, and sumptuously laid to sleep;
rises, is saluted, and after the malmsey, or some well-spiced
bruage, and better breakfasted, than He whose morning appetite would have gladly fed on green figs between Bethany
and Jerusalem, his religion walks abroad at eight, and leaves
his kind entertainer in the shop trading all day without his
religion.

Another sort there be, who when they hear that all things
40 shall be ordered, all things regulated and settled; nothing
written but what passes through the custom-house of certain

JOHN MILTON

publicans that have the tonnaging and poundaging of all free-
spoken truth, will straight give themselves up into your hands,
make them and cut them out what religion ye please: there be
delights, there be recreations and jolly pastimes, that will fetch
the day about from sun to sun, and rock the tedious year as in
a delightful dream. What need they torture their heads with
that which others have taken so strictly, and so unalterably into
their own purveying? These are the fruits which a dull ease
and cessation of our knowledge will bring forth among the
10 people. How goodly, and how to be wished were such an obe-
dient unanimity as this! What a fine conformity would it starch
us all into! Doubtless a staunch and solid piece of framework,
as any January could freeze together.

Lords and commons of England! consider what nation it is
whereof ye are, and whereof ye are the governors: a nation not
slow and dull, but of a quick, ingenious, and piercing spirit;
acute to invent, subtile and sinewy to discourse, not beneath
the reach of any point the highest that human capacity can soar
to.... Behold now this vast city, a city of refuge, the mansion-
20 house of liberty, encompassed and surrounded with his protection; the shop of war hath not there more anvils and hammers
working, to fashion out the plates and instruments of armed
justice in defence of beleagured truth, than there be pens and
heads there, sitting by their studious lamps, musing, searching,
revolving new notions and ideas wherewith to present, as with
their homage and their fealty, the approaching reformation:
others as fast reading, trying all things, assenting to the force
of reason and convincement.
    What could a man require more from a nation so pliant and
30 so prone to seek after knowledge? What wants there to such
a towardly and pregnant soil, but wise and faithful labourers,
to make a knowing people, a nation of prophets, of sages, and
of worthies? We reckon more than five months yet to harvest;
there need not be five weeks, had we but eyes to lift up, the
fields are white already. Where there is much desire to learn,
there of necessity will be much arguing, much writing, many
opinions; for opinion in good men is but knowledge in the
making. Under these fantastic terrors of sect and schism, we
wrong the earnest and zealous thirst after knowledge and under-
40 standing, which God hath stirred up in this city. What some

lament of, we rather should rejoice at, should rather praise this pious forwardness among men, to reassume the ill-deputed care of their religion into their own hands again. A little generous prudence, a little forbearance of one another, and some grain of charity might win all these diligencies to join and unite into one general and brotherly search after truth.

And that we are to hope better of all these supposed sects and schisms, and that we shall not need that solicitude, honest perhaps, though overtimorous, of them that vex in this behalf,
10 but shall laugh in the end at those malicious applauders of our differences, I have these reasons to persuade me.

First, when a city shall be as it were besieged and blocked about, her navigable river infested, inroads and incursions round, defiance and battle oft rumoured to be marching up, even to her walls and suburb trenches; that then the people, or the greater part, more than at other times, wholly taken up with the study of highest and most important matters to be reformed, should be disputing, reasoning, reading, inventing, discoursing, even to a rarity and admiration, things not before discoursed
20 or written of, argues first a singular good will, contentedness, and confidence in your prudent foresight, and safe government, lords and commons; and from thence derives itself to a gallant bravery and well-grounded contempt of their enemies, as if there were no small number of as great spirits among us, as his was who, when Rome was nigh besieged by Hannibal, being in the city, bought that piece of ground at no cheap rate whereon Hannibal himself encamped his own regiment.

Next, it is a lively and cheerful presage of our happy success and victory. For as in a body when the blood is fresh, the spirits
30 pure and vigorous, not only to vital, but to rational faculties, and those in the acutest and the pertest operations of wit and subtlety, it argues in what good plight and constitution the body is; so when the cheerfulness of the people is so sprightly up, as that it has not only wherewith to guard well its own freedom and safety, but to spare, and to bestow upon the solidest and sublimest points of controversy and new invention, it betokens us not degenerated, nor drooping to a fatal decay, by casting off the old and wrinkled skin of corruption to outlive these pangs, and wax young again, entering the glorious ways of
40 truth and prosperous virtue, destined to become great and

honourable in these latter ages. Methinks I see in my mind a noble and puissant nation rousing herself like a strong man after sleep, and shaking her invincible locks: methinks I see her as an eagle mewing her mighty youth, and kindling her un-dazzled eyes at the full midday beam; purging and unscaling her long-abused sight at the fountain itself of heavenly radiance; while the whole noise of timorous and flocking birds, with those also that love the twilight, flutter about, amazed at what she means, and in their envious gabble would prognosticate a
10 year of sects and schisms.

What should ye do then, should ye suppress all this flowery crop of knowledge and new light sprung up and yet springing daily in this city? Should ye set an oligarchy of twenty engros-sers over it, to bring a famine upon our minds again, when we shall know nothing but what is measured to us by their bushel? Believe it, lords and commons! they who counsel ye to such a suppressing, do as good as bid ye suppress yourselves; and I will soon show how. If it be desired to know the immediate cause of all this free writing and free speaking, there cannot be
20 assigned a truer than your own mild, and free, and humane government; it is the liberty, lords and commons, which your own valorous and happy counsels have purchased us; liberty which is the nurse of all great wits: this is that which hath rari-fied and enlightened our spirits like the influence of heaven: this is that which hath enfranchised, enlarged, and lifted up our apprehensions degrees above themselves. Ye cannot make us now less capable, less knowing, less eagerly pursuing of the truth, unless ye first make yourselves, that made us so, less the lovers, less the founders of our true liberty. We can grow ignor-
30 ant again, brutish, formal, and slavish, as ye found us; but you then must first become that which ye cannot be, oppressive, arbitrary, and tyrannous, as they were from whom ye have freed us. That our hearts are now more capacious, our thoughts more erected to the search and expectation of greatest and exactest things, is the issue of your own virtue propagated in us; ye cannot suppress that unless ye reinforce an abrogated and merci-less law, that fathers may dispatch at will their own children. And who shall then stick closest to ye and excite others? Not he who takes up arms for coat and conduct, and his four
40 nobles of Danegelt. Although I dispraise not the defence of just immunities, yet love my peace better, if that were all. Give

me the liberty to know, to utter, and to argue freely according
to conscience, above all liberties.

From *An Apology for Smectymnuus* (1641)

[*Milton's reasons for writing this pamphlet*] And here let me have
pardon, readers, if the remembrance of that which he hath
licensed himself to utter contemptuously of those reverend men,
provoke me to do that over again, which some expect I should
excuse as too freely done, since I have two provocations—his
latest insulting in his short answer, and their final patience. I
had no fear, but that the authors of *Smectymnuus*, to all the shew
10 of solidity, which the Remonstrant could bring, were prepared
both with skill and purpose to return a sufficing answer, and
were able enough to lay the dust and pudder in antiquity, which
he and his, out of stratagem, are wont to raise. But when I saw
his weak arguments headed with sharp taunts, and that his
design was, if he could not refute them, yet at least with quips
and snapping adages to vapour them out, which they, bent only
upon the business, were minded to let pass; by how much I
saw them taking little thought for their own injuries, I must
confess I took it as my part the less to endure that my respected
20 friends, through their own unnecessary patience, should thus
lie at the mercy of a coy flirting style; to be girded with frumps
and curtal gibes, by one who makes sentences by the statute, as
if all above three inches long were confiscate. To me it seemed
an indignity, that whom his whole wisdom could not move
from their place, them his impetuous folly should presume to
ride over.

[*Defence of the personal attack made on him*] Nevertheless, since
I dare not wish to pass this life unpersecuted of slanderous
tongues, for God hath told us that to be generally praised is
30 woeful, I shall rely on his promise to free the innocent from
causeless aspersions: whereof nothing sooner can assure me,
than if I shall feel him now assisting me in the just vindication
of myself, which yet I could defer, it being more meet, that to
those other matters of public debatement in this book I should
give attendance first, but that I fear it would but harm the truth
for me to reason in her behalf, so long as I should suffer my
honest estimation to lie unpurged from these insolent suspicions.

JOHN MILTON

And if I shall be large, or unwonted in justifying myself to
those who know me not, for else it would be needless, let them
consider that a short slander will ofttimes reach further than
a long apology; and that he who will do justly to all men, must
begin from knowing how, if it so happen, to be not unjust to
himself. I must be thought, if this libeller (for now he shows
himself to be so) can find belief, after an inordinate and riotous
youth spent at the university, to have been at length 'vomited
out thence.' For which commodious lie, that he may be encouraged in the trade another time, I thank him; for it hath
given me an apt occasion to acknowledge publicly with all
grateful mind, that more than ordinary favour and respect,
which I found above any of my equals at the hands of those
courteous and learned men, the fellows of that college wherein
I spent some years: who at my parting, after I had taken two
degrees, as the manner is, signified many ways how much better
it would content them that I would stay; as by many letters full
of kindness and loving respect, both before that time, and long
after, I was assured of their singular good affection towards me.
Which being likewise propense to all such as were for their
studious and civil life worthy of esteem, I could not wrong
their judgments and upright intentions, so much as to think I
had that regard from them for other cause, than that I might
be still encouraged to proceed in the honest and laudable courses,
of which they apprehended I had given good proof. And to
those ingenuous and friendly men, who were ever the coun-
tenancers of virtuous and hopeful wits, I wish the best and
happiest things, that friends in absence wish one to another.
As for the common approbation or dislike of that place, as
now it is, that I should esteem or disesteem myself, or any
other the more for that, too simple and too credulous is the
confuter, if he think to obtain with me, or any right discerner.
Of small practice were that physician, who could not judge by
what both she or her sister hath of long time vomited, that the
worser stuff she strongly keeps in her stomach, but the better
she is ever kecking at, and is queasy. She vomits now out of
sickness; but ere it will be well with her, she must vomit by
strong physic. In the meantime that suburb sink, as this rude
scavenger calls it, and more than scurrilously taunts it with the
plague, having a worse plague in his middle entrail, that suburb
wherein I dwell shall be in my account a more honourable place

184

than his university. Which as in the time of her better health, and mine own younger judgment, I never greatly admired, so now much less. But he follows me to the city, still usurping and forging beyond his book notice, which only he affirms to have had; 'and where my morning haunts are, he wisses not.' It is wonder that, being so rare an alchymist of slander, he could not extract that, as well as the university vomit, and the suburb sink which his art could distil so cunningly; but because his lembec fails him to give him and envy the more vexation, I will
10 tell him.

Those morning haunts are where they should be, at home; not sleeping, or concocting the surfeits of an irregular feast, but up and stirring, in winter often ere the sound of any bell awake men to labour, or to devotion; in summer as oft with the bird that first rouses, or not much tardier, to read good authors, or cause them to be read, till the attention be weary, or memory have its full fraught: then, with useful and generous labours preserving the body's health and hardiness to render lightsome, clear, and not lumpish obedience to the mind, to the
20 cause of religion, and our country's liberty, when it shall require firm hearts in sound bodies to stand and cover their stations, rather than to see the ruin of our protestation, and the inforcement of a slavish life.

These are the morning practices: proceed now to the afternoon; 'in playhouses,' he says, 'and the bordelloes.' Your intelligence, unfaithful spy of Canaan? He gives in his evidence, that 'there he hath traced me.' Take him at his word, readers; but let him bring good sureties ere ye dismiss him, that while he pretended to dog others, he did not turn in for his own plea-
30 sure: for so much in effect he concludes against himself, not contented to be caught in every other gin, but he must be such a novice as to be still hampered in his own hemp. In the *Animadversions*, saith he, I find the mention of old cloaks, false beards, night-walkers and salt lotion; therefore, the animadverter haunts playhouses and bordelloes; for if he did not, how could he speak of such gear? Now that he may know what it is to be a child, and yet to meddle with edged tools, I turn his antistrophon upon his own head; the confuter knows that these things are the furniture of playhouses and bordelloes, therefore, by the same
40 reason, 'the confuter himself hath been traced in those places.' Was it such a dissolute speech, telling of some politicians

who were wont to eavesdrop in disguises, to say they were often liable to a nightwalking cudgeller, or the emptying of a urinal? What if I had written as your friend the author of the aforesaid mime, *Mundus alter et idem*, to have been ravished like some young Cephalus or Hylas, by a troop of camping housewives in Viraginea, and that he was there forced to swear himself an uxorious varlet; then after a long servitude to have come into Aphrodisia that pleasant country, that gave such a sweet smell to his nostrils among the shameless courtezans of Desver-
10 gonia? Surely he would have then concluded me as constant at the bordello, as the galley-slave at his oar.

But since there is such necessity to the hearsay of a tire, a periwig, or a vizard, that plays must have been seen, what difficulty was there in that? when in the colleges so many of the young divines, and those in next aptitude to divinity, have been seen so often upon the stage, writhing and unboning their clergy limbs to all the antic and dishonest gestures of Trinculoes, buffoons, and bawds; prostituting the shame of that ministry, which either they had, or were nigh having, to the eyes of
20 courtiers and court ladies, with their grooms and mademoiselles. There, while they acted and overacted, among other young scholars, I was a spectator; they thought themselves gallant men, and I thought them fools; they made sport, and I laughed; they mispronounced, and I misliked; and, to make up the atticism, they were out, and I hissed. Judge now whether so many good textmen were not sufficient to instruct me of false beards and vizards, without more expositors; and how can this confuter take the face to object to me the seeing of that which his reverend prelates allow, and incite their young disciples to
30 act? For if it be unlawful to sit and behold a mercenary comedian personating that which is least unseemly for a hireling to do, how much more blameful is it to endure the sight of as vile things acted by persons either entered, or presently to enter into the ministry; and how much more foul and ignominious for them to be the actors!

[*The Humanizing Effects of Literature*] I had my time, readers, as others have, who have good learning bestowed upon them, to be sent to those places where, the opinion was, it might be soonest attained; and as the manner is, was not unstudied in
40 those authors which are most commended. Whereof some were

grave orators and historians, whose matter methought I loved indeed, but as my age then was, so I understood them; others were the smooth elegiac poets, whereof the schools are not scarce. . . . And long it was not after, when I was confirmed in this opinion, that he who would not be frustrate of his hope to write well hereafter in laudable things, ought himself to be a true poem; that is, a composition and pattern of the best and honourablest things; not presuming to sing high praises of heroic men, or famous cities, unless he have in himself the experience and the practice of all that which is praiseworthy.
10 These reasonings, together with a certain niceness of nature, an honest haughtiness, and self-esteem either of what I was, or what I might be, (which let envy call pride,) and lastly that modesty, whereof, though not in the title-page, yet here I may be excused to make some beseeming profession; all these uniting the supply of their natural aid together, kept me still above those low descents of mind, beneath which he must deject and plunge himself, that can agree to saleable and unlawful prostitutions.

Next, (for hear me out now, readers,) that I may tell ye
20 whither my younger feet wandered; I betook me among those lofty fables and romances, which recount in solemn cantos the deeds of knighthood founded by our victorious kings, and from hence had in renown over all Christendom. There I read it in the oath of every knight, that he should defend to the expense of his best blood, or of his life, if it so befell him, the honour and chastity of virgin or matron; from whence even then I learned what a noble virtue chastity sure must be, to the defence of which so many worthies, by such a dear adventure of themselves, had sworn. And if I whom both for the pleasing sound of their
30 numerous writing, which in imitation I found most easy, and most agreeable to nature's part in me, and for their matter, which what it is, there be few who know not, I was so allured to read, that no recreation came to me better welcome. For that it was then those years with me which are excused, though they be least severe, I may be saved the labour to remember ye. Whence having observed them to account it the chief glory of their wit, in that they were ablest to judge, to praise, and by that could esteem themselves worthiest to love those high perfections, which under one or other name they took to celebrate;
40 I thought with myself by every instinct and presage of nature, which is not wont to be false, that what emboldened them to

this task, might with such diligence as they used embolden me; and that what judgment, wit, or elegance was my share, would herein best appear, and best value itself, by how much more wisely, and with more love of virtue I should choose (let rude ears be absent) the object of not unlike praises. For albeit these thoughts to some will seem virtuous and commendable, to others only pardonable, to a third sort perhaps idle; yet the mentioning of them now will end in serious.

Nor blame it, readers, in those years to propose to them-
10 selves such a reward, as the noblest dispositions above other things in this life have sometimes preferred: whereof not to be sensible when good and fair in one person meet, argues both a gross and shallow judgment, and withal an ungentle and swain-ish breast. For by the firm settling of these persuasions, I be-came, to my best memory, so much a proficient, that if I found those authors anywhere speaking unworthy things of them-selves, or unchaste of those names which before they had ex-tolled; this effect it wrought with me, from that time forward their art I still applauded, but the men I deplored; and above
20 them all, preferred the two famous renowners of Beatrice and Laura, who never write but honour of them to whom they devote their verse, displaying sublime and pure thoughts, without transgression. And long it was not after, when I was confirmed in this found in the story afterward, any of them, by word or deed, breaking that oath, I judged it the same fault of the poet, as that which is attributed to Homer, to have written indecent things of the gods. Only this my mind gave me, that every free and gentle spirit, without that oath, ought to be born a knight, nor needed to expect the gilt spur, or the laying
30 of a sword upon his shoulder to stir him up both by his counsel and his arms, to secure and protect the weakness of any at-tempted chastity. So that even these books, which to many others have been the fuel of wantonness and loose living, I cannot think how, unless by divine indulgence, proved to me so many incitements, as you have heard, to the love and steadfast obser-vation of that virtue which abhors the society of bordelloes.

Thus, from the laureat fraternity of poets, riper years and the ceaseless round of study and reading led me to the shady spaces of philosophy; but chiefly to the divine volumes of Plato,
40 and his equal Xenophon: where, if I should tell ye what I learnt of chastity and love, I mean that which is truly so, whose charm-

ing cup is only virtue, which she bears in her hand to those who are worthy; (the rest are cheated with a thick intoxicating potion, which a certain sorceress, the abuser of love's name, carries about;) and how the first and chiefest office of love begins and ends in the soul, producing those happy twins of her divine generation, knowledge and virtue. With such abstracted sublimities as these, it might be worth your listening, readers, as I may one day hope to have ye in a still time, when there shall be no chiding; not in these noises, the adversary, as ye know,

10 barking at the door, or searching for me at the bordelloes, where it may be he has lost himself, and raps up without pity the sage and rheumatic old prelates, with all her young Corinthian laity, to inquire for such a one.

IX
Thomas Traherne
1637?–74

In the seventeenth century religious prose existed in many
forms outside the sermon, from commentary on Scripture to
topical controversy to meditations and prayers and to a few
great works of fiction, notably *Pilgrim's Progress* (which is not
represented here, partly because it seems unsuitable to excerpt-
ing, and also as Bunyan's qualities are (happily) generally ap-
preciated). Little of this prose is now read and not much has
been written about it, but some of its manifestations have been
explored. The meditative tradition, whose effect of poetry has
been well studied by L. L. Martz, exerted some influence on
prose. 'Meditation' is a process having a well-defined religious
(and literary) structure by which the author leads himself and
his readers towards an ever deeper contemplation of God.
That pioneering and influential writer Joseph Hall published
in 1606 his *Meditations and Vowes, Divine and Morall*, a series of
separate paragraphs (arranged in three 'centuries', or groups
of one hundred) which are designed not so much to reveal
Hall's own thoughts as to offer reflections on life which become
a model for the reader:

> There is nothing more odious than fruitless old age. Now
> (for that no tree bears fruit in Autumn unless it blossom in
> the Spring) to the end that my age may be profitable, and
> laden with ripe fruit; I will endeavour that my youth may be
> studious and flowered with the blossoms of learning and
> observation. (I, 54)

> Every sickness is a little death. I will be content to die oft,
> I may once die well. (II, 8)

In the same first-person future-tense form are many of the paragraphs in Owen Felltham's *Resolves, Divine, Moral and Political*
(1628; two centuries), such as this concluding sequence to
'Perfection':

> Nature hath in herself treasure enough to please a man;
> religion, a Christian: the last begets fear; the other, love;

together, admiration, reverence. I will like, I will love them
single; but conjoined, I will affect and honour. (CIII)

Hall's is the briefer form, Felltham's nearer the essay; both
include such typical stylistic devices as witty imagery and aphorisms (Hall described his *Meditations* as 'homely aphorisms');
but although both have some imaginative touches, neither is a
substantial literary achievement.

The prose work in this genre that most demands serious consideration is Traherne's, to which he gave no title—in the manuscript another hand has added the title 'Centuries of Meditations', and although now known simply as *Centuries* its kinship
with the work of Hall and Felltham is clear. Traherne seems to
have begun writing it in about 1664, and he completed four
centuries, and ten meditations in the fifth before stopping,
having written '11' on the next page. The work is better
structured than its apparently random shape would suggest:
it is designed overall to express Traherne's concept of 'Felicity',
the state of happiness or beatitude in which the soul regains its
lost innocence and creates an earthly paradise. Within this movement much space is given to defining the nature of Divine Love
and its availability to man, as to outlining the principles of
felicity and the stages by which we can reach it. The model for
the work is St Augustine's *Confessions*, and Louis Martz has
clarified its relation to that source as to the meditative method
expounded by St Bonaventure in his treatise *The Mind's Road to
God*. Professor Martz (whose account must be read by anyone
seriously interested in Traherne) has given a useful explanation
of the presence of so much repetition in both Augustine and
Traherne: it 'represents the essential mode of tentative explora-
tion, the varied efforts of approach, the pursuit of ever-new
beginnings, that constitute the basic attitudes of both these
seekers after Truth'. Both writers scatter their ideas, drawing
some together at this point, others before, others after, so creating a kind of fantasia effect which should reach ever nearer the
ultimate truth.

A complete and sustained reading of the *Centuries* and the
analysis of the religious states presented in it are tasks for the
critic and divine. But that artificial construct of non-specialisms,
the common reader, can appreciate something of the art of
Traherne without much additional knowledge. Traherne's

innovation in the form of the meditation (or perhaps his revival of it after Augustine) was to anchor it in his own experience. Although he continues the tradition of Hall and Felltham in making his 'resolve' public, in making it an exhortation to the reader to action: 'Let this therefore be the first principle of your soul. That to have no principles, or to live beside them is equally miserable. And that philosophers are not those that speak, but do great things.' (IV, 2—a statement of principle developed from the secular tradition of the 'active life') he goes on to exploit the personal nature of the form by making it a confession of his own experiences. Thus in order to describe what the state of Felicity is like he writes that remarkable sequence of spiritual autobiography at the opening of the Third Century:

> Will you see the infancy of this sublime and celestial great-ness? Those pure and virgin apprehensions I had from the womb, and that divine light wherewith I was born, are the best unto this day, wherein I can see the universe. . . . All things were spotless and pure and glorious: yea, and infi-nitely mine, and joyful and precious. . . . All time was eternity, and a perpetual sabbath. . . . The corn was orient and im-mortal wheat, which should never be reaped, nor was ever sown. I thought it had stood from everlasting to everlasting. The dust and stones of the street were as precious gold.

This is indeed paradise—no death, no *meum* and *tuum*, all pro-perty in common (the features of classical pastoral are here made Christian) and a persistent, glowing sense of wonder. It has been traditional to compare this visionary perception of childhood innocence with Wordsworth's *Immortality Ode* and with Blake's *Songs of Innocence and Experience*, but while it lacks the literary mastery of those two works it seems to me to exceed them in the brightness and solidity of its landscape—it is an authentic vision. Certainly it resembles those two in that the state does not persist, and Traherne records the descent into fallen man with a bitter brevity: 'With much ado I was cor-rupted; and made to learn the dirty devices of this world.'

These visions of paradise are communicated to us in lan-guage of purity, simplicity, artlessness; the sentence structure and syntax fulfil the most elementary functions, and the only deviations from this straightforward simplicity are an unpredictable brevity of utterance which catches the speed of transitions in Traherne's meditation, and the emotional stress recorded by the psalm-like incantations (such as the sequence in III, 3 beginning 'The streets were mine, the temple was mine . . .'). The images are the most striking literary feature—condensed, microcosmic, pellucid, light-giving. 'Felicity is a bird of paradise so strange, that it is impossible to fly among men without losing some feathers were she not immortal'; 'The most tempestous weather is the best seed time. A Christian is an oak flourishing in Winter'; 'The Cross is the abyss of Wonders, the centre of desires, the school of virtues, the house of wisdom, the throne of love, the theatre of joys and the place of sorrows'; in loving we both give and receive—'thus we see the seeds of eternity sparkling in our natures'; 'love is a phoenix that will revive in its own ashes, inherit death, and smell sweetly in the grave'. The best comment on the thought and style of Traherne would seem to be by Blake: he had the ability

> To see a World in a Grain of Sand
> And a Heaven in a Wild Flower,
> Hold Infinity in the palm of your hand
> And eternity in an hour.

These are indeed 'Auguries of Innocence'.

From *The Centuries* (*c.* 1664)

The First Century

1

An empty book is like an Infant's Soul, in which anything may be written. It is capable of all things, but containeth nothing. I have a mind to fill this with profitable wonders. And since Love made you put it into my hands I will fill it with those Truths you love without knowing them: and with those things which, if it be possible, shall shew my Love; to you, in communicating most enriching Truths: to Truth, in exalting her beauties in such a Soul.

2

10 Do not wonder that I promise to fill it with those Truths you love, but know not; for though it be a maxim in the schools

that there is no Love of a thing unknown, yet I have found that things unknown have a secret influence on the soul, and like the centre of the earth unseen violently attract it. We love we know not what, and therefore everything allures us. As iron at a distance is drawn by the loadstone, there being some invisible communications between them, so is there in us a world of Love to somewhat, though we know not what in the world that should be. There are invisible ways of conveyance by which some great thing doth touch our souls, and at a distance is drawn by the
10 loadstone, there being some invisible communications between them, so is there in us a world of Love to somewhat, though we know not what in the world that should be. There are invisible ways of conveyance by which some great thing doth touch our souls, and by which we tend to it. Do you not feel yourself drawn by the expectation and desire of some Great Thing?

3

I will open my mouth in Parables, I will utter things that have been kept secret from the foundation of the world. Things strange yet common, incredible, yet known; most high, yet plain; infinitely profitable, but not esteemed. Is it not a great thing that you
20 should be Heir of the World? Is it not a great enriching verity? In which the fellowship of the Mystery which from the beginning of the World hath been hid in God lies concealed! The thing hath been from the Creation of the World, but hath not so been explained as that the interior Beauty should be understood. It is my design therefore in such a plain manner to unfold it that my friendship may appear in making you possessor of the whole world.

4

I will not by the noise of bloody wars and the dethroning of kings advance you to glory: but by the gentle ways of peace
30 and love. As a deep friendship meditates and intends the deepest designs for the advancement of its objects, so doth it shew itself in choosing the sweetest and most delightful methods, whereby not to weary but please the person it desireth to advance. Where Love administers physic, its tenderness is expressed in balms and cordials. It hateth corrosives, and is rich in its administrations. Even so, God designing to show His

Love in exalting you hath chosen the ways of ease and repose by which you should ascend. And I after His similitude will lead you into paths plain and familiar, where all envy, rapine, bloodshed, complaint and malice shall be far removed; and nothing appear but contentment and thanksgiving. Yet shall the end be so glorious that angels durst not hope for so great a one till they had seen it.

7

To contemn the world and to enjoy the world are things contrary to each other. How then can we contemn the world, which we are born to enjoy? Truly there are two worlds. One was made by God, the other by men. That made by God was great and beautiful. Before the Fall it was Adam's joy and the Temple of his Glory. That made by men is a Babel of Confusions: Invented Riches, Pomps and Vanities, brought in by Sin. Give all (saith Thomas à Kempis) for all. Leave the one that you may enjoy the other.

55

The contemplation of Eternity maketh the Soul immortal. Whose glory it is, that it can see before and after its existence into endless spaces. Its Sight is its presence. And therefore in the presence of the understanding endless, because its Sight is so. O what glorious creatures should we be could we be present in spirit with all Eternity! How wise, would we esteem this presence of the understanding, to be more real than that of our bodies! When my soul is in Eden with our first parents, I myself am there in a blessed manner. When I walk with Enoch, and see his translation, I am transported with him. The present age is too little to contain it. I can visit Noah in his ark, and swim upon the waters of the deluge. I can see Moses with his rod, and the children of Israel passing through the sea; I can enter into Aaron's Tabernacle, and admire the mysteries of the holy place. I can travel over the Land of Canaan, and see it overflowing with milk and honey; I can visit Solomon in his glory, and go into his temple, and view the sitting of his servants, and admire the magnificence and glory of his kingdom. No creature but one like unto the Holy Angels can see into all ages. Sure this power was not given in vain, but for some wonderful purpose;

worthy of itself to enjoy and fathom. Would men consider what
God hath done, they would be ravished in spirit with the glory
of His doings. For Heaven and Earth are full of the majesty of
His glory. And how happy would men be could they see and
enjoy it! But above all these our Saviour's cross is the throne
of delights. That Centre of Eternity, that Tree of Life in the
midst of the Paradise of God!

60

The Cross of Christ is the Jacob's ladder by which we ascend
into the highest heavens. There we see joyful Patriarchs,
10 expecting Saints, Prophets ministering. Apostles publishing,
and Doctors teaching, all Nations concentering, and Angels
praising. That Cross is a tree set on fire with invisible flame,
that illuminateth all the world. The flame is Love: the Love in
His bosom who died on it. In the light of which we see how to
possess all the things in Heaven and Earth after His similitude.
For He that suffered on it was the Son of God as you are: tho'
He seemed only a mortal man. He had acquaintance and relations as you have, but He was a lover of Men and Angels. Was
He not the Son of God; and Heir of the whole world? To this
20 poor, bleeding, naked Man did all the corn and wine, and oil,
and gold and silver in the world minister in an invisible manner,
even as He was exposed lying and dying upon the Cross.

The Second Century

54

Love is infinitely delightful to its object, and the more violent
the more glorious. It is infinitely high, nothing can hurt it.
And infinitely great in all extremes: of beauty and excellency.
Excess is its true moderation, activity its rest, and burning
fervency its only refreshment. Nothing is more glorious yet
nothing more humble; nothing more precious, yet nothing
more cheap; nothing more familiar, yet nothing so inaccessible;
30 nothing more nice, yet nothing more laborious; nothing more
liberal, yet nothing more covetous. It doth all things for its

object's sake, yet it is the most self-ended thing in the whole world; for of all things in nature it can least endure to be displeased. Since therefore it containeth so many miracles it may well contain this one more, that it maketh every one greatest, and among lovers every one is supreme and sovereign.

57

Love is so vastly delightful in the Lover, because it is the communication of His Goodness. For the natural end of Goodness is to be enjoyed: it desireth to be another's happiness. Which Goodness of God is so deeply implanted in our natures, that we never enjoy ourselves but when we are the joy of others. Of all our desires the strongest is to be good to others. We delight in receiving, more in giving. We love to be rich, but then it is that we thereby might be more greatly delightful. Thus we see the seeds of Eternity sparkling in our natures.

67

Suppose a river, or a drop of water, an apple or a sand, an ear of corn, or an herb: God knoweth infinite excellencies in it more than we: He seeth how it relateth to angels and men; how it proceedeth from the most perfect Lover to the most perfectly Beloved; how it representeth all His attributes; how it conduceth in its place, by the best of means to the best of ends: and for this cause it cannot be beloved too much. God the Author and God the End is to be beloved in it; Angels and men are to be beloved in it; and it is highly to be esteemed for all their sakes. O what a treasure is every sand when truly understood! Who can love anything that God made too much? What a world would this be, were everything beloved as it ought to be!

The Third Century

1

Will you see the infancy of this sublime and celestial greatness? Those pure and virgin apprehensions I had from the womb, and that divine light wherewith I was born are the best unto this day, wherein I can see the Universe. By the Gift of God they attended me into the world, and by His special favour I remember them till now. Verily they seem the greatest gifts His wisdom could bestow, for without them all other gifts had been dead and vain. They are unattainable by book, and therefore I will teach them by experience. Pray for them earnestly: for they will make you angelical, and wholly celestial. Certainly Adam in Paradise had not more sweet and curious apprehensions of, the world, than I when I was a child.

2

10   All appeared new, and strange at first, inexpressibly rare and delightful and beautiful. I was a little stranger, which at my entrance into the world was saluted and surrounded with innumerable joys. My knowledge was Divine. I knew by intuition those things which since my Apostasy, I collected again by the highest reason. My very ignorance was advantageous. I seemed as one brought into the Estate of Innocence. All things were spotless and pure and glorious: yea, and infinitely mine, and joyful and precious. I knew not that there were any sins, or complaints or laws. I dreamed not of poverties, contentions
20   or vices. All tears and quarrels were hidden from mine eyes. Everything was at rest, free and immortal. I knew nothing of sickness or death or rents or exaction, either for tribute or bread. In the absence of these I was entertained like an Angel with the works of God in their splendour and glory, I saw all in the peace of Eden; Heaven and Earth did sing my Creator's praises, and could not make more melody to Adam, than to me. All Time was Eternity, and a perpetual Sabbath. Is it not strange, that an infant should be heir of the whole World, and see those mysteries which the books of the learned never unfold?

3

30   The corn was orient and immortal wheat, which never should be reaped, nor was ever sown. I thought it had stood from everlasting to everlasting. The dust and stones of the street were as precious as gold: the gates were at first the end of the world. The green trees when I saw them first through one of the gates transported and ravished me, their sweetness and unusual beauty made my heart to leap, and almost mad with ecstasy,

they were such strange and wonderful things. The Men! O
what venerable and reverend creatures did the aged seem!
Immortal Cherubims! And young men glittering and sparkling
Angels, and maids strange seraphic pieces of life and beauty!
Boys and girls tumbling in the street, and playing, were moving
jewels. I knew not that they were born or should die; But all
things abided eternally as they were in their proper places.
Eternity was manifest in the Light of the Day, and something
infinite behind everything appeared: which talked with my
10 expectation and moved my desire. The city seemed to stand in
Eden, or to be built in Heaven. The streets were mine, the
temple was mine, the people were mine, their clothes and gold
and silver were mine, as much as their sparkling eyes, fair skins
and ruddy faces. The skies were mine, and so were the sun and
moon and stars, and all the World was mine; and I the only
spectator and enjoyer of it. I knew no churlish proprieties, nor
bounds, nor divisions: but all proprieties and divisions were
mine: all treasures and the possessors of them. So that with
much ado I was corrupted, and made to learn the dirty devices
20 of this world. Which now I unlearn, and become, as it were, a
little child again that I may enter into the Kingdom of God.

5

Our Saviour's meaning, when He said, *He must be born again
and become a little child that will enter into the Kingdom of Heaven* is
deeper far than is generally believed. It is not only in a careless
reliance upon Divine Providence, that we are to become little
children, or in the feebleness and shortness of our anger and
simplicity of our passions, but in the peace and purity of all our
soul. Which purity also is a deeper thing than is commonly
apprehended. For we must disrobe ourselves of all false colours,
30 and unclothe our souls of evil habits; all our thoughts must be
infant-like and clear; the powers of our soul free from the leaven
of this world, and disentangled from men's conceits and customs. Grit in the eye or yellow jaundice will not let a man see
those objects truly that are before it. And therefore it is requisite
that we should be as very strangers to the thoughts, customs,
and opinions of men in this world, as if we were but little
children. So those things would appear to us only which do to
children when they are first born. Ambitions, trades, luxuries,

inordinate affections, casual and accidental riches invented
since the fall, would be gone, and only those things appear,
which did to Adam in Paradise, in the same light and in the
same colours: God in His works, Glory in the light, Love in
our parents, men, ourselves, and the face of Heaven: Every
man naturally seeing those things, to the enjoyment of which
he is naturally born.

9

It was a difficult matter to persuade me that the tinselled
ware upon a hobby-horse was a fine thing. They did impose
10 upon me, and obtrude their gifts that made me believe a ribbon
or a feather curious. I could not see where was the curiousness
or fineness: And to teach me that a purse of gold was at any
value seemed impossible, the art by which it becomes so, and
the reasons for which it is accounted so, were so deep and hidden to my inexperience. So that Nature is still nearest to natural
things, and farthest off from preternatural; and to esteem that
the reproach of Nature, is an error in them only who are unac-
quainted with it. Natural things are glorious, and to know
them glorious: but to call things preternatural, natural, mon-
20 strous. Yet all they do it, who esteem gold, silver, houses, lands,
clothes, &c., the riches of Nature, which are indeed the riches
of invention. Nature knows no such riches: but art and error
make them. Not the God of Nature, but Sin only was the parent
of them. The riches of Nature are our Souls and Bodies, with
all their faculties, senses, and endowments. And it had been
the easiest thing in the whole world to teach me that all felicity
consisted in the enjoyment of all the world, that it was prepared
for me before I was born, and that nothing was more divine
and beautiful.

10

30 Thoughts are the most present things to thoughts, and of the
most powerful influence. My soul was only apt and disposed to
great things; but souls to souls are like apples to apples, one
being rotten rots another. When I began to speak and go,
nothing began to be present to me, but what was present to me
in their thoughts. Nor was anything present to me any other
way, than it was so to them. The glass of imagination was the

only mirror, wherein anything was represented or appeared to me. All things were absent which they talked not of. So I began among my play-fellows to prize a drum, a fine coat, a penny, a gilded book, &c., who before never dreamed of any such wealth. Goodly objects to drown all the knowledge of Heaven and Earth! As for the Heavens and the Sun and Stars they disappeared, and were no more unto me than the bare walls. So that the strange riches of man's invention quite overcame the riches of Nature, being learned more laboriously and in the
10 second place.

II

By this let nurses, and those parents that desire Holy Children learn to make them possessors of Heaven and Earth betimes; to remove silly objects from before them, to magnify nothing but what is great indeed, and to talk of God to them, and of His works and ways before they can either speak or go. For nothing is so easy as to teach the truth because the nature of the thing confirms the doctrine: As when we say the sun is glorious, a man is a beautiful creature, sovereign over beasts and fowls and fishes, the stars minister unto us, the world was made
20 for you, &c. But to say this house is yours, and these lands are another man's, and this bauble is a jewel and this gew-gaw a fine thing, this rattle makes music, &c., is deadly barbarous and uncouth to a little child; and makes him suspect all you say, because the nature of the thing contradicts your words. Yet doth that blot out all noble and divine ideas, dissettle his foundation, render him uncertain in all things, and divide him from God. To teach him those objects are little vanities, and that though God made them, by the ministry of man, yet better and more glorious things are more to be esteemed, is natural
30 and easy.

The Fourth Century

61

Since Love will thrust in itself as the greatest of all principles, let us at last willingly allow it room. I was once a stranger to it, now I am familiar with it as a daily acquaintance. 'Tis the only heir and benefactor of the world. It seems it will break in everywhere, as that without which the world could not be enjoyed. Nay as that without which it would not be worthy to be enjoyed. For it was beautified by love, and commandeth the love of a Donor to us. Love is a Phoenix that will revive in its own ashes, inherit death, and smell sweetly in the grave.

94

Having once studied these principles you are eternally to practise them. You are to warm yourselves at these fires, and to have recourse to them every day. When you think not of these things you are in the dark. And if you would walk in the
10 light of them, you must frequently meditate. These principles are like seed in the ground, they must continually be visited with heavenly influences, or else your life will be a barren field. Perhaps they might be cast into better frame, and more curiously expressed; but if well cultivated they will be as fruitful, as if every husk were a golden rind. It is the substance that is in them that is productive of joy and good to all.

95

It is an indelible principle of Eternal truth, that practice and exercise is the Life of all. Should God give you worlds, and laws, and treasures, and worlds upon worlds, and Himself also
20 in the Divinest manner, if you will be lazy and not meditate, you lose all. The soul is made for action, and cannot rest till it be employed. Idleness is its rust. Unless it will up and think and taste and see, all is in vain. Worlds of beauty and treasure and felicity may be round about it, and itself desolate. If therefore you would be happy, your life must be as full of operation as God of treasure. Your operation shall be treasure to Him, as His operation is delightful to you.

The Fifth Century

7

Eternity is a mysterious absence of times and ages: an endless length of ages always present, and for ever perfect. For as there
30 is an immovable space wherein all finite spaces are enclosed,

and all motions carried on and performed; so is there an immovable duration, that contains and measures all moving durations. Without which first the last could not be; no more than finite places, and bodies moving without infinite space. All ages being but successions correspondent to those parts of the Eternity wherein they abide, and filling no more of it, than ages can do. Whether they are commensurate with it or no, is difficult to determine. But the infinite immovable duration is Eternity, the place and duration of all things, even of infinite
10 space itself: the cause and end, the author and beautifier, the life and perfection of all.

8

Eternity magnifies our joys exceedingly, for whereas things in themselves began, and quickly end; before they came, were never in being; do service but for few moments; and after they are gone pass away and leave us for ever, Eternity retains the moments of their beginning and ending within itself: and from everlasting to everlasting those things were in their times and places before God, and in all their circumstances eternally will be, serving Him in those moments wherein they existed, to
20 those intents and purposes for which they were created. The swiftest thought is present with Him eternally: the creation and the day of judgment, His first consultation, choice and determination, the result and end of all just now in full perfection, ever beginning, ever passing, ever ending: with all the intervals of space between things and things: As if those objects that arise many thousand years one after the other were all together. We also were ourselves before God eternally; and have the joy of seeing ourselves eternally beloved and eternally blessed, and infinitely enjoying all the parts of our blessedness; in all the
30 durations of eternity appearing at once before ourselves, when perfectly consummate in the Kingdom of Light and Glory. The smallest thing by the influence of eternity, is made infinite and eternal. We pass through a standing continent or region of ages, that are already before us, glorious and perfect while we come to them. Like men in a ship we pass forward, the shores and marks seeming to go backward, though we move and they stand still. We are not with them in our progressive motion, but prevent the swiftness of our course, and are present with

them in our understandings. Like the sun we dart our rays before us, and occupy those spaces with light and contemplation which we move towards, but possess not with our bodies. And seeing all things in the light of Divine knowledge, eternally serving God, rejoice unspeakably in that service, and enjoy it all.

9

His omnipresence is our ample territory or field of joys, a transparent temple of infinite lustre, a strong tower of defence, a castle of repose, a bulwark of security, a palace of delights, an immediate help, and a present refuge in the needful time of trouble, a broad and a vast extent of fame and glory, a theatre of infinite excellency, an infinite ocean by means whereof every action, word, and thought is immediately diffused like a drop of wine in a pail of water, and everywhere present, everywhere seen and known, infinitely delighted in, as well as filling infinite spaces. It is the Spirit that pervades all His works, the life and soul of the universe, that in every point of space from the centre to the heavens, in every kingdom in the world, in every city, in every wilderness, in every house, every soul, every creature, in all the parts of His infinity and eternity sees our persons, loves our virtues, inspires us with itself, and crowns our actions with praise and glory. It makes our honour infinite in extent, our glory immense, and our happiness eternal. The rays of our light are by this means darted from everlasting to everlasting. This spiritual region makes us infinitely present with God, Angels, and Men in all places from the utmost bounds of the everlasting hills, throughout all the unwearied durations of His endless infinity, and gives us the sense and feeling of all the delights and praises we occasion, as well as of all the beauties and powers, and pleasures and glories which God enjoyeth or createth.

10

Our Bridegroom and our King being everywhere, our Lover and Defender watchfully governing all worlds, no danger or enemy can arise to hurt us, but is immediately prevented and suppressed, in all the spaces beyond the utmost borders of those unknown habitations which He possesseth. Delights of inestimable value are there preparing, for everything is present by its own existence. The essence of God therefore being all light and knowledge, love and goodness, care and providence, felicity and glory, a pure and simple act, it is present in its operations, and by those acts which it eternally exerteth is wholly busied in all parts and places of His dominion, perfecting and completing our bliss and happiness.

X
Reform in Prose Style and the Royal Society

The great variety and exuberance shown so far in seventeenth-century prose is part of the literary energy of the Renaissance, which expressed itself both through imagery and through inventiveness in syntax. But as the climate of taste gradually changed both details of style came in for criticism and ultimately for reform. The trend is a general one (it is not sufficiently organized to be called a 'movement') and thanks to the work of Richard Foster Jones[1] three centres can be detected within it. First there is the overall reaction against the inventiveness of Elizabethan and Jacobean language with its tendency to pack language full of meaning and wit, the ability (seen at both ends of the literary scale, as say, Lancelot Andrewes against Nashe) to sustain a condensed and total exploitation of words. This concentration could not be imitated, for those two writers and others such as Sidney in the intensely logical yet intensely poetic prose of the *Arcadia*, had in effect reached the absolute limits of language, and no one could copy or even learn from them (this is perhaps one explanation of the absence of major fiction for the rest of the century until the new mode of Defoe). The only reaction could be away from concentration or complexity, and it was made energetically—as, to give one example, in the universal dislike of puns in Elizabethan and Jacobean literature, especially in sermons and the drama. Dryden, Addison, and Dr Johnson are the best-known representatives of this distrust of punning, but it stretches nearly 150 years, as far as Coleridge and Macaulay.

The second reactionary trend was that of the New Science, stemming from Bacon, and enormously amplifying his plea that the purely philological interests of traditional post-Aristotelian science, based on written authorities and textbooks, should be totally destroyed, and that man should inspect things in nature, and reproduce his findings in language that was itself thing-like. But in amplifying Bacon the leaders of this reaction

[1] See his classic essays collected in the volume presented to him, *The Seventeenth Century, from Bacon to Pope*, second edition, O.U.P., 1965.

crudified him. He had insisted that this absolute plainness of style was only to be used for collecting data from the physical world and for recording the progress of experiments, and that for normal communication and especially for purposes of persuasion such as winning an audience for science it was absolutely essential to use metaphor, simile, and all the imaginative resources of language (indeed he had gone so far as to argue, rightly, that the process of analogy was a fundamental part of man's ability to create mental concepts). In place of these crucial distinctions the proponents of experimental science urged that *all* language was to be purged of metaphor and reduced to a naked simplicity. This movement eventually resulted in half a dozen schemes for founding a 'Real Character' or 'Universal Language', in which words would be replaced by signs, symbols, or even numbers. The futility of such schemes was exposed once and for all by Swift in that wonderful passage in *Gulliver's Travels* (Book 3, chapter 5) where in the 'School of Languages' of the Royal Society of Lagado the sages walked around carrying 'bundles of *things*' on their backs, and Swift blandly pretends not to notice the impracticabilities which are glaringly obvious to us all.

But the attack on metaphor is not simply a scientism; the Church also supported it, for as Professor Jones was the first to show, the imaginative flights and syntactical extremes of Andrewes and Donne were severely attacked, and a new, chaste, tempered, plain style was called for, which scorned images, preferred short sentences, and equated plainness with sincerity, rhetoric with deceit. This ecclesiastical revisionism is not, as one might at first expect, the product of Puritan plainness, but rather of the Established Church, the university-trained Protestants and Congregationalists. Paradoxically it was this fashion-conscious party, attuned to the movements of taste, which opposed metaphor, and not the Puritans, who continued in the old-fashioned modes of similitude and allegory (most notably in *Pilgrim's Progress*) and who defended metaphor both in practice and in theory (the most accessible theoretical document is Bunyan's 'Apology for his Book'). To the modern reader they seem the only ray of hope. But it was the Puritans closest to the Church who persisted in the traditional styles: those connected with the political and educational reforms planned by the Parliamentarians in fact argued the same case as the Royalist and Church party were to take up still more strongly. I mention this fact to ensure that we guard against reducing these critics of style all to one head, be it on political or religious grounds: thus one of the most violent opponents of metaphor was, as we have seen, that arch-Royalist Hobbes. Although there are three main movements the current of feeling is surprisingly general.

It would take too much time to chart the changing attitudes to metaphor, and the task has already been done in a very scholarly way by R. F. Jones, although it can be argued that he has not always drawn the right critical deductions. Briefly, the most interesting literary phenomenon is the fact that, like Hobbes, the critics of metaphor used metaphor to damn itself, and that their images develop their own conventions and show a gradual change. Metaphor is most commonly a 'mist', a 'cloud' which darkens knowledge: this is an absolute (and it must be said arbitrary) reversal of two thousand years of literature, for since Aristotle metaphor has been held to be the chief mode of illumination in an argument. Now suddenly it is an eclipse. An equally strong set of images was based on the old idea that rhetoric was an ornament, like cosmetics or fine clothes —'garnished out with flaunting affected eloquence'; not to 'disfigure the face of truth by daubing it over with the paint of language' (all sorts of naïve assumptions are revealed there); the 'varnish of fine metaphors and glittering allusions'. The corollary of this type of imagery is that the critics of metaphor will want to strip off the paint and clothes, and indeed the cant phrase which is on everyone's lips is that of showing 'the naked Truth'. One wit applies the cosmetic metaphors as the patches which people put on their cheeks to hide some defect in the skin. How wrong he was. But the attack continued, and there was even a skirmish over the existence of metaphors in the Bible, which to my mind the Puritans won convincingly.

Two documents best illustrate this reaction, and as it happens both come from the Royal Society. This great scientific institution (still in existence, and although no longer a centre for research, still the most prestigious scientific body in England, the election to a Fellowship—F.R.S.—being a high honour for any scientist today) was founded in 1662 along the lines of the research academy described by Bacon in his *New Atlantis*. It never became an actual research institute with laboratories and its own experimental staff, but it held regular meetings and published a journal of *Transactions* which printed the scientific articles submitted by its members. The Royal Society (its first patron was Charles II) caught an existing interest and magnified it enormously.[1] It was the flowering of a movement which had begun in the 1600s with the foundation of Gresham's College in London (an institution devoted to practical science, such as mathematics, astronomy, and engineering) and which continued with a research group in Oxford inspired by Bacon's call for a new experimental science. Its prestige gave it a considerable influence in many spheres of thought; on the literary side it set up a committee to reform the English language (the poets Cowley and Dryden were on it), and it was particularly concerned about the proper style for English prose. Thus, it is not surprising that the first of these two documents, an excerpt from the official *History of the Royal Society* by Bishop Thomas Sprat, constitutes what amounts to a manifesto for the New Style, in which all the elements distinguished here can be clearly seen. Secondly, an actual example of reform at work, again unearthed by the late R. F. Jones: a young member of the society was Joseph Glanvill (1636–80), who took part in both religious and scientific controversy. In 1661 he wrote a book called *The Vanity of Dogmatizing*; in 1676 he reissued it with sweeping stylistic revisions (as he wrote, his present taste in style was 'more gratified with manly sense, flowing in a natural and unaffected eloquence, than in the music and curiosity of fine metaphors and dancing periods'). The alterations certainly conform to Sprat's call to reject all 'amplifications' of style, and their comparison would make an excellent essay in Practical Criticism. I will prejudge neither the conduct of that exercise, nor its final conclusion as to the relative literary merits of the two versions. The change is by any standards remarkable, forming a concrete demonstration of the reaction which from many sides assaulted the fundamental imaginative resources of English prose.

[1] The account of its formation given by Christopher Hill in his *Intellectual Origins of the English Revolution*, O.U.P., 1965, overstresses the Puritan connection, and needs to be corrected by the more Baconian approach of Marjorie Purver, *The Royal Society: Concept and Creation*, Routledge, 1967.

THOMAS SPRAT (1635–1713)

From *A History of the Royal Society* (1667)

There is one thing more about which the Society has been
most solicitous; and that is, the manner of their discourse:
which unless they had been very watchful to keep in due temper, the whole spirit and vigour of their design had been soon
eaten out by the luxury and redundance of speech. The ill
effects of this superfluity of talking have already overwhelmed
most other arts and professions; inasmuch, that when I consider the means of happy living, and the causes of their corruption, I can hardly forbear recanting what I said before, and con-
10 cluding that eloquence ought to be banished out of all civil
societies, as a thing fatal to peace and good manners. To this
opinion I should wholly incline; if I did not find that it is a
weapon which may be as easily procured by bad men as good:
and that, if these should only cast it away, and those retain it;
the naked innocence of virtue would be upon all occasions
exposed to the armed malice of the wicked. This is the chief
reason that should now keep up the ornaments of speaking in
any request; since they are so much degenerated from their
original usefulness. They were at first, no doubt, an admirable
20 instrument in the hands of wise men; when they were only employed to describe goodness, honesty, obedience, in larger,
fairer, and more moving images: to represent truth, clothed with
bodies; and to bring knowledge back again to our very senses,
from whence it was at first derived to our understandings. But
now they are generally changed to worse uses: they make the
fancy disgust the best things, if they come sound and unadorned;
they are in open defiance against reason, professing not to hold
much correspondence with that; but with its slaves, the passions: they give the mind a motion too changeable and bewitch-
30 ing to consist with right practice. Who can behold without in-
dignation how many mists and uncertainties these specious
tropes and figures have brought on our knowledge? How many
rewards, which are due to more profitable and difficult arts, have
been still snatched away by the easy vanity of fine speaking?
For, now I am warmed with this just anger, I cannot withhold
myself from betraying the shallowness of all these seeming
mysteries, upon which we writers, and speakers, look so big.

And, in few words, I dare say that of all the studies of men, nothing may be sooner obtained than this vicious abundance of phrase, this trick of metaphors, this volubility of tongue, which makes so great a noise in the world. But I spend words in vain; for the evil is now so inveterate, that it is hard to know whom to blame, or where to begin to reform. We all value one another so much upon this beautiful deceit, and labour so long after it in the years of our education, that we cannot but ever after think kinder of it than it deserves. And indeed, in most
10 other parts of learning, I look upon it as a thing almost utterly desperate in its cure: and I think it may be placed among those general mischiefs, such as the dissension of Christian princes, the want of practice in religion, and the like, which have been so long spoken against that men are become insensible about them; every one shifting off the fault from himself to others; and so they are only made bare common-places of complaint. It will suffice my present purpose to point out what has been done by the Royal Society towards the correcting of its excesses in natural philosophy; to which it is, of all others, a most pro-
20 fessed enemy.

They have therefore been most rigorous in putting in execution the only remedy that can be found for this extravagance, and that has been, a constant resolution to reject all the amplifications, digressions, and swellings of style; to return back to the primitive purity, and shortness, when men delivered so many things, almost in an equal number of words. They have exacted from all their members a close, naked, natural way of speaking; positive expressions; clear senses; a native easiness: bringing all things as near the mathematical plainness as they can; and pre-
30 ferring the language of artizans, countrymen, and merchants, before that of wits or scholars.

JOSEPH GLANVILL (1636–80)

From *The Vanity of Dogmatizing*

(*a*) [*1661*] That all bodies both animal, vegetable, and inanimate, are form'd out of such particles of matter, which by reason of their figures, will not cohere or lie together, but in such an order as is necessary to such a specifical formation, and that therein they naturally of themselves concure and reside, is a pretty conceit, and there are experiments that credit it. If after a decoction of herbs in a Winter-night, we expose the liquor to the frigid air; we may observe in the morning under a crust of ice, the perfect appearance both in figure, and colour, of the plants that were taken from it. But if we break the aqueous crystal, those pretty images disappear and are present[ly] dissolved.

Now these airy vegetables are presumed to have been made, by the relics of these plantal emissions whose avolation was prevented by the condensed inclosure. And therefore playing
10 up and down for a while within their liquid prison, they at last settle together in their natural order, and the atoms of each part finding out their proper place, at length rest in their methodical situation, till by breaking the ice they are disturbed, and those counterfeit compositions are scattered into their first Indivisibles.

[*1676*] And there is an experiment ... That after a decoction of herbs in a frosty night, the shape of the plants will appear under the ice in the morning: which images are supposed to be made by the congregated effluvia of the plants themselves, which
20 loosely wandering up and down in the water, at last settle in their natural place and order, and so make up an appearance of the herbs from whence they were emitted.

(*b*) [*1661*] Nor is the composition of our bodies the only wonder; we are as much nonplussed by the most contemptible worm and plant we tread on. How is a drop of dew organized into an insect, or a lump of clay into animal perfections? How are the glories of the field spun, and by what pencil are they limned in their unaffected bravery? By whose directions is the nutriment so regularly distributed unto the respective parts, and
30 how are they kept to their specific uniformities? If we attempt mechanical solutions, we shall never give an account, why the woodcock doth not sometimes borrow colours of the Mag-pie, why the lily doth not exchange with the daisy, or why it is not sometimes painted with a blush of the rose? Can unguided matter keep it self to such exact conformities, as not in the least spot to vary from the species? That divers limners at a distance without either copy, or design, should draw the same picture to an undistinguishable exactness, both in form, colour, and

features; this is more conceivable, than that matter, which is so diversified both in quantity, quality, motion, site, and infinite other circumstances, should frame it self so absolutely according to the idea of it and its kind. And though the fury of that Appelles, who threw his pencil in a desperate rage upon the picture he had essayed to draw, once casually effected those lively representations, which his Art could not describe; yet 'tis not likely, that one of a thousand such precipitancies should be crowned with so unexpected an issue. For though blind mat-
10 ter might reach some elegancies in individual effects; yet specific conformities can be no unadvised productions, but in greatest likelihood, are regulated by the immediate efficiency of some knowing agent.

[*1676*] Blind matter may produce an elegant effect for once, by a great chance; as the painter accidentally gave the grace to his picture, by throwing his pencil in rage, and disorder upon it; but then constant uniformities, and determinations to a kind, can be no results of unguided motions.

XI
John Dryden
1631–1700

The most distinguished exemplar of the new style is John
Dryden. He shared the general reaction against the wit of the
Elizabethans and Jacobeans—in fact he is one of the most
vigorous critics of the 'luxuriant fancy' of the last age, as in one
of the excerpts chosen here. Although outside the ecclesiastical movement he was certainly in tune with the aims of the
third of the reactionary centres, the new science, for he was
himself a member of the Royal Society (until expelled for not
paying his subscription) and he was one of its abortive committee to reform the English language. The scientific influence
was indeed a strong one, for as Dr Johnson first observed in a
brilliant critique, Dryden not only uses images frequently but
bases many of them on scientific analogies:

> His works abound with knowledge, and sparkle with illus-
> trations. There is scarcely any science or faculty that does not
> supply him with occasional images and lucky similitudes;
> every page discovers a mind very widely acquainted both
> with art and nature, and in full possession of great stores of
> intellectual wealth.

But the scientific influence is not the only one: in Dryden's
case, to reach a full understanding of his style one would also
have to consider the social circumstances of post-Restoration
London; the extent to which the Court really influenced taste
('The Court', Dryden wrote, 'is the best and surest judge of
writing'); the influence of drama on society and vice versa; the
importance of conversation, in literature as in life; and the
whole conscious refinement of taste. The results of this conscious gentility are obvious everywhere, and in the first excerpt
here Dryden rather arrogantly criticizes the age of Jonson and
Shakespeare for being 'unpolished', not 'courtly', having 'less
of gallantry than in ours', reaching a ridiculous literary conclusion in attacking Jonson for daring to show 'Cob and Tib'
on the stage, for 'Gentlemen will now be entertained with the
follies of each other'.

This conscious refinement of the subject-matter and style of literature has its consequences for prose. The English gentle-man has always abhorred fuss and technicality: 'good breeding' is often a kind of inverted snobbery which takes care to dress in simple clothes and use simple ideas. Thus Dryden writes that

> wit is best conveyed to us in the most easy language; and is most to be admired when a great thought comes dressed in words so commonly received that it is understood by the meanest apprehensions, as the best meat is the most easily digested.

So prose must limit itself to simple words and simple sentences; the tradition of syntactical symmetry is totally abandoned for a smooth, easy, conversational style. All Dryden's sentences are easily spoken (so are Milton's), but spoken in a smooth, polite tone of voice: it is not 'conversational' in the slangy or spark-ling sense, those extremes wonderfully recorded by the dia-logue of Restoration drama; rather it is the sort of formal conversation that a group of gentleman-scholars might indulge in if they knew that their words were being recorded for pos-terity. Dryden often addresses his patron of the moment (those courtly nonentities whose literary powers he always fulsomely praises) in clipped but respectful phrases:

> I am still speaking to you, my Lord, though in all probability you are already out of hearing. Nothing which my meanness can produce is worthy of this long attention.

One of these addresses, the late *Preface to Virgil* (and the later the work, the more casual and unbuttoned it is, the more creased are the trousers, the more worn the jacket), gives a clue to the peculiarly disorganized nature of Dryden's prose:

> In this address to your Lordship, I design not a Treatise of Heroic Poetry, but write in a loose, epistolary way. . . . I have taken up, laid down, and resumed as often as I pleased, the same subject . . .

and elsewhere he writes that 'the nature of a preface is rambling, never wholly out of the way, nor in it'.

Most of Dryden's prose consists of prefaces to his own work or defences of it, and is thus taken up with the particular issue

H   215

of the moment. A recurrent one is his need to defend his own plays and those of his time against the giants of the last age, which results in several derogatory estimates of Shakespeare, such as the rather silly pursuit of a critical antithesis given here. The desultory, dilatory nature of these prefaces encourages Dryden to amble along in a chatty way, and the general temperature of the discussion is enervatingly low: all is cool, reasonable, disengaged in a gentlemanly way. As far as syntax goes, in abandoning syntactical symmetry Dryden might be called the father of modern prose, but in its place he has no comparable positive resource to offer, nor indeed has prose discovered one since then. Dryden's virtues in the shape or form of prose are the faintly negative ones of clarity and smoothness, negative in the sense that although they cause him to avoid such faults as clumsiness or ambiguity, they do not aid any definite literary or imaginative development: they make for clear and elegant but neutral communication. Thus at the level of the physical shape of prose on the page or in the ear Dryden has no expressive resources, and below the level of imagery he can only use sarcasm or professions of sincerity. The movement of his prose is smooth and without hindrance (as any page will show) but it has disarmed itself of its weapons.

Happily, although Dryden was theoretically committed to the removal of imagery from prose, in practice he used it constantly, and indeed it is his only weapon for expressing praise or blame (the fact that he was so dependent on it shows again the folly of trying to ban metaphor). In the early works his images are indeed very witty, rather like the conceits in his poetry at this time, but in the mature style they are used in a fluent way to illuminate the argument:

> We cannot read a verse of Cleveland's without making a face at it, as if every word were a pill to swallow: he gives us many times a hard nut to break our teeth, without a kernel for our pains.
> For criticism is now become mere hangman's work, and meddles only with the faults of authors.

Many of these clarificatory images are used for literary topics: to those who would make too strict laws for the poet he says: 'You would have him follow nature, but he must follow her on foot: you have dismounted him from his Pegasus.' They are

witty and perceptive—'for many a fair precept in poetry is like
a seeming demonstration in the mathematics: very specious in
the diagram, but failing in the mechanic operation'; 'Wit,
which is a kind of Mercury with wings fastened to his head and
heels, can fly but slow in a damp air.' But they are also rather
thin, well-disciplined to the context, and without much emotional or imaginative weight behind them. To apply a pragma-
tic but not invalid test, few of them either move you or stick in
your memory. But they are used, despite the manifesto against
metaphor, and indeed throughout his career, so to be fair to
Dryden I have taken the second excerpt from one of his most
vigorous pieces of prose, the *Preface to Virgil*, where he is evidently much more engaged with his argument than elsewhere
and uses a flow of both witty and illuminating images—the
reader can make up his own mind as to their other qualities.
To my mind this is Dryden's writing at its best.

From *An Essay on the Dramatic Poetry of the Last Age* (1672)

There is yet another way of improving language, which poets
especially have practised in all ages: that is, by applying received
words to a new signification. And this, I believe, is meant by
Horace, in that precept which is so variously construed by
expositors:

> dixeris egregie, notum si callida verbum
> reddiderit junctura novum.

And, in this way, he himself had a particular happiness: using
all the tropes, and particularly metaphors, with that grace
10 which is observable in his Odes, where the beauty of expression
is often greater than that of thought; as in that one example,
amongst an infinite number of others: *et vultus nimium lubricus
aspici*.
  And therefore, though he innovated little, he may justly be
called a great refiner of the Roman tongue. This choice of
words, and heightening of their natural signification, was observed in him by the writers of the following ages: for Petronius
says of him, *et Horatii curiosa felicitas*. By this graffing, as I may
call it, on old words, has our tongue been beautified by the
20 three forementioned poets, Shakespeare, Fletcher, and Jonson:
whose excellencies I can never enough admire. And in this

JOHN DRYDEN

they have been followed especially by Sir John Suckling and
Mr Waller, who refined upon them. Neither have they who
succeeded them been wanting in their endeavours to adorn our
mother tongue: but it is not so lawful for me to praise my living
contemporaries as to admire my dead predecessors.

I should now speak of the refinement of wit; but I have been
so large on the former subject that I am forced to contract myself in this. I will therefore only observe to you that the wit of
the last age was yet more incorrect than their language. Shake-
10 speare, who many times has written better than any poet in any
language, is yet so far from writing wit always, or expressing
that wit according to the dignity of the subject, that he writes
in many places below the dullest writer of ours, or of any precedent age. Never did any author precipitate himself from such
heights of thought to so low expressions as he often does. He
is the very Janus of poets; he wears almost everywhere two
faces; and you have scarce begun to admire the one, ere you
despise the other. Neither is the luxuriance of Fletcher (which
his friends have taxed in him) a less fault than the carelessness
20 of Shakespeare. He does not well always; and, when he does,
he is a true Englishman; he knows not when to give over. If
he wakes in one scene, he commonly slumbers in another; and
if he pleases you in the first three acts, he is frequently so tired
with his labour that he goes heavily in the fourth, and sinks
under his burden in the fifth.

For Ben Jonson, the most judicious of poets, he always writ
properly, and as the character required; and I will not contest
farther with my friends who call that wit: it being very certain
that even folly itself, well represented, is wit in a larger significa-
30 tion; and that there is fancy as well as judgment in it, though
not so much or noble: because all poetry being imitation, that
of folly is a lower exercise of fancy, though perhaps as difficult
as the other, for 'tis a kind of looking downward in the poet,
and representing that part of mankind which is below him.

In these low characters of vice and folly lay the excellency of
that inimitable writer; who, when at any time he aimed at wit
in the stricter sense, that is, sharpness of conceit, was forced
either to borrow from the Ancients, as to my knowledge he did
very much from Plautus; or, when he trusted himself alone,
40 often fell into meanness of expression. Nay, he was not free
from the lowest and most grovelling kind of wit, which we call

clenches, of which *Every Man in His Humour* is infinitely full. And, which is worse, the wittiest persons in the drama speak them. His other comedies are not exempted from them. Will you give me leave to name some few? Asper, in which character he personates himself (and he neither was, nor thought himself, a fool), exclaiming against the ignorant judges of the age, speaks thus:

> How monstrous and detested is't, to see
> A fellow that has neither art nor brain,
> Sit like an Aristarchus, or stark-ass,
> Taking men's lines, with a tobacco face,
> In snuff, &c.

And presently after: 'I mar'le whose wit 'twas to put a prologue in yond sackbut's mouth. They might well think he would be out of tune, and yet you'd play upon him too.' Will you have another of the same stamp? 'O, I cannot abide these limbs of satin, or rather Satan.'

But it may be you will object that this was Asper, Macilente, or Carlo Buffone: you shall, therefore, hear him speak in his own person, and that in the two last lines or sting of an epigram. 'Tis inscribed to Fine Grand who, he says, was indebted to him for many things which he reckons there; and concludes thus:

> Forty things more, dear Grand, which you know true,
> For which, or pay me quickly, or I'll pay you.

This was then the mode of wit, the vice of the age, and not Ben Jonson's. For you see, a little before him, that admirable wit Sir Philip Sidney perpetually playing with his words. In his time, I believe, it ascended first into the pulpit, where (if you will give me leave to clench too) it yet finds the benefit of its clergy. For they are commonly the first corrupters of eloquence, and the last reformed from vicious oratory; as a famous Italian has observed before me, in his *Treatise of the Corruption of the Italian Tongue*, which he principally ascribes to priests and preaching friars.

But, to conclude with what brevity I can, I will only add this, in defence of our present writers, that, if they reach not some excellencies of Ben Jonson (which no age, I am confident, ever shall) yet, at least, they are above that meanness of thought which I have taxed, and which is frequent in him.

That the wit of this age is much more courtly may easily be proved by viewing the characters of gentlemen which were written in the last. First, for Jonson, Truewit in the *Silent Woman* was his masterpiece. And Truewit was a scholar-like kind of man, a gentleman with an allay of pedantry, a man who seems mortified to the world by much reading. The best of his discourse is drawn not from the knowledge of the town, but books. And, in short, he would be a fine gentleman in an university. Shakespeare showed the best of his skill in his Mercutio;
10 and he said himself that he was forced to kill him in the third act, to prevent being killed by him. But, for my part, I cannot find he was so dangerous a person: I see nothing in him but what was so exceeding harmless that he might have lived to the end of the play, and died in his bed, without offence to any man.

Fletcher's Don John is our only bugbear; and yet I may affirm, without suspicion of flattery, that he now speaks better, and that his character is maintained with much more vigour in the fourth and fifth acts than it was by Fletcher in the three former. I have always acknowledged the wit of our predecessors,
20 with all the veneration which becomes me; but, I am sure, their wit was not that of gentlemen; there was ever somewhat that was ill-bred and clownish in it, and which confessed the conversation of the authors.

And this leads me to the last and greatest advantage of our writing, which proceeds from conversation. In the age wherein those poets lived, there was less of gallantry than in ours; neither did they keep the best company of theirs. Their fortune has been much like that of Epicurus, in the retirement of his gardens: to live almost unknown, and to be celebrated after
30 their decease. I cannot find that any of them were conversant in courts, except Ben Jonson: and his genius lay not so much that way as to make an improvement by it. Greatness was not then so easy of access, nor conversation so free, as now it is. I cannot, therefore, conceive it any insolence to affirm that, by the knowledge and pattern of their wit who writ before us, and by the advantage of our own conversation, the discourse and raillery of our comedies excel what has been written by them. And this will be denied by none but some few old fellows who value themselves on their acquaintance with the Blackfriars;
40 who, because they saw their plays, would pretend a right to judge ours. The memory of these grave gentlemen is their only

plea for being wits. They can tell a story of Ben Jonson, and perhaps have had fancy enough to give a supper in Apollo that they might be called his sons; and, because they were drawn in to be laughed at in those times, they think themselves now sufficiently entitled to laugh at ours. Learning I never saw in any of them, and wit no more than they could remember. In short, they were unlucky to have been bred in an unpolished age, and more unlucky to live to a refined one. They have lasted beyond their own, and are cast behind ours: and not contented to have 10 known little at the age of twenty, they boast of their ignorance at threescore.

Now, if any ask me whence it is that our conversation is so much refined, I must freely, and without flattery, ascribe it to the Court; and, in it, particularly to the King, whose example gives a law to it. His own misfortunes, and the nation's, afforded him an opportunity which is rarely allowed to sovereign princes, I mean of travelling, and being conversant in the most polished courts of Europe; and thereby of cultivating a spirit which was formed by nature to receive the impressions 20 of a gallant and generous education. At his return, he found a nation lost as much in barbarism as in rebellion. And as the excellency of his nature forgave the one, so the excellency of his manners reformed the other. The desire of imitating so great a pattern first wakened the dull and heavy spirits of the English from their natural reservedness, loosened them from their stiff forms of conversation, and made them easy and pliant to each other in discourse. Thus, insensibly, our way of living became more free: and the fire of the English wit, which was before stifled under a constrained, melancholy way of breeding, began 30 first to display its force, by mixing the solidity of our nation with the air and gaiety of our neighbours. This being granted to be true, it would be a wonder if the poets, whose work is imitation, should be the only persons in three kingdoms who should not receive advantage by it; or if they should not more easily imitate the wit and conversation of the present age than of the past.

Let us therefore admire the beauties and the heights of Shakespeare, without falling after him into a carelessness and (as I may call it) a lethargy of thought, for whole scenes to-40 gether. Let us imitate, as we are able, the quickness and easiness of Fletcher, without proposing him as a pattern to us, either in the

redundancy of his matter, or the incorrectness of his language.
Let us admire his wit and sharpness of conceit; but let us at the
same time acknowledge that it was seldom so fixed, and made
proper to his characters, as that the same things might not be
spoken by any person in the play. Let us applaud his scenes of
love; but let us confess that he understood not either greatness
or perfect honour in the parts of any of his women. In fine, let
us allow that he had so much fancy as when he pleased he could
write wit: but that he wanted so much judgment as seldom to
10 have written humour, or described a pleasant folly. Let us
ascribe to Jonson the height and accuracy of judgment in the
ordering of his plots, his choice of characters, and maintaining
what he had chosen to the end. But let us not think him a perfect pattern of imitation; except it be in his humour: for love,
which is the foundation of all comedies in other languages, is
scarcely mentioned in any of his plays. And for humour itself,
the poets of this age will be more wary than to imitate the meanness of his persons. Gentlemen will now be entertained with the
follies of each other: and though they allow Cob and Tib to
20 speak properly, yet they are not much pleased with their tankard
or with their rags: and surely their conversation can be no jest
to them on the theatre, when they would avoid it in the street.

To conclude all, let us render to our predecessors what is
their due, without confining ourselves to a servile imitation of
all they writ: and, without assuming to ourselves the title of
better poets, let us ascribe to the gallantry and civility of our
age the advantage which we have above them; and to our knowledge of the customs and manners of it, the happiness we have
to please beyond them.

From *The Preface to Virgil* (1697)

30 Long before I undertook this work I was no stranger to the
original. I had also studied Virgil's design, his disposition of it,
his manners, his judicious management of the figures, the sober
retrenchments of his sense, which always leaves somewhat to
gratify our imagination, on which it may enlarge at pleasure;
but, above all, the elegance of his expressions and the harmony
of his numbers. For, as I have said in a former dissertation,
the words are in poetry what the colours are in painting; if the
design be good, and the draught be true, the colouring is the

first beauty that strikes the eye. Spenser and Milton are, in English, what Virgil and Horace are in Latin; and I have endeavoured to form my style by imitating their masters. I will farther own to you, my Lord, that my chief ambition is to please those readers who have discernment enough to prefer Virgil before any other poet in the Latin tongue. Such spirits as he desired to please, such would I choose for my judges, and would stand or fall by them alone. Segrais has distinguished the readers of poetry according to their capacity of judging, into
10 three classes (he might have said the same of writers too, if he had pleased): in the lowest form he places those whom he calls *les petits esprits*, such things as are our upper-gallery audience in a playhouse, who like nothing but the husk and rind of wit; prefer a quibble, a conceit, an epigram, before solid sense and elegant expression. These are mob readers: if Virgil and Martial stood for Parliament-men, we know already who would carry it. But, though they make the greatest appearance in the field, and cry the loudest, the best on't is, they are but a sort of French Huguenots, or Dutch boors, brought over in herds, but not
20 naturalized; who have not land of two pounds *per annum* in Parnassus, and therefore are not privileged to poll. Their authors are of the same level, fit to represent them on a mountebank's stage, or to be masters of the ceremonies in a beargarden. Yet these are they who have the most admirers. But it often happens to their mortification that, as their readers improve their stock of sense (as they may by reading better books, and by conversation with men of judgment), they soon forsake them; and when the torrent from the mountains falls no more, the swelling writer is reduced into his shallow bed, like the
30 Mançanares at Madrid, with scarce water to moisten his own pebbles. There are a middle sort of readers (as we hold there is a middle state of souls), such as have a farther insight than the former, yet have not the capacity of judging right; for I speak not of those who are bribed by a party, and know better if they were not corrupted; but I mean a company of warm young men who are not yet arrived so far as to discern the difference betwixt fustian, or ostentatious sentences, and the true sublime. These are above liking Martial, or Owen's Epigrams, but they would certainly set Virgil below Statius or Lucan. I need not say their
40 poets are of the same paste with their admirers. They affect greatness in all they write, but 'tis a bladdered greatness, like

that of the vain man whom Seneca describes: an ill habit of
body, full of humours, and swelled with dropsy. Even these too
desert their authors, as their judgment ripens.

... But having before observed that Virgil endeavours to be
short, and at the same time elegant, I pursue the excellence and
forsake the brevity: for there he is like ambergris, a rich perfume, but of so close and glutinous a body that it must be opened
with inferior scents of musk or civet, or the sweetness will not
be drawn out into another language.

10 On the whole matter, I thought fit to steer betwixt the two
extremes of paraphrase and literal translation; to keep as near
my author as I could, without losing all his graces, the most
eminent of which are in the beauty of his words; and those words,
I must add, are always figurative. Such of these as would retain
their elegance in our tongue, I have endeavoured to graff on it;
but most of them are of necessity to be lost, because they will
not shine in any but their own. Virgil has some times two of
them in a line; but the scantiness of our heroic verse is not
capable of receiving more than one; and that too must expiate
20 for many others which have none. Such is the difference of the
languages, or such my want of skill in choosing words.

... On these considerations I have shunned hemistichs; not
being willing to imitate Virgil to a fault, like Alexander's courtiers, who affected to hold their necks awry, because he could
not help it. I am confident your Lordship is by this time of my
opinion, and that you will look on those half lines hereafter as
the imperfect products of a hasty Muse; like the frogs and ser-
pents in the Nile, part of them kindled into life, and part a lump
of unformed, unanimated mud.

30 I am sensible that many of my whole verses are as imperfect
as those halves, for want of time to digest them better: but give
me leave to make the excuse of Boccace who, when he was up-
braided that some of his novels had not the spirit of the rest,
returned this answer, that Charlemain, who made the Paladins,
was never able to raise an army of them. The leaders may be
heroes, but the multitude must consist of common men.

I am also bound to tell your Lordship, in my own defence,
that, from the beginning of the First Georgic to the end of the
last Æneid, I found the difficulty of translation growing on me
40 in every succeeding book. For Virgil, above all poets, had a
stock, which I may call almost inexhaustible, of figurative, ele-

gant, and sounding words. I, who inherit but a small portion of his genius, and write in a language so much inferior to the Latin, have found it very painful to vary phrases, when the same sense returns upon me. Even he himself, whether out of necessity or choice, has often expressed the same thing in the same words, and often repeated two or three whole verses which he had used before. Words are not so easily coined as money; and yet we see that the credit not only of banks but of exchequers cracks when little comes in and much goes out. Virgil called upon me
10 in every line for some new word: and I paid so long, that I was almost bankrupt; so that the latter end must needs be more burdensome than the beginning or the middle; and, consequently, the Twelfth Æneid cost me double the time of the first and second. What had become of me, if Virgil had taxed me with another book? I had certainly been reduced to pay the public in hammered money, for want of milled; that is, in the same old words which I had used before: and the receivers must have been forced to have taken any thing, where there was so little to be had.
20 Besides this difficulty (with which I have struggled, and made a shift to pass it over), there is one remaining which is insuperable to all translators. We are bound to our author's sense, though with the latitudes already mentioned; for I think it not so sacred as that one iota must not be added or diminished, on pain of an anathema. But slaves we are, and labour on another man's plantation; we dress the vineyard, but the wine is the owner's: if the soil be sometimes barren, then we are sure of being scourged: if it be fruitful, and our care succeeds, we are not thanked; for the proud reader will only say, the poor drudge
30 has done his duty. But this is nothing to what follows; for being obliged to make his sense intelligible, we are forced to untune our own verses, that we may give his meaning to the reader. He who invents is master of his thoughts and words: he can turn and vary them as he pleases, till he renders them harmonious; but the wretched translator has no such privilege: for being tied to the thoughts, he must make what music he can in the expression; and, for this reason, it cannot always be so sweet as that of the original.

Afterword

Looking back over seventeenth-century English prose from the point of view of Dryden is a rather melancholy task. A reaction was fought, and won, against the full resources of prose as used in the Renaissance, and the resulting style had much less imaginative potential. Some of the causes of the reaction are evident, others obscure, and until we know more about it we must not simplify it to any one source. Critics have always been too quick in finding explanations for the exceedingly complex shifts of taste within or between 'periods', and the most difficult of all relationships to make is that between 'ideas' and 'style': various writers share the same intellectual outlook but write in a totally different way; others conform to a current style or fashion from quite diverse positions. So none of the old explanations, such as the spread of scepticism, or Jacobean melancholy, or the influence of Seneca or Ramus, will do. Nor is the reaction purely 'literary' or purely 'social': some of its manifestations are social (the court of Charles II, the scientific movement) but not restricted to any sect, creed, or political party. The overall movement seems to be within taste, loosely defined as a reaction against the supercharged use of language at the turn of the century. Perhaps all that one can conclude here is that in our literature periods of excellence in one mode or genre have been followed by periods of almost totally opposed reaction which led to the development of some other genre: as in the interaction between the drama and poetry from Marlowe to Pope, or between the novel and poetry in the eighteenth and nineteenth centuries.

But although such general speculations are not open to proof or disproof, there will surely be general agreement that the prose at the end of this period is very different from that of the beginning, is, in a word, thinner. When we think back from the smooth clarity of Dryden's syntax to the variety of expressive resources revealed by the Character writers' sparkling wit on the one hand and on the other Bacon's use of syntactical symmetry to enact stylistically the rise and fall of Ciceronianism, or the way

in which Ralegh and Donne constructed such cataclysmic cata-
logues of human evil through parallelism and climax, then we
must agree that 'a great prince in prison lies'. If we think of the
intellectual and emotional scope of metaphor, ranging from
Bacon's mockery of the narcissistic and futile proceedings of
scholasticism to his great praise of learning; or the different
shades of melancholy in Ralegh and Sir Thomas Browne; or the
extremes of joy and despair in Lancelot Andrewes and Donne,
or the even greater range in Milton, from gutter warfare to the
awakening of a New Jerusalem; when we think of the inward
particularity of the images in Lancelot Andrewes, or their solid
boldness in Milton, or their luminous visionary quality in
Traherne—then the pert, tamed images of Dryden seem like
little glow-worms each giving off the prescribed quantity of
light before moving on. There is no need to indulge in nostalgia
for 'the world we have lost', because in our own reading we
can enter the world of our choice, but the change is still a sad
one. And although I do not deny that the achievements of
eighteenth-century prose are not negligible (especially those of
Swift and Dr Johnson), they consist of the intelligent application of a limited range of imaginative literary resources: the
great flexibility and power which the medium acquired in the
Renaissance have been cast off. Prose is now a tidier but a
smaller thing.

Notes

SIR FRANCIS BACON
The Advancement of Learning

p. 15, l. 9 'the state and virtue': 'the' is used where we would now use 'its'; 'state' here has the sense 'original condition'.

l. 22 'curious', 'curiousity': careful to excess, over-fastidious.

l. 24 'distemper': disease.

l. 28 Martin Luther (1483–1546): the great German religious leader, father of the Reformation. In his controversy with Rome and the decadent Church (corrupted at the material level by fraud and greed, and at the theological level by its use of the futile hair-splitting logical processes of medieval scholasticism) Luther found no assistance in contemporary culture and turned to the Classics for help.

p. 16, l. 3 'solitude': his solitary, unaided position.

l. 9 'exquisite': elaborate, minute.

l. 31 'affectionate': zealous, devoted.

l. 31 'copie': Latin *copia*, copiousness.

l. 36 'tropes and figures': the traditional two-part classification of the figures of rhetoric. Tropes involve a change of meaning or application (as in metaphor), figures of disposition (as in various types of repetition, echo-effects, etc.).

ll. 39–p. 17, l. 2 The identities of the writers whom Bacon singles out as the leaders of Ciceronianism are: *Orsorius* (*d.* 1580), Bishop of Silves in Algarves and a historian, whose redundant style was criticized by Ascham in *The Scholemaster*; *Sturmius* (1507–89), Professor at Paris and Strasbourg, wrote commentaries on the Rhetorics of Cicero and Hermogenes (a Greek rhetorician of the second century A.D., who laid much emphasis on style) and was known as 'the German Cicero'; Nicholas *Carr* (1523–68) succeeded Sir John Cheke at Cambridge as Regius Professor of Greek in 1547; Roger *Ascham* (1515–68), tutor to Queen Elizabeth and an influential educationalist, frequently praised Cicero in his writing.

p. 17, l. 18 'limned book': illustrated book, the first letter of official documents or manuscripts being often elaborated with large flourishes and decorations.

l. 20 'Pygmalion's frenzy': in Greek mythology Pygmalion was a sculptor who fell in love with a statue which he had made.

l. 32 'just period': mere eloquence satisfies men's minds too soon, before their thoughts reach a proper (i.e. solid, dependable) conclusion.

p. 18, l. 6 St. Paul: 1 Timothy vi. 20

l. 8 'respective': relevant to.

l. 8 'extensive': may be extended to.

l. 13 'strictness of positions': dogmatic assertions, inflexible arguments.

l. 19 'vermiculate': wormlike, wormy.

p. 19, l. 21 'cavillation': hair-splitting objection.

l. 30 'proportionable': adequate.

l. 36 'all out of their way . . .': 'they are all wrong who never agree'.

l. 37 'digladiation': wrangling, controversy (as with swords).

p. 20, l. 5 'fierce with dark keeping': this refers either to the belief that animals were thought to be fierce with being kept in the dark, or to the Elizabethan treatment for madmen, keeping them 'in a dark room and bound', as in the trick played upon Malvolio in Shakespeare's *Twelfth Night*.

l. 10 'unequal': uneven, and so, distorting.

l. 24 *Percontatorem . . .*: 'I flee the inquisitive man, for he is also a gossip', Horace, Epistles i. 18; 69.

l. 37 'levity': frivolity, unseasonable jocularity. Bacon argues that increased knowledge and experience remove superficial reactions and give man a true perspective and a critical spirit of inquiry. In the following paragraph 'It' as the subject of sentences refers to 'a true proficiency in liberal learning'.

p. 21, l. 9 'advise': consider, reflect; by the analogy with a puppet-show (which was a novelty in England at this time) Bacon points to that increased ability to penetrate appearances which knowledge gives.

l. 10 'motion': a puppet-show.

l. 14 'for a passage': for a pass or ford, which on Alexander's scale of military conquests would be a trivial achievement.

p. 22, l. 5 'exculceration': an ulcer.

l. 7 *'rationem totius'*: the end of all (Ecclesiastes xii. 13), the aim to which the whole process is directed.

p. 23, l. 27 'Homer hath given more men their livings': it was one of the humanists' common arguments in praise of literature that it gave immortality both to the author and to his subject—Homer still supports more men than ever the Roman emperors did. Compare Ben Jonson's *Epistle to Elizabeth, Countess of Rutland*, lines 53 ff.

> . . . There were brave men, before
> Ajax, or Idomen, or all the store,
> That Homer brought to Troy; yet none so live:
> Because they lack'd the sacred pen; could give
> Like life unto them.

l. 38 'exceed the senses': exceed the pleasure of the senses.

p. 24, l. 3 'deceits of pleasure': deceptive, unreal pleasures.

l. 11 Lucretius, *De rerum natura* ii. 1–10.

l. 37 'leese of': cannot but lose some of the life and truth.

p. 25, l. 9 'some of the philosophers': Aristotle and his followers.

l. 32 *Agrippina*: mother of the Emperor Nero, who had her executed in A.D. 59 so that he could marry Poppaea. Compare the versions of the story in Monteverdi's *L'Incoronazione di Poppaea* and Racine's *Britannicus*.

l. 34 *Ulysses*: in Book Five of the *Odyssey* Homer tells how Ulysses insists on leaving the beautiful nymph Calypso (despite promises of immortality) to continue his voyage back to Ithaca and his wife Penelope.

l. 36 'figure': emblem, type.

l. 40 *'Justificata'*: Matthew xi. 19, quoted from the Vulgate.

p. 26, l. 2 'which . . . which': there is a little confusion of construction here, the first 'which' referring to 'arts' and the second to 'judgment'. (Aldis Wright.) This section includes a highly technical review of some of the theoretical procedures in traditional logic, and I have not attempted to explain all the issues involved because the real interest of this section is Bacon's formulation of the fallacies inherent in the human mind (p. 28 ff). But I have preferred to include the section leading up to it in order to give the full context, even at the cost of puzzling non-logicians. Some of the main terms are:

'syllogism': 'an argument expressed in the form of two propositions called the premisses, containing a common or middle term, with a third proposition called the conclusion, resulting necessarily from the other two' (*O.E.D.*).

'*elench*': a logical refutation, a sophistical argument, hence a fallacy.

'redargution': refutation, disproof.

'categories or predicaments': the Greek and Latin words for Aristotle's concept of 'existences', an enumeration of all things capable of being named.

p. 28, l. 17 'glass': mirror, although Bacon now applies the analogy with such a fluid use of metaphors (from magic, trapping, infection) that it is impossible to detach the various strands of literal meaning.

l. 21 'false appearances': in the Latin translation, *idola*, which Bacon later calls 'the idols of the tribe'.

l. 38 'eccentrics': according to the Ptolemaic system of astronomy, these were the supposed circular orbits described by the planets about the earth, which was not in the centre. Bacon did not accept the new Copernican theories.

p. 29, l. 5 '*communis mensura*': the Greek philosopher Protagoras affirmed that man is the measure of all things.

l. 7 'Anthropomorphites': a philosophical sect which held that God was of human shape, and interpreted literally all the passages in the Scripture in which mention is made of his eye, ear, arm, or hand. Epicurus (341–270 B.C.) is guilty, according to Bacon of the more general weakness of anthropomorphism, attributing human form to the Deity.

l. 12 'Ædilis': A Roman magistrate in charge of temples, buildings, and the public games, including the *ludi scenici* or dramatic representations; their officers decorated the Forum and its vicinity with statues and various ornaments during festive occasions. By this witty and recondite analogy Bacon points to the human brain's desire for uniformity: if man had had to arrange the stars he would have done so in an orderly not a random manner.

l. 16 'frets': figures in architecture, used in ornamenting the roofs of houses, formed by small fillets intersecting each other at right-angles.

l. 17 'posture': the relative disposition of the various parts of anything.

l. 22 Plato: in the *Republic*, the opening of Book Seven.

l. 27 'complexion': the constitution both of mind and body ('personality' is perhaps the nearest modern equivalent).

l. 30 'peccant': morbid, unhealthy.

l. 38 'Tartar's': the Tartars (or inhabitants of Central Asia—Turks, Mongols, etc.) were famous for being able to ride horseback and shoot their arrows behind them at the enemy pursuing; the custom is more familiar in the expression 'Parthian dart' (the Parthians were another Asian tribe with the same tactic), as in Shakespeare's *Antony and Cleopatra* III.i.1.

The Essays
Of Truth

l. 12 'Pilate': John xviii. 38.

l. 13 'giddiness': variability, inconstancy.

l. 14 'affecting': striving for.

l. 22 'One of the Grecians': probably Lucian.

l. 25 'poets': in the controversy over the function of poetry in the Elizabethan age one of the Puritans' arguments against poets was that they were liars: the argument was vigorously disproved by Sir Philip Sidney in his *Apology for Poetry*.

l. 28 'mummeries': 'play-acting', display (like 'triumphs').

l. 29 'daintily': elegantly.

l. 31 'carbuncle': a reddish precious stone.

p. 31, l. 1 'One of the Fathers': probably St Augustine.

l. 16 'The poet': Lucretius (*c.* 98–55 B.C.) who transmitted the atomic philosophy of Leucippus and the Epicurean.

l. 20 *'adventures'*: fortunes.

l. 22 'not to be commanded': unconquerable.

l. 31 'allay': alloy.

l. 37 Montaigne (1533–92), in his *Essais* III. 18.

p. 32, l. 4 'foretold': Luke xviii. 8.

Of Adversity

l. 6 Seneca (*c.* 3 B.C.–A.D. 65). Roman statesman, stoic philosopher, and dramatist, in his *Epistulae* VII. 4. 329.

l. 18 'mystery': hidden significance.

l. 23 'in a mean': in a moderate manner.

l. 36 'sad': serious, here 'dark-coloured'.

l. 40 'incensed': burned—Bacon is referring to the methods of producing perfume from herbs and spices.

Of Goodness and Goodness of Nature

p. 33, l. 1 'affecting of the weal of men': working for human welfare.

l. 17 Busbechius: a Flemish scholar of the sixteenth century who was ambassador at Constantinople and recorded this incident from his experiences there.

l. 22 'doctors': i.e. teachers. Machiavelli (1469–1527) the Florentine statesman and writer whose study of *The Prince* had an enormous influence throughout the Renaissance, and whose attempt to reduce history to a series of maxims or general rules about political behaviour was an inspiration to Bacon's theory of the aphorism. The reference here is to his *Discorsi* II. 2.

p. 34, l. 10 'frowardness': perversity.

l. 11 'difficilness': stubbornness.

l. 13 'on the loading part': always aggravating.

l. 14 'Lazarus': Luke xvi. 21.

l. 17 'Timon': the greatest of all misanthropes (man-haters) spoke to the Athenians, according to Plutarch, as follows: 'My Lords of Athens, I have a little yard in my house where there groweth a fig tree, on the which many citizens have hanged themselves; and because I mean to make some building on the place, I thought good to let you all understand it, that before the fig tree be cut down, if any of you be desperate, you may there in time go hang yourselves': see Shakespeare's *Timon of Athens* V. ii.

l. 19 'politiques': politicians.

l. 20 'knee timber': crooked timber.

l. 24 'his heart is no island cut off from other lands, but a continent that joins to them': perhaps an echo of Donne's image: 'No man is an island, entire of itself; every man is a piece of the Continent, a part of the main' (*Devotions* xvii).

l. 26 'tree': the balsam genus.

l. 32 '*anathema*': (cf. Romans ix. 3)—a curse, especially the Christian curse of damnation.

Of Wisdom for a Man's Self

l. 35 'shrewd': mischievous.

l. 39 'centre': referring to the Ptolemaic theory that the planets revolved around the stationary earth. Bacon develops the analogy a few sentences later in the term 'eccentric': not having the same centre.

p. 35, l. 25 'and it were': even if only (to further their own petty aims at the expense of great ones).

l. 41 'pinioned': to cut the pinion (terminal segment) of a bird's wing, to prevent it from flying. Bacon uses imagery very fluently throughout the essay, and in this condensed metaphor he subtly insinuates that the self-preserving aims of such self-lovers in the end defeat themselves. The bird image seems to fit the sequence of animal imagery with which he expresses his contempt of selfish and evil behaviour: here foxes, the false tears of crocodiles, rats, and in the previous essay man without goodness is 'a kind of vermin'.

SIR WALTER RALEGH

p. 42, l. 16 'Hermes': Hermes Trismegistus ('thrice great Hermes') was the name given by the Neoplatonists (a school of philosophy which had an enormous revival in the Italian Renaissance) to the Egyptian god Thoth, thought to be identical with the Greek god Hermes, and from the third century A.D. the name was applied to the author of various Neoplatonic writings. For an interesting account of this cult especially as applied to painting see Edgar Wind, *Pagan. Mysteries in the Renaissance*, 1958; Pelican, 1967.

p. 43, l. 31 'tempered': mixed; well applied via 'mortar' and 'blood' to Ralegh's image of the ruin of buildings.

p. 44, l. 30 Casaubon (1559–1614) the great Renaissance classical scholar who ended his life in England and was buried in Westminster Abbey.

p. 45, l. 14 '*spretæque injuria formæ*': 'the affront to her slighted beauty' (Virgil).

p. 46, l. 27 'post': a type of noticeboard often used in Elizabethan London for official notices, or for advertising books (their title-pages would often be posted up).

p. 49, l. 30 '*non obstante*': ('not being in the way'): the first two words of a clause formerly used in statutes and letters patent, which conveyed a licence from the King notwithstanding any statute to the contrary.

p. 51, l. 15 'this terrible sentence': Galatians vi. 7.

l. 18 Louis the Eleventh (1423–83) King of France from 1461 on, combined ruthlessness towards his enemies with extreme religiosity.

p. 53, l. 5 'black swans': a proverbial phrase for something extremely rare (or non-existent).

l. 31 'Cineas to Pyrrhus': Cineas was a Thessalian, a minister of state and friend to Pyrrhus, King of Epirus in the third century B.C. Sent to Rome to force a peace he advised the King that to fight the Romans would be like fighting the devil.

p. 55, l. 23 '*Hic jacet*': 'here lies', the first two words of a Latin epitaph: hence any epitaph.

The Character Writers

JOSEPH HALL

p. 61, l. 19 'hale': to pull, drag out.

l. 36 'low roof': not vain or ostentatious.

p. 62, l. 1 'press': printing-press—but in the dazzling series of abusive images and puns with which this Character opens Hall combines several meanings: the surface one, 'the press hath left his head empty', is sufficiently amusing with its picture of the ostentatious writer so anxious to get his wit into print that he empties his head of all its contents: but it contains a submerged image of 'press' like a lemon-squeezer. A further pun on 'borrow' hits the plagiarism of such petty wits.

l. 10 'parieting': walling, within which 'glazing' means inserting the glass for windows.

l. 15 'a bare head': with the hat removed as a sign of respect (as he thinks, for himself).

l. 17 'ordinary': public meal or eating-house.

l. 23 'endorsed with his own style': perhaps means 'written with his own pen', that is addressed to himself by himself; or 'fully listing his titles'.

l. 39 'picks his teeth': the toothpick was a fashionable trademark of the traveller or experienced man of the world (see Shakespeare's 'character' of such an affected person, *King John* I. i. 189–205): thus this show-off uses one even though he has not just finished a meal.

p. 63, l. 4 'messes': courses or dishes at a meal.

l. 4 'how rich his coat is': coat of arms.

SIR THOMAS OVERBURY

A Courtier

l. 29 'loves nothing': note the surprise cut-off which the parallel structure ('nothing but') engineers to reinforce the sense.

l. 30 'censure': here 'judgment, opinion', which thus has to be 'charged' or reloaded like a gun with more news.

l. 31 'fish-like': he dies for lack of his normal sustenance.

l. 33 'spheres': a pun on planetary influence as seen here ('he is to be found only about princes').

l. 35 'Paul's': the old cathedral of St Paul's (burnt down in the Great Fire of 1666) which—like most churches in the sixteenth and seventeenth centuries—was a place where the fashionable people strolled and much business was transacted.

A Fine Gentleman

p. 64, l. 1 'Cinnamon': the tree of which the inner bark is dried in the sun and then ground up to make a spice—a very witty analogy for this foppish dedication to clothes.

l. 4 'bolstering and bombasting': types of padding in garments used to give the figure a better shape—thus, as the rest of the sentence reveals, he has purchased 'legs' (perhaps artificial calf-muscles) and 'straightness'.

l. 7 'Euphues': Lyly's ornate romance, which for a time was the mark of highest breeding in court circles, but which had been mocked in the 1590s (as in Shakespeare's *Henry IV*) and was now very much out of date.

l. 9 'Birchin Lane': this was the part of London where secondhand clothes shops were situated (compare the last sentence with its 'broker's shop' full of cast-off fashions).

l. 10 'Salamander': a lizard-like animal then thought to live in, or to be able to endure, fire.

l. 17 'galliard': a Renaissance dance, which this fop presumably dances to his own whistling.

l. 18 'calendar of ten years': either 'a record of the last ten years' (and so, of immediate events and fashions only), or 'will only last ten years'—the verbal ambiguities which the character writers exploited makes a single definition often difficult.

l. 19 'ushering': a menial attendant.

l. 24 'fantasticness': whimsicality, a state of irrational and impulsive behaviour.

A Puritan

A devasting picture of religious hypocrisy, which in its concentration ranks with the more extended exposures by Ben Jonson in *The Alchemist* and *Bartholomew Fair*. Some of the densely-packed allusions are mysterious, but the general picture is like Jonson's, mocking the discrepancy between the extreme Puritan's profession of piety and his real greed.

l. 27 'rabies': canine madness, hydrophobia.

l. 31 'Bragger': a mock-personification of the vice of boasting.

l. 32 'costive': constipated (leading to the pun on 'hidebound', which bears this sense in addition to its normal one).

l. 34 'non residents': clergymen culpably absent from their parishes.

p. 65, l. 8 'lousy': infected by vermin, here representing controversy, with perhaps a further allusion to the Puritans' views about a clergymen's proper dress.

l. 14 'clyster-pipe': an enema, or the syringe used to inject a medicine into the rectum.

JOHN EARLE
A Bowl-Alley

l. 28 Bowling was a favourite Elizabethan pastime and often involved gambling.

l. 31 'Schools': university disputations, and from this point Earle makes a series of witty puns on bowls taken from general argument: thus 'hair's breath' is normally used for the very small difference separating two parties, and here it represents the bowls; again 'a straw' is both the small point which could settle a greater, and a means of measuring the distance between the bowls.

l. 32 'antic': a performer who plays a grotesque part, a clown, mountebank, etc. (this is what in *Hamlet* is called 'an antic disposition').

l. 36 'beadsmen': those who pray for the soul of another.

p. 66, l. 2 'humours': the four temperaments (melancholic, sanguine, choleric, phlegmatic).

l. 7 'wrong-biassed': having made the wrong allowance for the bias (a tendency to adopt a curved path because of the weight placed within it on one side) of the bowl's path. The final series of brilliant puns develop this analogy, and to understand it one must know what the technical terms mean: I borrow the explanation given in his edition by H. Osborne:
'*Mistress*: in bowls the "mistress", or as it is now called the "jack", is the small bowl at which the others are aimed: *Fortune*: in apposition to Mistress. Fortune is the mistress (jack) of the world. *Spited*: regarded with spite or annoyance. *Toucher*: a technical term for the ball which is closest to the jack. Thus in only a few sentences, by an ingenious use of his image, Earle constructs a whole allegory of the workings of Court.'

An Antiquary

l. 11 'his maw': its maw, that is the stomach of 'time past', from which this student of the past drags his main interest. The antiquary is a scholar dedicated to preserving the past in all spheres—here a mixture of archaeology, numismatics, bibliography, biology and everything else old (Sir Thomas Browne is not entirely exempt from the satire here). Earle's wit is to take his passion for the past over the present to the stage at which he is completely out of touch with the present (e.g. having more Roman or Hebrew coins than current English ones), and gently to insinuate that the passion is not a very discriminating one: reading only illegible inscriptions; preferring cobwebby and dusty manuscripts—where the dust by making 'a parenthesis between syllable' is likely to cause some remarkable misreadings in the text!

l. 24 'cozen'; cheat, deceive.

l. 33 'Tully': Marcus Tullius Cicero, this familiar form for Cicero was widely used at that time.

l. 35 'charnel house': a cemetery or sepulchre.

l. 38 'criticism': 'his breeches are out of fashion as a criticism of his own age' (Osborne), but I suspect another pun somewhere here. The last sentence is typical of Earle both in its wit and in its gentle humour and humanity.

A She Precise Hypocrite

The female version of Overbury's Puritan, with some overlapping details and even more pungent wit.

p. 67, l. 7 'taken a toy': perhaps 'taken a liking to', found entertaining.

l. 9 'stomacher': the front of the doublet.

l. 9 'Geneva print': an allusion to the smallness of type used in books printed at Geneva (the home of Calvinism, and thus the Paradise for English Puritans), but also a pun on the Puritans' fanatical love of austere dress. As Philip Bliss noted in his 1811 edition of Earle, 'Strict devotees were, I believe, noted for the smallness and precision of their ruffs, which were termed *in print* from the exactness of the folds'.

l. 12 'Whore of Babylon': the usual abusive name for Rome as the centre of Roman Catholicism.

l. 13 'virginity' refers to the celibacy of nuns as a catholic belief, the Puritans scorning even the marriage-ring as a 'Papist' invention.

l. 13 'tribe': as Mr Osborne well observed, 'The use of the word "tribe" subtly implies that the Puritan custom is on a level with the marital habits of savages, or possibly of the gypsies'.

l. 19 'lecturers' were lay-preachers, who often preached at the week-day service (or 'exercise') and were very popular with the most devoted 'sermon tasters'. Every single detail satirizes the fanatical zeal of Puritans—their opposition to the Virgin Mary as a symbol of Popery, their ridiculous fashion of using scriptural names, their hatred of music and musical instruments as an unpardonably ornate adjunct to church worship, their excessive use—and misuse, of the Scripture.

p. 68, l. 1 *The Practice of Piety* (1612) by Lewis Bayly, was a very popular devotional manual.

l. 3 'Brownist', a follower of Robert Browne, an extreme separatist.

l. 5 'a capon's wing': the wing of a large cock—the wit lies in the ambiguity of the verb position in the sentence: at first sight one thinks that someone has thrown the wing at her, but we then realize that she is eating it greedily (an even more devasting crossing of our expectations is that later: 'Her conscience is like others' lust, never satisfied').

l. 13 'Scotus': John Duns Scotus (1265–1305), nicknamed *Doctor Subtilis*, one of the most ingenious of all the scholastic logicians.

l. 15 'maypole': the Puritans were notoriously opposed to May games (again an ambiguity in this sentence: 'more than her husband').

l. 16 'Phineas' act': Numbers xxv. 7; 8 Phineas expressed God's disapproval of how the Israelites were consorting with the women and idols of the Moabites by taking a javelin and killing one of the couples: by this extreme of zealous behaviour Earle satirizes the imbalance of the Puritans towards music and indeed everything else.

A Suspicious or Jealous Man

l. 19 'watches himself a mischief': is on the look-out for any insult or injury done to him, and so, it is hinted, causes the mischief (thus later: 'not a jest thrown out, but he will make it hit him').

l. 19 'leer eye': a side glance; a roll of the eye expressive of slyness or (here 'and') malignity. The second half of

this Character is a very compelling analysis of the
psychology of self-hurt through excessive self-defence.

LANCELOT ANDREWES

p. 75, l. 2 'the nobleman': Acts viii. 34.

p. 76, l. 13 'Edom': the district south of Palestine, between the
Dead Sea and the Gulf of Akaba, the inhabitants of
which were regarded by the Israelites as a 'brother'
people. Bozrah was its chief city.

p. 77, l. 13 *'formosus in stola'*: Andrewes frequently refers to the details of his text in the Latin Vulgate version which is also
quoted at the head of the sermon. Many of the quotations within inverted commas are of relevant biblical
texts, and I have not reproduced the references (which
will be found in other editions of Andrewes) since the
purpose of this anthology is literary not theological.

l. 26 'all to': entirely.

p. 78, l. 14 'ghostly': spiritual.

p. 80, l. 7 *'habeas corpus'*: 'thou (shalt) have the body (i.e. in
court)': a writ which requires that the body of a person
restrained of liberty should be brought before the
judge or into court, that the lawfulness of the restraint
may be investigated and determined; *'habeas animam'*:
Andrewes applies the phrase to the soul as well.

l. 31 'the *chirographum contra nos*, the ragman roll': literally,
a statute which respected complaints of injuries, and
also such letters as contained self-accusations of crimes
committed against the state. See Colossians ii. 14.

p. 81, l. 4 'debellation': subjugation.

l. 21 'foil': a fall, check.

p. 87, l. 3 *'consummatum est'*: 'it is finished', the Vulgate text for
Christ's dying words on the cross. (John, xix. 30.)

p. 89, l. 15 *'dibaphus'*: double dyed, once with scarlet and then
with purple.

p. 91, l. 25 'Paschal lamb': the lamb slain and eaten at the Pass-
over: applied to Christ, and hence *Agnus Dei*, the lamb
of God. Possibly also meant in the literal sense 'our
Easter food'.

JOHN DONNE

p. 97, l. 9 'cerecloth': a cloth smeared or impregnated with wax:
used as a plaster in surgery, and (on a larger scale) as
a winding-sheet.

p. 98, l. 6 'gomer' or 'omer': a Hebrew measure of capacity:
hence a container.

p. 99, l. 38 'comminatory': denunciatory.
p. 100, l. 1 'commonitory': serving to admonish, correct.
l. 27 'As soon as I hear God say': the first example is from Job i. 1, the second from 1 Samuel (xiii) iii. 14.
p. 101, l. 26 'that plant': the plant *Litho spermus*, which is described by Pliny, Book 27, § 11; Donne's knowledge of 'hairy hearts' also comes from Pliny and Plutarch. If this recondite knowledge of abnormalities in nature now seems to us to smack of the 'unnatural natural history' of Euphuism, we should remember that the greatest and most critical minds of the Renaissance—Bacon, Montaigne, Shakespeare, Milton—also believed what they read in Pliny.
l. 38 'petrifaction': making stonelike (the vision of the seven Angels that follows is taken from Revelation xvi).
p. 102, l. 8 'talent': an ancient denomination of weight.
l. 17 'spital': a house or hospital for people suffering from foul diseases.
l. 30 'serenity': not only 'calmness', but also the state of fair and clear weather (without cloud or rain or wind).
p. 105, l. 8 'contumacy': perverse and obstinate resistance of authority.
l. 23 'recusant': a dissenter who refused to attend services of the Church of England (used especially of Roman Catholics).
l. 23 'libertine': free-thinker, sceptic.
l. 24 'separatist': one who belongs to a religious community separated from the Church or from a particular church.
p. 106, l. 19 Epictetus (A.D. 60–140) an eminent Stoic philosopher.
l. 23 'the School': the schoolmen, the scholastic philosophers, and theologians collectively.
p. 110, l. 11 'inchoations': beginnings, origins.
l. 11 'consummations': completions.
p. 111, l. 5 'spangled': to adorn as with spangles to cause to glitter.
l. 19 'cuirass': a piece of armour consisting of a breastplate and a backplate.
p. 114, l. 21 'lees': the sediment from wine and other liquids.

THOMAS HOBBES

p. 123, l. 4 'Cadmus': According to Greek mythology, Cadmus 'is said to have civilized the Boeotians and to have taught them the use of letters. Here the myth is a reflection of

241

historical fact, for the Greek alphabet is largely derived from Phoenician script' (*Oxford Companion to Classical Literature*, ed. Sir Paul Harvey).

p. 124, l. 15 '*entity* . . .': here Hobbes mocks the phraseology of schoolmen, as he does again below.

p. 127, l. 35 'cast up': add up.

p. 128, l. 19 'Thomas': Thomas Aquinas (*c*. 1225–74) the greatest of scholastic philosophers.

p. 130, l. 35 'affections': passions, appetites.

p. 131, l. 31 '*paction*': a bargain, agreement, contract.

p. 132, l. 26 'play . . . –trump': an analogy from card games where one suit is chosen as trumps and has precedence over the others.

p. 133, l. 26 '*accident*': a term in logic for an attribute which is not part of the essence, hence a non-determinant factor.

p. 136, l. 11 'perspicuous': transparent, hence 'clearly expressed', lucid. In this passage Hobbes seems to be using the word to mean almost 'light-giving', in opposition to the so-called 'mists' of metaphor.

l. 12 'snuffed': to have freed a candle from the snuff: hence to make clearer or brighter.

l. 13 'pace': here means 'method', the 'action of stepping'.

p. 138, l. 10 'bile': boil.

p. 142, l. 38 '*ghostly*': spiritual.

p. 145, l. 15 'ague': a malarial fever, with paroxysms, consisting of a cold, a hot, and a sweating stage.

l. 27 'pleurisy': inflammation of the pleura (a membrane enveloping the lungs), sometimes with effusion of fluid into the pleural cavity, and usually producing pains (here 'stitches') in the chest or side.

p. 146, l. 22 '*ascarides*': intestinal threadworms.

l. 25 '*wen*': tumour, boil.

SIR THOMAS BROWNE
Religio Medici

p. 152, l. 23 'Oedipus': a character in Greek mythology and the hero of Sophocles play *Oedipus Tyrannus*: presumably Browne is referring to his great intellectual powers, shown in his solving the riddle of the Sphinx.

p. 153, l. 1 'epicycle': a small circle, having its centre on the circumference of another circle.

l. 9 'the river Arethusa': supposed to lose itself in the earth in Greece but to reappear in Sicily.

l. 15 'Arians': followers of the doctrines of Arius (a presbyter of Alexandria in the fourth century A.D.) that Christ was not of the same substance or essence as God.

l. 17 'propense': liable to, prone to.

l. 34 'pia mater': the membrane enveloping the brain: the brain.

l. 38 '*O altitudo*': the Vulgate text for Romans xi. 33: 'O the depth of the riches both of the wisdom and knowledge of God! how unsearchable are his judgments....'

p. 154, l. 3 'Tertullian' (born *c.* A.D. 150): one of the greatest of the early Christian writers in Latin; '*Certum est ...*': 'it is certain because it is impossible'.

l. 30 'Hermes': Trismegistus, who defined God as 'a sphere whose centre is everywhere and whose circumference nowhere'.

l. 36 'the text': Genesis ii. 7: 'And the Lord God formed man of the dust of the ground.'

l. 37 'played the sensible operator': 'moulded man from a material substance' (Winny).

p. 155, l. 2 'affections': attributes, that is those of immortality and incorruptibility.

l. 7 Paracelsus (*c.* 1490–1541), the German physician and alchemist who had an enormous reputation during the Renaissance, whose work ranged from accurate observation of nature to an inflated mystical philosophy.

l. 11 'antimetathesis': a rhetorical figure involving the juxtaposed inversion of an antithesis: related to the figure *antimetabole* (later known as *chiasmus*); here the sentence means 'by the act of creating, grace is poured on the world'.

l. 12 'St Augustine' (354–430): one of the great fathers of the Latin Church who was a teacher of rhetoric before his conversion; best known for his works *The City of God* and his *Confessions*.

l. 18 'monstrous productions': this section shows Browne's speculative and curious nature in a rather incongruous light.

l. 27 'crasis': the mixture of different elements in the constitution of the body, hence 'temperament'.

p. 156, l. 4 'elemental': made out of the four elements.

l. 8 'anthropophagi': man-eaters, cannibals (referred to by Shakespeare as one of the marvels which Othello recounted to Desdemona).

l. 10 Browne here develops a paradox which (to reverse his terms) is 'not literally but metaphorically true'.

l. 14 Pythagoras: Greek philosopher of the sixth century B.C., one of whose chief doctrines was that of metempsychosis (the passing of the soul after death into some other body)—thus Lot's wife was transformed into a pillar of salt for looking back at Sodom; for the transformation of Nebuchadnezzar see Daniel iv. 33.

p. 157, l. 39 'microcosm': the 'little world' of human nature: man as an epitome of the macrocosm or 'great world' of the universe.

p. 158, l. 13 'secundine': the placenta.

l. 15 'Paul': cf. II Corinthians xii. 4.

l. 27 '*Est mutatio . . .*': 'there is a final transformation by which that noble extract of the microcosm is brought to perfection' (Winny).

p. 159, l. 4 '*Quantum mutatus ab illo*': 'how much changed from his former self'—alluding to the shade of Hector whom Aeneas encountered in Hades, *Aeneid* 2. 274.

l. 20 'Diogenes': 'he willed his friend not to bury him but to hang him up with a staff in his hand to frighten off crows' (1643 edition, note).

l. 21 'rodomontado': an extravagantly arrogant or boastful speech.

l. 30 'jubilee': the Jewish computation for fifty years.

l. 31 'Saturn': the planet Saturn was thought to make his revolution once in thirty years.

l. 36 'canicular': the dog-days during the hottest season when dogs might run mad: hence 'prime of life'.

l. 38 'pantaloon': the Venetian character in Italian comedy, a foolish old man wearing pantaloons (peculiar trousers, often with ribbons) spectacles, and slippers.

p. 160, l. 15 'incurvate': to bring into a curved shape; here: accentuate, confirm.

l. 27 'figures in arithmetic': indices which raise a figure to a greater power (e.g. 2^3).

l. 39 'Aeson's bath': the process by which Medea restored Aeson (the father of Jason, he who recovered the golden fleece) to youth by boiling him in a cauldron with magic herbs.

p. 161, l. 2 'radical humour': in medieval philosophy, the moisture naturally inherent in all plants and animals, its presence there being a necessary condition of their vitality.

l. 5 'found themselves': base their arguments.

l. 8 'glome or bottom': a ball or clue of yarn: here 'hidden thread', an image caught up again in the last sentences.

l. 19 'antipathies': natural incompatibilities, marvels, esoteric knowledge.

Urn-Burial
(No attempt is made here to gloss every name or allusion: a useful edition which performs this function is by W. Murison.)

l. 30 'specious': splendid.

l. 32 'diuturnity': long duration.

l. 34 '*Sic ego . . .*': Tibullus III. ii. 26: 'Tis thus that I, when turned to bones, should wish to be laid to rest.'

p. 162, l. 13 'Moses his man': cf. Psalms xc: 10.

l. 16 'a span long . . . long finger': Browne here plays on the common image for the shortness of human life (a span being the distance from the tip of the thumb to the tip of the little finger) and joins it to the 'ancient arithmetic of the hand, wherein the little finger of the right hand contracted, signified an hundred' (Browne's marginal note in the first edition).

l. 24 'Alcmena's nights': one night as long as three.

l. 27 'mal-content': discontent.

l. 34 'ossuaries': a receptacles for the bones of the dead: bone-urns.

l. 36 'proprietaries': owners.

p. 163, l. 1 'pyramidally': like the mummies (embalmed bodies) preserved in pyramids.

l. 8 'Atropos': one of the three fates who carried a shears to cut the thread of life.

l. 11 'the probable meridian of time': 'i.e. halfway between Creation and the Last Day. Creation was held to have been 4,000 years before Christ and the Last Day was expected to be 2,000 years after Christ' (Murison). Hence 'the prophecy of Elias' below was that the world would last only six thousand years.

l. 23 'one face of Janus': the past and future are out of proportion.

l. 36 'the mortal right-lined-circle': Browne's note is 'Θ The character of death', referring to the tradition by which the letter theta Θ, which is the initial of the Greek θάνατος, 'death', came to be used as a symbol for death.

l. 40 'scarce forty years': Browne adds the note: 'Old ones being taken up, and other bodies laid under them'.

p. 164, l. 1 'Gruter' (1560–1627): an eminent Dutch scholar who compiled an important list of classical inscriptions.

l. 9 'Cardan' (1501–76): a versatile Renaissance scientist.

l. 13 'entelechia': the informing spirit, the soul.

l. 21 'Herostratus': in 356 B.C. he determined to achieve endless fame by burning the temple of Diana, one of the seven wonders of the world.

l. 22 'Adrian's horse', Borysthenes, was given both a monument and an epitaph.

l. 34 'the first story': 'before the flood' as Browne notes: cf. Genesis iv-v.

l. 37 'equinox': the mid-point, when past and future would be equal.

l. 39 'Lucina': the moon-goddess or light-bringer, invoked in childbirth as the bringer of light.

l. 41 'winter arches': the arcs, in the astronomical sense.

p. 165, l. 10 'callosities': insensibility, hardness to suffering.

p. 166, l. 1 'perspectives': telescopes.

l. 1 'spots': sun-spots.

l. 23 'Sardanapalus': King of Assyria, besieged in Nineveh for two years, and 876 B.C. unable to endure it any longer ordered a general conflagration of himself and all his possessions.

l. 27 'Five languages': the epitaph on the Emperor Gordianus, killed in A.D. 244 by his own soldiers, was written in Greek, Latin, Persian, Hebrew, and Egyptian.

l. 35 'in the decretory term': at the day of judgment.

p. 167, l. 12 'Isaiah': cf. chapter xiv, verses 9 ff.

l. 18 'diminish their diameters': shrink in comparison with, until they become 'angles of contingency', the infinitesimal angles between the circumference of a circle and its tangent.

l. 24 'Christian annihilation . . .': terms from Christian mysticism for the process by which the mystic is united with God.

l. 30 'Chymera's': wild, unfounded fancies.

l. 32 'metaphysics . . .': Christian theology.

l. 35 'St Innocents Church-yard': Browne adds the note: 'In Paris, where bodies soon consume', unlike 'the sands of Egypt' which would preserve bodies by their heat.

l. 37 'moles of Adrianus': 'A stately mausoleum (= Moles, in Latin) built by Adrianus in Rome, where now standeth the Castle of St Angelo', the opposite extreme from 'six foot', the standard size grave.

l. 39 Lucan (A.D. 39–65) from his *Pharsalia* vii. 809 ff:

'Whether it is decay that consumes the dead body or
whether it is the funeral pyre, matters not at all.'

JOHN MILTON

Areopagitica

p. 174, l. 7 'dragon's teeth': the teeth of the dragon were sown by
its slayer, King Cadmus, and from them up sprang a
band of armed warriors whom he defeated by throwing a stone among them, so provoking them to fight
and kill each other until only five were left.

l. 20 'spill': to destroy.

l. 23 'impression': the total number of copies of a book
printed at one time (in the Elizabethan period, about
1,200 copies).

l. 25 'fifth essence': the first four (earth, water, air, fire) are
'elemental', belonging to the elements of the material
world; the fifth, the quintessence is ethereal—from it
are formed the stars (cf. *Paradise Lost* III. 714–18).

l. 32 'the inquisition': started in 1231 by Pope Honorius
III, and flourished throughout Europe in Catholic
countries, most violently in Spain. There follows a
compact survey of censorship since Greece.

l. 35 'Eusebius' (*c.* 264–360): the 'father of ecclesiastical
history', and Bishop of Caesarea: the story is in his
History VII. vi.

l. 37 'Dionysius': Bishop of Alexandria, A.D. 247–65.

p. 175, l. 8 'apostle': the two references to St Paul are to 1 Thessalonians v, 21 and Titus i, 15.

l. 22 'concoction': digestion.

l. 28 'Mr Selden': John Selden (1584–1654), the great English lawyer, legal historian, and parliamentarian.

p. 176, l. 2 'omer': as in Donne, the Hebrew measure of quantity—
here the amount of manna which Moses was com-
mended to ration to the Israelites daily (Exodus xvi.
16).

l. 18 'St Paul's converts': see Acts xix. 19.

l. 28 'Psyche': Venus, as part of the abuse she visited upon
her daughter-in-law made her sort a vast quantity of
different types of grain into the same piles (wheat,
barley, etc.).

p. 177, l. 8 'blank': pale or colourless.

l. 8 'excremental': external, superficial.

l. 10 'Spenser': see the *Faerie Queene* II. viii; in fact the
Palmer [= Reason] does not accompany Guyon to the

Cave of Mammon, a detail which Spenser intended to
show that temperance alone is a sufficient power to
withstand temptation of greed, although he is needed
as defence in Acrasia's Bower of Bliss (xii).

l. 22 'Atlantic and Utopian politics': the imaginary commonwealths described by Plato in his *Critias* (describing the Kingdom of Atlantis) and More's *Utopia*:
Milton seems to have missed the point in his zeal to
recommend the active life.

l. 30 'Plato there mentions': *Republic* iv. 424–33.

l. 38 'pittance': ration, allowance.

l. 40 'gramercy': thanks.

p. 178, l. 5 'motions': puppet-shows.

p. 179, l. 2 'complexion': 'personality' or 'character'.

l. 7 'assembly': Presbyterians pervailed in the Assembly of
Divines, which was then sitting at Westminster.

l. 12 'professors': 'persons professing religious (and presumably Protestant) faith' (Hughes); [=Puritans].

l. 13 'Loretto': the shrine near Ancona in Italy worshipped
by pilgrims since 1294, and supposed to contain
the house in which Mary was born and Jesus conceived.

l. 15 'piddling': insignificant, paltry.

l. 16 'mysteries': trades.

l. 16 'skill': contrive.

l. 21 'factor': agent (Milton uses a sarcastic parody of trade
jargon in this fable of the busy tradesman who hires
a dog to do his barking for him).

l. 28 'dividual': separable.

l. 33 'malmsey': a sweet wine.

l. 35 'green figs': eaten by Christ on his way to Jerusalem
(Mark xi. 12–13).

p. 180, l. 22 'plates': armour of plate mail—'the flourishing condition of the arms industry was due to the state of the
Civil War' (Sirluck).

l. 33 'five months': Milton here paraphrases Christ's words
to the disciples whom he sent to preach to the Jews
(John iv. 35).

p. 181, l. 15 'suburb trenches': in 1643 the City of London erected
fortifications in a twelve-mile radius in the suburbs,
to repel royalist invasions.

l. 19 'admiration': here 'astonishment'.

p. 182, l. 4 'mewing': moulting. Milton here alludes to stories of
eagles in their old age flying straight into the sun's
rays to burn the mist from their eyes and to singe their

wings before plunging thrice into a fountain from which they emerge with renewed plumage and restored vision (Hughes).

l. 9 'prognosticate': infer, deduce, prophecy.

l. 13 'oligarchy of . . . engrossers': the powerful rule of the censors.

l. 36 'abrogated': repealed, as was the case with the absolute legal power which the Roman father had over his children.

l. 39 'coat and conduct': a form of taxation 'originally levied to pay for clothing and transporting feudal troops in the king's service, and revived by Charles I in his effort to obtain funds without a parliamentary grant' (Hughes).

l. 40 'noble': a coin worth 6s. 8d.

l. 40 'Danegelt': money raised by taxation in England to buy off the Danish invaders of the Saxon kingdoms.

Apology for Smectymnuus

p. 183, l. 3 'Smectymnuus' was the name under which five Presbyterian ministers published in 1641 a pamphlet attacking episcopacy; the name was formed by combining the initials of their names—Stephen Marshal, Edmund Calamy, Thomas Young, Matthew Newcomen, and William Spurstowe. It was answered by Joseph Hall, and several other pamphlets were published during the controversy, which seems to have been ended by Milton's Apology.

l. 4 'he': the author of the Modest Confutation ('the Remonstrant' elsewhere) who Milton thinks to be either Joseph Hall or his son Edward.

l. 12 'dust and pudder': 'bustle, confusion'; a 'pudder' or 'pother' is a choking, dust-filled smoke.

l. 16 'vapour': to put a person off by talking big—to defeat by specious rhetoric.

l. 21 'flirting': scoffing.

l. 21 'frumps': jeers, mocking speeches.

l. 22 'curtal': brief, cut off, docked.

l. 24 'whom': those whom.

l. 30 'woeful': 'woe unto you, when all men shall speak well of you' (Luke vi. 26).

p. 184, l. 8 'vomited': in the Lent Term of 1626 Milton was rusticated (temporarily 'sent down' as a punishment) from Cambridge for some trivial offence.

l. 13 'equals': contemporaries, fellow-students.

l. 34 'her sister': Oxford.

l. 36 'kecking': to make a sound as if to vomit, to retch.

l. 38 'suburb sink': the *Confutation* had accused Milton of haunting immoral places in the London suburbs, as he says below, playhouses and 'bordelloes' (brothels).

p. 185, l. 3 'usurping': to make arrogant pretensions.

l. 9 'lembec': alembic or still.

l. 12 'concocting': digesting.

l. 26 'Canaan': the spies sent by Moses into Canaan returned 'bringing up a slander on the land' (Numbers xiv. 36).

l. 31 'gin': 'trap or snare', as in the vigorous phrase which follows 'hamper'd in his own hemp'—caught in his own trap.

l. 37 'antistrophon': a rhetorical figure which turns an argument back upon an opponent.

p. 186, l. 4 *Mundus alter et idem*: the title of Hall's early work (1605, translated in 1608 as *The Discovery of a New World*), which Milton has previously savagely mocked. The names are in fact Hall's own: a land of viragos (*Viraginea*), a land of erotic romance (*Aphrodisia*), and a city of debauchery (*Desvergognia*).

l. 5 'Cephalus or Hylas': beautiful youths in classical mythology.

l. 12 'tire': costume.

l. 13 'periwig': wig.

l. 13 'vizard': mask: theatrical properties which Hall had accused Milton of being familiar with.

l. 17 'Trinculo': the drunken jester in Shakespeare's *The Tempest*, but as M. Y. Hughes has shown, more likely to be the rustic character in Thomas Tomkys's *Albumazar*, a play acted at Trinity, Cambridge, in 1614.

l. 25 'atticism': a well-turned phrase; Milton here imitates a passage in Demosthenes' oration *On the Crown*.

p. 187, l. 3 'elegiac poets': especially Ovid.

l. 28 'dear': hard, severe.

l. 30 'numerous': rhythmic, metrical.

p. 188, l. 20 'Beatrice and Laura': the heroines of Dante and Petrarch.

l. 26 'Homer': the 'fault' is that found by Plato (*Republic* 377 e), that Homer drew morally unsatisfactory portraits of the gods.

l. 37 'laureat': worthy of the Muses' crown.

l. 40 'Xenophon': the contemporary ('equal') of Plato: famous in the Renaissance (cf. Sidney's *Apology for*

Poetry) for his *Cyropædia*, an account of the education
of the Emperor Cyrus which was regarded as a model
for moral and physical training.

p. 189, l. 3 'sorceress': Circe.

l. 12 'Corinthians': a name for prostitutes ('Prelatess':
bawd) which goes back to antiquity, deriving from the
licentious manners of that town. It is used in Shakespeare's *Henry IV*.

THOMAS TRAHERNE

p. 193, l. 1 I, 1. 'An empty book is like an Infant's Soul. . .':
editors cite the opening of the first Character in Earle's
Microcosmography, A Child: 'His soul is yet a white
paper unscribbled with observations of the world,
wherewith at length it becomes a blurred notebook.'

p. 194, l. 5 I, 2. 'loadstone': the magnet.

l. 16 I, 3. 'Parables': cf. Matthew xiii. 35.

l. 20 'Heir of the world': cf. Romans iv. 13.

p. 195, l. 15 I, 7. 'Thomas à Kempis': *The Imitation of Christ* III. v:
'Love gives all for all.'

l. 17 I, 55. H. M. Margoliouth makes an interesting comparison with a passage in Blake's *Vision of the Last
Judgment*: 'If the Spectator could enter into these
Images in his Imagination, approaching them on the
Fiery Chariot of his Contemplative Thought, if he
could Enter into Noah's Rainbow or into his bosom,
or could make a Friend & Companion of one of these
Images of wonder, which always intreats him to leave
mortal things (as he must know), then would he arise
from his Grave, then would he meet the Lord in the
Air & then he would be happy.' See the notes to his
edition (listed in 'Further Reading'). The similarity is,
I suppose, due to the common fund of Christian and
Neoplatonic mysticism on which both poets are
drawing.

p. 196, l. 23 II, 54. This is one of the few meditations where
Traherne uses symmetrical syntax, and the effect is to
heighten the ecstatic note.

l. 30 'nice': fastidious.

p. 198, l. 10 III, 2. Compare this meditation with Traherne's poems
'The Salutation', 'Wonder', 'Eden', 'Innocence', 'The
Apostacy'.

l. 30 III, 3. 'orient': radiant, 'like the dawn', shining red.

l. 33 'gates': these were the five gates of the walled city of

Hereford, near which Traherne was born. Margoliouth notes that 'The ravishment was, of course, not because the child Traherne had never before seen green trees, but because of his first sight of them framed in the gateway—a visionary Sight. . . .'

l. 16 'proprieties': properties.

p. 200, l. 9 III, 9. 'Hobby-horse': a stick with a horse's head which children bestride as if it were a horse (Traherne's was decorated with tinsel).

l. 11 'curious': valuable, precious.

l. 16 'preternatural': beyond, surpassing the ordinary course of nature.

p. 201, l. 21 III, 11. 'gew-gaw': a gaudy trifle, bauble.

p. 202, l. 14 IV, 94. 'curiously': carefully, attractively.

l. 21 IV, 95. 'The soul is made for action': beneath the unique and personal nature of Traherne's vision one sees glimpses of orthodox Christianity, here the need for good works in the active life.

p. 204, l. 11 V, 9. 'theatre': Traherne seems to be using the word in its classical sense, an open-air amphitheatre (as in the preceding clause, 'a broad and a vast extent of . . . glory'). The repetition of 'every' here has the same ecstatic climactic effect as Donne's use of 'joy' and 'heaven' in the conclusion to his sermon.

JOHN DRYDEN
A Defence of the Epilogue

p. 217, l. 4 'Horace': *Ars Poetica,* lines 47–8: 'You will speak well if a fresh setting restores new force to a familiar word.'

l. 12 *'et vultus'*: Horace, *Odes* I. xix. 8: 'her face too dangerous to gaze on'.

l. 17 'Petronius': *Satyricon*, 118: 'the studied felicity of Horace'.

l. 18 'graffing': grafting, an image from gardening.

l. 20 'Fletcher': John Fletcher (1579–1625) a Jacobean playwright best known for his collaboration with Francis Beaumont (1584–1616); much admired after the Restoration for his pathos and wit. Sir John Suckling (1609–42) and Edmund Waller (1606–87) were two lyric poets of the so-called 'Cavalier' school who occupied the same positions of admired predecessors in poetry that Beaumont and Fletcher did in drama.

p. 218, l. 6 'refinement of wit': for the complex associations of the important term 'wit' see George Watson's notes to

his Everyman edition and the illuminating essay by
C. S. Lewis in his *Studies in Words*, C.U.P., 1960.

p. 219, l. 4 'Asper': in *Every Man Out of His Humour*, Induction,
lines 177–81; the next two quotations are from the
Prologue to the play and from IV. iv. Dryden is here
objecting to the traditional forms of puns, either when
the two words are almost alike in sound though different in sense (here 'Ari-starchus or stark-ass', 'satin-
Satan') or where they are identical but involve a change
of meaning, as in the later example: 'or pay me quickly,
or I'll pay you' (Jonson's *Epigrams* lxxiii. 21–2). Sidney
used puns for both serious and humorous functions in
the *Arcadia* as in *Astrophel and Stella*.

l. 29 'clench': to pun.

l. 31 'a famous Italian': not yet identified.

p. 220, l. 15 'Don John': the hero of Fletcher's play *The Chances*.

l. 39 'the Blackfriars': the indoor theatre of Shakespeare's
troupe, built in 1596 by Richard Burbage, and demolished about fifteen years before Dryden writes this.

p. 221, l. 2 the 'Apollo': a large upstairs room in the Devil
Tavern at Temple Bar, and the haunt of Ben Jonson
and his 'sons', the younger poets who were his protégés.

p. 222, l. 19 'Cob and Tib': characters in Jonson's *Every Man in
His Humour* (Cob is a water-bearer, Tib his wife); thus
general names for low-class characters.

The Preface to the Aeneis

l. 30 'no stranger': George Watson notes that 'Dryden had
translated the fourth and ninth Eclogues for *Miscellany
Poems* (1684), four passages from the *Aeneid* in the
Sylvae (1685), and the third Georgic in the fourth
Miscellany (1694). All those drafts were incorporated,
with revisions, in the complete Virgil of 1697.'

p. 223, l. 8 'Segrais': a French poet who had published a transla-
lation of the *Aeneid* in 1668 together with a critical
preface, which Dryden draws on heavily.

l. 20 '*per annum*': i.e. those ineligible to vote in parliamentary
elections.

l. 38 John Owen (1560–1622) published eleven books of
Latin epigrams between 1606 and 1613.

p. 224, l. 1 Seneca: in his *Epistulae morales* cxi.

l. 32 Boccaccio: in 'The Author's Conclusion' to *The
Decameron*.

Biographical Information

LANCELOT ANDREWES (1555–1626) was born in London, the eldest of thirteen children of middle-class parents (his father was a successful mariner who became a Master of Trinity House); educated at Merchant Taylors' School under the great schoolmaster Richard Mulcaster (who also taught Spenser) from 1565 to 1571, when he went up to Pembroke Hall, Cambridge, the college where he became a Fellow in 1575, and was Master from 1589 to 1605. His academic ability was high, especially in languages, and after being ordained in 1581 his rise within the Church was rapid: he aroused great interest as a preacher at Pembroke, was made Dean of Westminster in 1601, and became successively Bishop of Chichester (1605), Ely (1609), and Winchester (1618). He was revered for his great scholarship, being acquainted with all the great classical scholars in Europe, and was an influential member of the group of scholars and clergymen that produced the Authorized Version of the Bible in 1611. He was celebrated for his preaching and attracted great interest throughout his life, and a large number of testimonies on his death (including poems by Milton and Crashaw). The major collection of his work is the *XCVI Sermons* (1629).

SIR FRANCIS BACON (1561–1626) was born at York House in the Strand, youngest son of Sir Nicholas Bacon, Queen Elizabeth's first Lord Keeper; his mother was a very learned woman (she had the same tutor as King Edward VI) and educated Bacon herself before he went to Trinity College, Cambridge, in 1573, where, it is reported, he rebelled against the tyranny of Aristotle's philosophy. In 1576 he was entered at Gray's Inn, where his father had studied, before making a very distinguished career as a lawyer. Bacon was attached to the embassy in France from 1576 to 1579 when his father died, and as a younger son without a substantial inheritance he was forced to take up a professional career. His intellectual gifts helped him to remarkable progress as a lawyer: he became a barrister and then lecturer at Gray's Inn at a much younger age than was usual and later rose to be Solicitor-General in 1607, Attorney-General in 1613, Lord Keeper in 1617, and Lord Chancellor in 1618. He entered Parliament in 1584 and quickly established a reputation in the House and its committees for intellectual acumen and diplomacy, but his courage in opposing the Queen on a matter of principle (1593) brought him out of favour, and it was only after some years of King James's rule that he achieved the promotion he deserved. His philosophical ideas were first expounded in the 1590s, and with some shape in the *Advancement* (1605), a programme on which he was constantly elaborating, most notably in the *Novum Organum* (1620) and the *De Augmentis Scientiarum* (1623). He became Baron Verulam in 1618, and Viscount St Alban in 1621, but in the same year his political enemies seized the chance to accuse him of bribery (his servants had accepted presents, but Bacon had not allowed these to influence any of his legal decisions), and he was deposed from office. After his fall he dedicated himself to his literary and scientific work, producing his *History of Henry VII*, the first political–historical analysis in English, in the amazingly brief time of five months; as well as revising and expanding the *Essays* (1625; earlier versions 1597, 1612) he produced a vast number of works in his *Natural and Experimental History*. He died of a chill caught when making an experiment of stuffing chicken with snow, to see if refrigeration could preserve food. His extraordinary intellect gave him an outstanding position in several careers (he was, for example, the first to propose a logical and coherent system of jurisprudence for the English law), and after his death his ideas dominated seventeenth-century England and had an enormous influence throughout Europe in the eighteenth century and well into the nineteenth.

SIR THOMAS BROWNE (1605–82) was born in London and educated at Winchester (1616–23) and Oxford (1623–9), continuing his medical studies abroad, as was the custom then, at Montpellier, Padua, and Leyden (1631–4). For a short time he lived in Yorkshire, where *Religio Medici* was written; it was published without his permission in 1642, and the authorized text was issued the following year. In 1637 he settled at Norwich to practise his profession as doctor, marrying in 1641 (he had twelve children) and remaining there for the rest of his life.

Besides his medical work he sustained a keen interest in science and all natural curiosities, and although influenced by Bacon he did not develop beyond the master's own indiscriminate use of untested printed material. Both Bacon's *Natural History* (the *Sylva Sylvarum*) and Browne's *Vulgar Errors* (the *Pseudodoxia Epidemica*) are not what we would think of as 'scientific' works, but are more like medieval or even classical compilations of fabulous materials and marvels. Browne was famous as an antiquary, but never became a member of the Royal Society, perhaps because his style was too rich and poetic for their sober, non-digressive ideals.

JOHN DONNE (1573–1631) was the son of a prosperous London ironmonger; his mother was the granddaughter of Sir Thomas More's sister, Elizabeth Rastell, and she brought Donne up as a Catholic. He was for some time at Oxford and perhaps Cambridge too, before making the conventional move to 'the third great University of the realm', the Inns of Court, where he read widely, lived gaily, and wrote his greatest love poetry and satire (according to Ben Jonson, Donne wrote 'all his best pieces ere he was twenty-five years old'). He travelled abroad in the mid-nineties, and was on Essex's expeditions to Spain in 1596 and 1597; in 1598 he was made secretary to Sir Thomas Egerton, the Lord Keeper. A promising public career seemed open when in 1601 he made a secret marriage with Egerton's niece, Anne More, and her angry father caused Donne's imprisonment and dismissal. For the next fourteen years Donne and his ever-expanding family were dependent for money on a variety of patrons, especially the kind Sir Robert Drury, for the death of whose young daughter Anne he wrote a funeral elegy and the two great *Anniversaries* (1611–12). Donne seems to have become a nominal Anglican at about the turn of the century, and in 1615 he was ordained, being appointed Reader in Divinity at Lincoln's Inn from 1616 to 1622; in 1621 King James made him Dean of St Paul's and in 1624 vicar of St Dunstan's. In 1617 his wife, who had borne twelve children and lost five, died and Donne became an ascetic recluse, 'crucified to the world', and an evermore dedicated preacher who attracted a large and faithful congregation. Donne selected the best of his sermons for publication: *Eighty Sermons* were published in 1640, and *Fifty Sermons* in 1649. His earlier prose works include the *Paradoxes and Problems* and the *Devotions upon Emergent Occasions*.

JOHN DRYDEN (1631–1700) was born at Aldwinkle in North-amptonshire, being brought up in a Puritan environment (he later served Cromwell's chamberlain and in 1659 wrote his 'Heroic Stanzas' on the death of Cromwell). He was educated at Westminster under Busby, and went up to Trinity College, Cambridge, in May 1650, taking his degree in 1654, and per-haps staying in Cambridge to read before settling in London in 1657. Despite his Puritan beginnings he celebrated the Restoration of Charles II in *Astraea Redux*, 1660. In 1663 he married Lady Elizabeth Howard and had two sons. He became a Fellow of the Royal Society in 1662 and in 1663 a playwright by profession, producing between then and 1681 almost a play a year in the fashionable modes of heroic tragedy and bawdy society comedy. He was appointed Poet Laureate in 1668, and Historiographer in 1670, and engaged in literary controversies with Buckingham, Settle, and Rochester. His greatest period as a poet was from 1678 to 1682 when he produced his three satires, *Mac Flecknoe*, *Absolom and Achitophel*, and *The Medal*. In 1686 he was converted to Roman Catholicism and in 1687 published the long didactic poem *The Hind and the Pan-ther*, to justify his change; because of his religion he refused to take oaths at the Revolution in 1688, and was deprived of his official positions. In the last period of his life he again had to make a living by the pen, writing plays, odes, critical pre-faces, verse translations of Persius, Juvenal, Horace and, most celebrated, Virgil (1697, said to have earned him £1,200) and adaptations of Chaucer, Boccaccio, and Ovid. He was buried in Westminster Abbey, in Chaucer's grave.

JOHN EARLE (1601 ?–65), after being educated at Merton Col-lege, Oxford (where he became a Fellow in 1619), was one of the circle which gathered at Great Tew, near Oxford, for religious and literary discussions (it was led by Falkland, and its members included Owen Felltham and Edward Hyde, Earl of Claren-don). In 1641 he became tutor to Prince Charles, an attachment which lasted till his death, but during the Commonwealth period he was deprived of his preferments and exiled for sixteen years. At the Restoration he was made Dean of Westminster, then

Bishop of Worcester and later of Salisbury. In his life as in his work his quiet humanity won much affection.

JOSEPH HALL (1574–1656) had a distinguished career at Emmanuel College, Cambridge, and in his youth was one of the most versatile and experimental writers, producing the violent verse satires *Virgidemiarum* in 1597–8, and the prose satire *Mundus Alter et Idem* in 1605. He was an innovator in writing Characters, and also in religious–philosophical forms (he was a Christian stoic) such as the *Meditations* and *Epistles*. In 1608 he became a chaplain to Prince Henry, was made Bishop of Exeter in 1627, and of Norwich in 1641. As one of the most vigorous defenders of episcopacy he was punished by the parliamentarians, being forced into retirement in 1643, although he continued to write. He was friendly with both Donne and Sir Thomas Browne. His extraordinary literary development has yet to be properly studied.

THOMAS HOBBES (1588–1679) was born at Malmesbury, son of a Wiltshire parson, and learnt Latin and Greek at the age of six. Educated at Magdalen Hall, Oxford, from 1603 to 1608, and then became tutor and companion to the Cavendish family, an association which lasted for most of his life (between 1621 and 1626 he acted for some time as a secretary to Bacon, accompanying him in his walks and writing down any ideas that occurred to him). Hobbes made several tours on the Continent, and his friendship with such leading thinkers as Galileo, Gassendi, and Mersenne strengthened his radical attitudes. In 1640 he led the Royalist flight to Paris after the meeting of the Long Parliament, and for the next eleven years enjoyed his association there with the leading French intellectuals, but after publishing *Leviathan* in 1651 his anticlerical feelings led to him being accused of atheism, and he returned to England and submitted to the Government. After the Restoration he enjoyed more favour and Charles II protected him from Clarendon and the Church party and granted him a pension of £100 (which was never paid). His last years were spent in religious and philosophical controversies with Bishop Bramhall, Seth Ward, John Boyle, and John Wallis. Among a great number of philosophical and political works his remarkable vitality found the strength and skill at the age of seventy-five to make a translation of

Homer. One of the most penetrating minds of his own or any age.

JOHN MILTON (1608–74) was born in London, son of a prosperous scrivener who was also a composer and music-lover. Milton received his formal education at St Paul's School (c. 1620–5) and at Christ's College, Cambridge (1625–32), but he read very diligently on his own at all times, and after graduating spent the next six years at his father's house (in Horton, Buckinghamshire) in further reading and study, in which period he also wrote his first great English poems. He travelled on the Continent in 1638–9 but returned to England because of the threat of civil war (he had earlier abandoned his plan to take holy orders because he could not submit to the discipline of the Church). From 1641 to 1660 he was energetically occupied in defending the Puritan cause in a series of prose pamphlets, and in 1649 he was appointed Secretary for Foreign Tongues to the Council of State; his eyesight had begun to fail in 1644–5, and his labour in writing aggravated the condition until in 1652 he became completely blind. In the same year his first wife, Mary Powell died (she had married him in 1642 but as member of a Cavalier family was opposed to his political beliefs and soon deserted him; she returned in 1645, however, and they lived together until her death). In 1656 he married Katherine Woodcock but she died in 1658 (cf. the sonnet beginning 'Methinks I saw my late espoused saint'), and in 1663 he married his third wife, Elizabeth Minshull. At the Restoration Milton was in some danger as the apologist for the party that had killed Charles I, but after a few days imprisonment he was allowed to go free and was left in his peaceful old age to live a simple, godly, and sober life. By the laborious process of dictating to his wife and daughters Milton was still able to write poetry; and in the last fifteen years of his life he produced the three greatest poems of the seventeenth century, *Paradise Lost* (1667), *Paradise Regained*, and *Samson Agonistes* (1671). Although there has been a predictable reaction to the twentieth century against the Victorians' vague and undiscriminating praise of Milton, it is already evident that the current has moved back to considering him, after Shakespeare, the most complex and the most sustained of our major poets. His other many and various prose works include five pamphlets against prelacy

(1641–2); four on divorce (1643–5); the *Tenure of Kings and Magistrates* (1649); *Eikonoklastes* (1649); and *A Ready and Easy Way to Establish a Free Commonwealth* (1660).

SIR THOMAS OVERBURY (1581–1613) was educated at Oxford and the Middle Temple, and although he was quite satisfied with the aimless life of a courtier he showed definite literary talents. He became the confidant of Robert Carr, later Earl of Somerset, and for some years he shared his patron's prosperity at court, but when he opposed Carr's marriage with Frances Howard, Countess of Essex, he aroused the wrath of Carr and the Howards, who had Overbury imprisoned in the Tower and bribed his jailor to poison him. The truth only emerged later, and at the trial in 1615–16 Bacon delivered speeches for the prosecution of enormous force and eloquence; the Earl and Countess were convicted but their lives spared by the King. The second edition of his poem 'A Wife' (1614) included twenty-one characters by Overbury 'and other learned gentlemen his friends', and it went through several editions with considerable enlargements until by 1622 it numbered eighty-four characters—among the contributors were Webster, Dekker, and Donne.

SIR WALTER RALEGH (1552?–1618) was born at Hayes Barton in Devonshire, son of a country gentleman. Little is known of his early life, but at some stage he attended Oriel College, Oxford, and perhaps also the Middle Temple, and he fought in the French Wars and in Ireland, returning from there to Court in 1582. Then suddenly began his extraordinary rise to favour, and from 1582 to 1592 he was Elizabeth's reigning favourite, arbiter in all matters serious or trivial. He brought his downfall upon himself, for in 1592 he married one of the royal maids of honour, Elizabeth Throckmorton, and incurred the Queen's displeasure to such a degree that he was cast into the Tower; even after his release was not received at court for five years. In 1595 Ralegh made his famous expedition to Guiana (his own account of the voyage, *The Discovery of Guiana*, is one of the freshest of all Elizabethan travel writings), but his plans to colonize it were dismissed by the Queen; he achieved some recognition in 1596 with a brave expedition to Cadiz, and again in 1597 with the voyage to Azores. In 1601 he was made

Governor of Jersey, but it was an ephemeral success for with the accession of James he was immediately implicated in the alleged plot of Cobham and Brook to kill the King; there was no evidence against Ralegh and the trial was a disgrace, but he was nevertheless condemned to death and only spared at the last moment, and even when spared he was condemned to life imprisonment in the Tower. In 1616 he managed to get himself released to plunder the gold mines of Guiana, but the voyage was disastrous: the gold was not found, his son was killed by the Spaniards, and his friend Keymis killed himself. Ralegh's letter to his wife bearing the news is as unbearably moving as that to her on the eve of his threatened execution in 1603. This time James's advisers made no mistake and Ralegh was beheaded in 1618: a great and noble man, much lamented by his contemporaries, and even more by posterity. Under Elizabeth one of the greatest poets, and under James one of the greatest prose writers: in an age of versatile men only two or three surpassed him in his mastery of both media.

THOMAS TRAHERNE (1637?–74) was born in Hereford, the son of a poor shoemaker who died while Thomas and his brother Philip were small. They were brought up by a more prosperous relative, and from 1652 to 1656 he was at Brasenose College, Oxford, being ordained in 1660. The following year he became parish priest at Credenhill, a small parish near Hereford where he stayed until 1669, when he became chaplain to Sir Orlando Bridgman, Lord Keeper of the Great Seal, and held this post (living in London or at Sir Orlando's seat at Teddington) until his death. He was a very dedicated servant of God, but at the same time, in the words of a contemporary account, 'of a cheerful and sprightly temper ... affable and pleasant in conversation, ready to do all good offices to his friends, and charitable to the poor almost beyond his ability.' Apart from his poetry he wrote a treatise on *Christian Ethics* (1675) and nine *Thanksgivings*, composed in a psalm-like mixture of poetry and prose.

Further Reading

GENERAL

Intellectual and Literary Background

R. R. BOLGAR, *The Classical Heritage and its Beneficiaries* (Cambridge University Press, 1954; paperback, Harper Torchbooks). On the transmission of the classics through education; a wide-ranging but lucid study.

HARDIN CRAIG, *The Enchanted Glass: the Elizabethan mind in literature* (Blackwell, 1950). A classic account of intellectual assumptions and attitudes in the Renaissance.

E. R. CURTIUS, *European Literature and the Latin Middle Ages*, trans. W. R. Trask (Routledge, 1953; Harper paperbacks).

ROSEMUND TUVE, *Elizabethan and Metaphysical Imagery* (Chicago University Press, 1947), (paperback, Phoenix Books). A closely written and difficult book but very penetrating.

English Renaissance Prose

J. A. BARISH, *Ben Jonson and the Language of Prose Comedy* (Harvard University Press, 1960).

J. W. BLENCH, *Preaching in England; Late Fifteenth and Sixteenth Centuries* (Blackwell, 1964).

K. G. HAMILTON, *The Two Harmonies: poetry and prose in the seventeenth century* (Oxford University Press, 1963). Relies too much on the dubious theories of M. W. Croll and G. Williamson, and provides little analysis; but a useful outline.

R. FOSTER JONES, *The Seventeenth Century, Bacon to Pope* (Oxford University Press, 1965). Articles on 'Science and English prose style', 'Science and the English language', 'The attack on pulpit eloquence in the Restoration'.

BRIAN VICKERS, *The Artistry of Shakespeare's Prose* (Methuen, 1968).

GEORGE WILLIAMSON, *The Senecan Amble* (Faber, 1951). Contains useful material, but arranged to support a highly suspect thesis (derived from M. W. Croll) that most prose in the seventeenth century was written in the deliberately asymmetrical style, opposed to Ciceronian syntax. The actual analyses are equally sketchy (cf. those of Bacon).

F. WILSON, P. *Seventeenth-century Prose* (Cambridge University Press, 1961). Five lectures, clear and sound, but without much penetration.

INDIVIDUAL WRITERS

ANDREWES
Collected Sermons, ed. J. P. Wilson and J. Bliss, 5 vols. (Oxford University Press, 1841–54).
Selected Sermons, ed. G. M. Story (Oxford University Press, 1967). Twelve sermons, with useful introduction.
T. S. ELIOT, 'For Lancelot Andrewes' in *Selected Essays 1932–1960* (Faber, 1961).

BACON
Works, ed. James Spedding, 14 vols. (London, 1857–74).
Advancement of Learning and *Essays*, ed. W. A. Wright, 5th edn. (Oxford University Press, 1900). With copious notes.
R. FOSTER JONES, *Ancients and Moderns* (California University Press; Cambridge University Press, 1936), (paperback, 1965). Bacon's influence on the seventeenth century, with an excellent account of his philosophy.
ANNE RIGHTER, 'Francis Bacon' in *The English Mind*, ed. H. S. Davies and G. Watson (Cambridge University Press, 1964).
BRIAN VICKERS, *Francis Bacon and Renaissance Prose* (Cambridge University Press, 1968).

BROWNE
Works, ed. G. Keynes, 2nd edn. (Faber, 4 vols. 1964).
Religio Medici, ed. J. Winny (Cambridge University P ess, 1963).
Urne-Buriall, ed. W. Murison (Cambridge University Press, 1922, 1933).
JOAN BENNETT, *Sir Thomas Browne* (Cambridge University Press, 1962).
F. L. HUNTLEY, *Sir Thomas Browne* (University of Michigan Press; Cresset, 1962).

THE CHARACTER WRITERS

JOSEPH HALL, *Characters of Virtues and Vices*, ed. R. Kirk (Rutgers University Press, 1948).

The Overburian Characters, ed. W. Paylor (Oxford University Press, 1936).

JOHN EARLE, *Microcosmographie*, ed. H. Osborne (University Tutorial Press, 1933, 1964).

D. N. SMITH, *Characters of the Seventeenth Century* (Oxford University Press, 1918).

B. BOYCE, *The Theophrastan Character in England to 1642* (Harvard University Press, 1947).

DONNE

Collected Sermons, ed. E. N. Simpson and G. R. Potter, 10 vols. (California University Press and Cambridge University Press, 1953–?).

Selected Prose, ed. E. N. Simpson (Oxford University Press, 1967). Too many brief excerpts.

Selected Sermons, ed. T. Gill (New York, Living Age paperback, 1961). Nine largely complete sermons, but gushing introductions.

E. M. SIMPSON, *A Study of the Prose Works of John Donne*, 2nd edn. (Oxford University Press, 1948).

JOAN WEBBER, *Contrary Music: the prose style of John Donne* (Madison, Wisconsin, 1963).

DRYDEN

Critical Essays, ed. G. Watson, 2 vols. (Dent Everyman's Library, 1962).

A. BELJAME, *Men of Letters and the English Public in the Eighteenth Century (1660–1744)*, trans. E. O. Lorimer, (Routledge, 1948).

HOBBES

Leviathan, ed. M. Oakeshott (Blackwell, 1945).

R. PETERS, *Hobbes* (Penguin, 1956).

S. MINTZ, *The Hunting of Leviathan* (Cambridge University Press, 1962). The controversies about Hobbes.

MILTON

Complete Prose Works (Yale University Press, 1953–?). Copious notes and introductions.

Major Prose Works, ed. M. Y. Hughes (Odyssey Press, 1957). Admirably annotated; available either on its own or as part of a one-volume almost complete edition.

A. BARKER, *Milton and the Puritan Dilemma* (Toronto University Press, 1942).

RALEGH

History of the World (selections), ed. C. A. Patrides (Macmillan, forthcoming).

H. HAYDN, *The Counter-renaissance* (Scribner, 1950).

E. A. STRATHMANN, *Sir Walter Raleigh* (Columbia University Press, 1951).

PHILIP EDWARDS, *Sir Walter Raleigh* (Longmans, 1954).

TRAHERNE

Complete Works, ed. H. Margoliouth, 2 vols. (Oxford University Press, 1958).

Selections (including *Centuries*, complete), ed. A. Ridler (Oxford University Press; Standard Authors, 1966).

LOUIS MARTZ, *The Paradise Within* (Yale University Press; Oxford University Press, 1964).